Garfield
out to lunch

BY JIM DAVIS

Ballantine Books • New York

2006 Ballantine Books Trade Paperback Edition

Copyright © 1986, 2006 by PAWS, Inc. All Rights Reserved.
"GARFIELD" and the GARFIELD characters are trademarks of PAWS, Inc.

Published in the United States by Ballantine Books, an imprint of The Random House Publishing Group,
a division of Random House, Inc., New York.

Ballantine and colophon are registered trademarks of Random House, Inc.

Originally published in slightly different form in the United States by Ballantine Books, an imprint of
The Random House Publishing Group, a division of Random House, Inc., in 1986.

Library of Congress Control Number: 2006900498

ISBN 0-345-47562-3

Printed in the United States of America

www.ballantinebooks.com

9 8 7 6 5 4 3 2

First Colorized Edition

EARLIEST KNOWN GARFIELD!

Presented here for the first time anywhere is the earliest known Garfield strip.

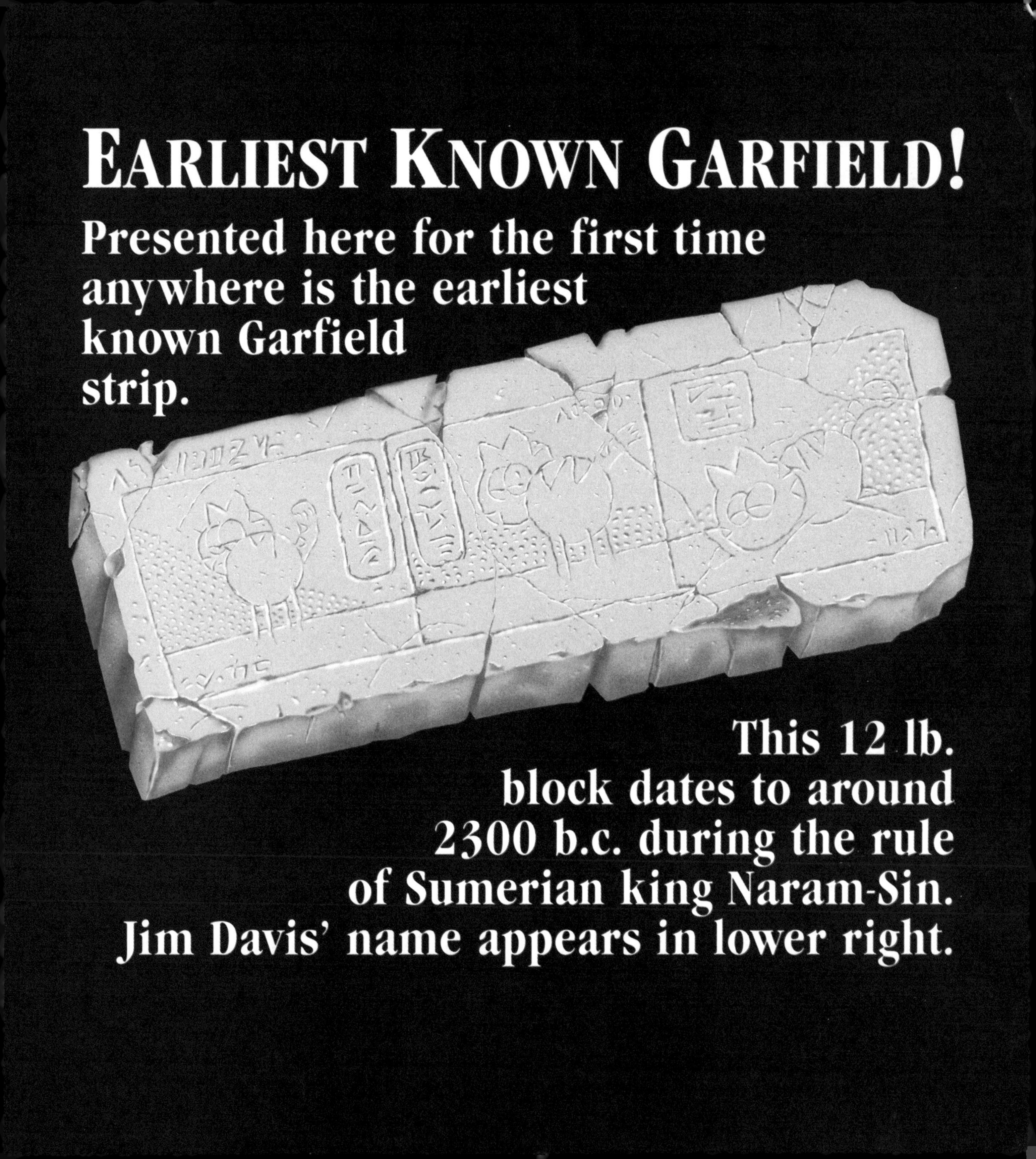

This 12 lb. block dates to around 2300 b.c. during the rule of Sumerian king Naram-Sin. Jim Davis' name appears in lower right.

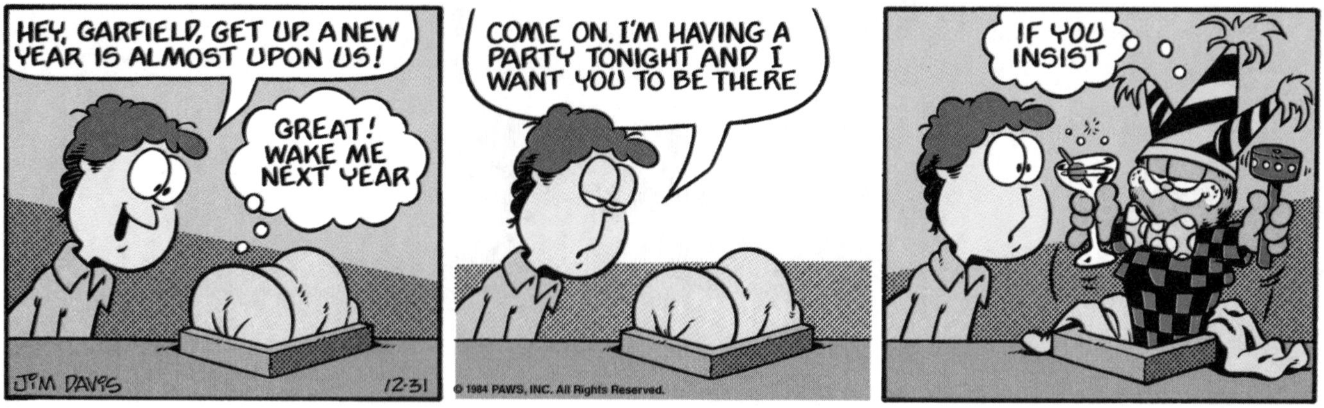
HEY, GARFIELD, GET UP. A NEW YEAR IS ALMOST UPON US!
GREAT! WAKE ME NEXT YEAR
JIM DAVIS 12-31
COME ON. I'M HAVING A PARTY TONIGHT AND I WANT YOU TO BE THERE
© 1984 PAWS, INC. All Rights Reserved.
IF YOU INSIST

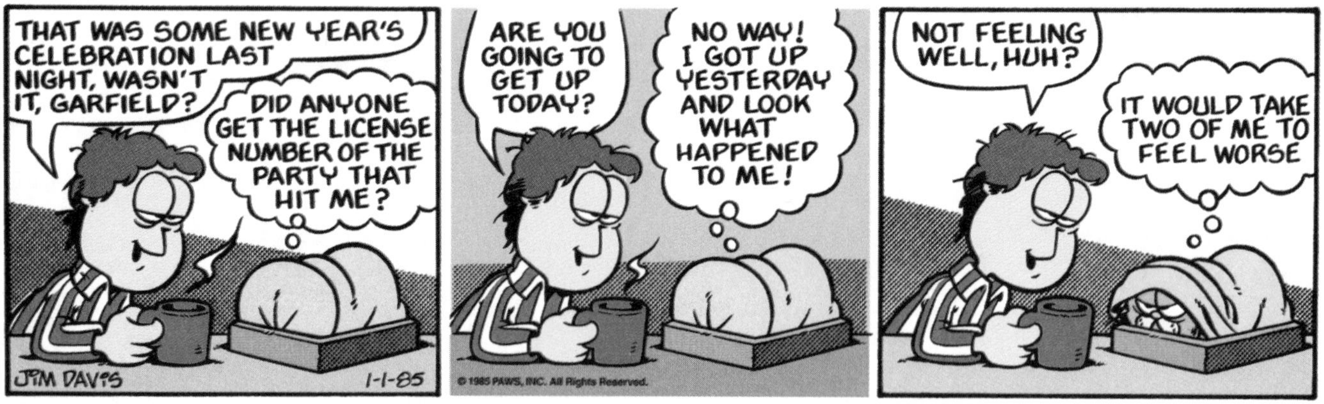
THAT WAS SOME NEW YEAR'S CELEBRATION LAST NIGHT, WASN'T IT, GARFIELD?
DID ANYONE GET THE LICENSE NUMBER OF THE PARTY THAT HIT ME?
JIM DAVIS 1-1-85
ARE YOU GOING TO GET UP TODAY?
NO WAY! I GOT UP YESTERDAY AND LOOK WHAT HAPPENED TO ME!
© 1985 PAWS, INC. All Rights Reserved.
NOT FEELING WELL, HUH?
IT WOULD TAKE TWO OF ME TO FEEL WORSE

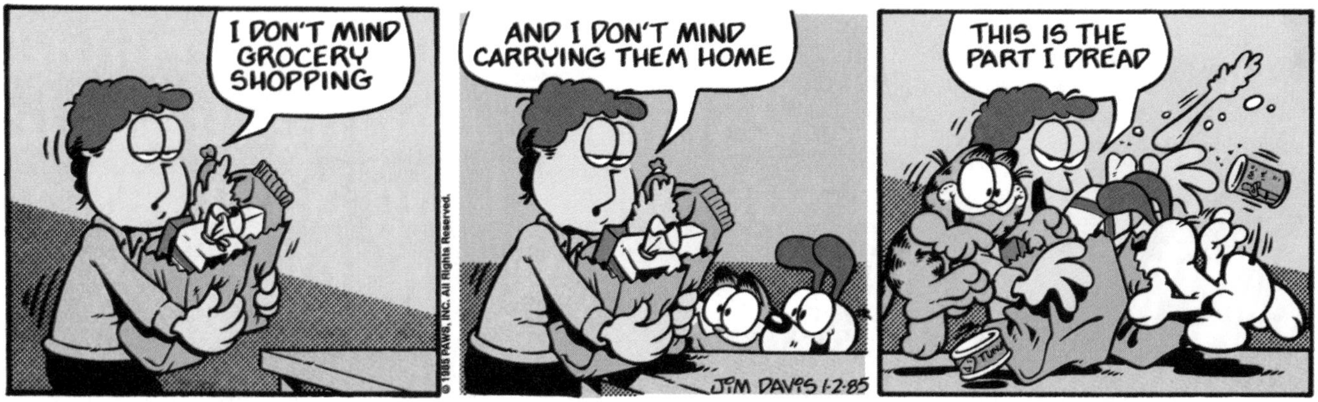
I DON'T MIND GROCERY SHOPPING
© 1985 PAWS, INC. All Rights Reserved.
AND I DON'T MIND CARRYING THEM HOME
JIM DAVIS 1-2-85
THIS IS THE PART I DREAD

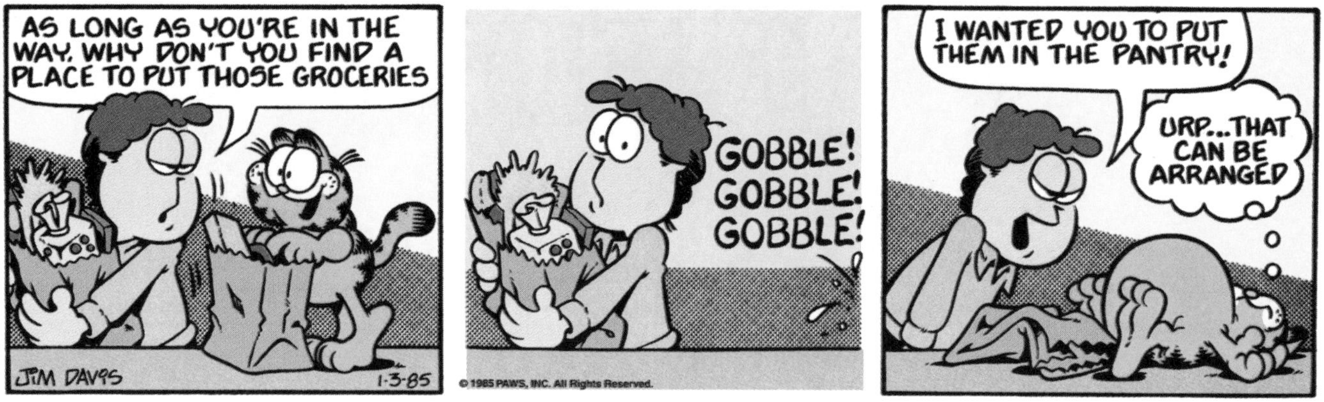
AS LONG AS YOU'RE IN THE WAY, WHY DON'T YOU FIND A PLACE TO PUT THOSE GROCERIES
JIM DAVIS
1-3-85
GOBBLE! GOBBLE! GOBBLE!
© 1985 PAWS, INC. All Rights Reserved.
I WANTED YOU TO PUT THEM IN THE PANTRY!
URP...THAT CAN BE ARRANGED

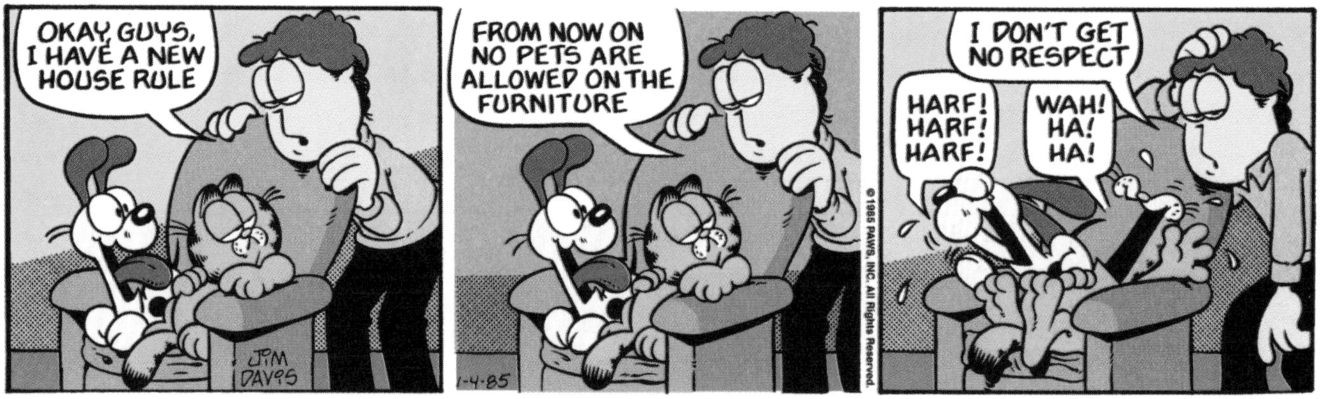
OKAY, GUYS, I HAVE A NEW HOUSE RULE
JIM DAVIS
FROM NOW ON NO PETS ARE ALLOWED ON THE FURNITURE
1-4-85
© 1985 PAWS, INC. All Rights Reserved.
I DON'T GET NO RESPECT
HARF! HARF! HARF!
WAH! HA! HA!

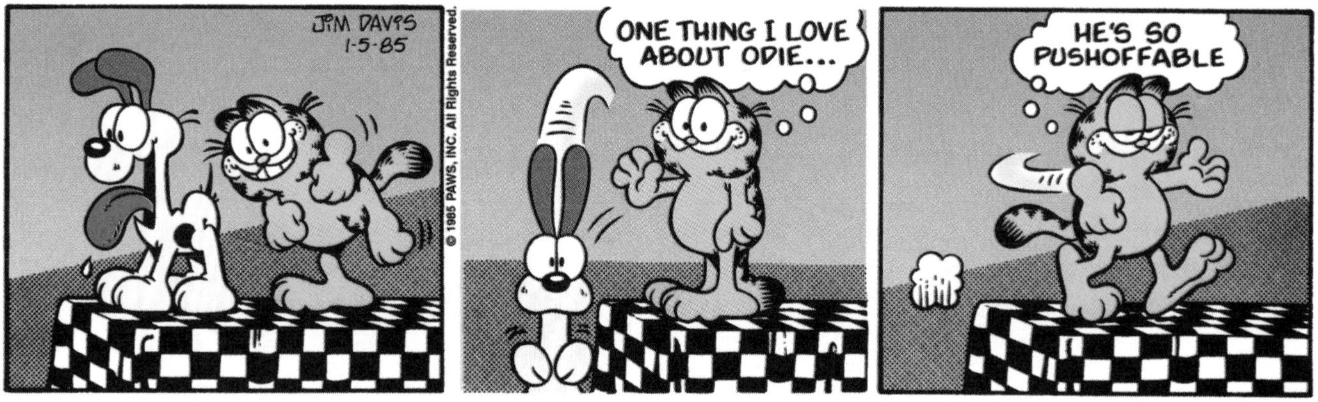
JIM DAVIS
1-5-85
© 1985 PAWS, INC. All Rights Reserved.
ONE THING I LOVE ABOUT ODIE...
HE'S SO PUSHOFFABLE

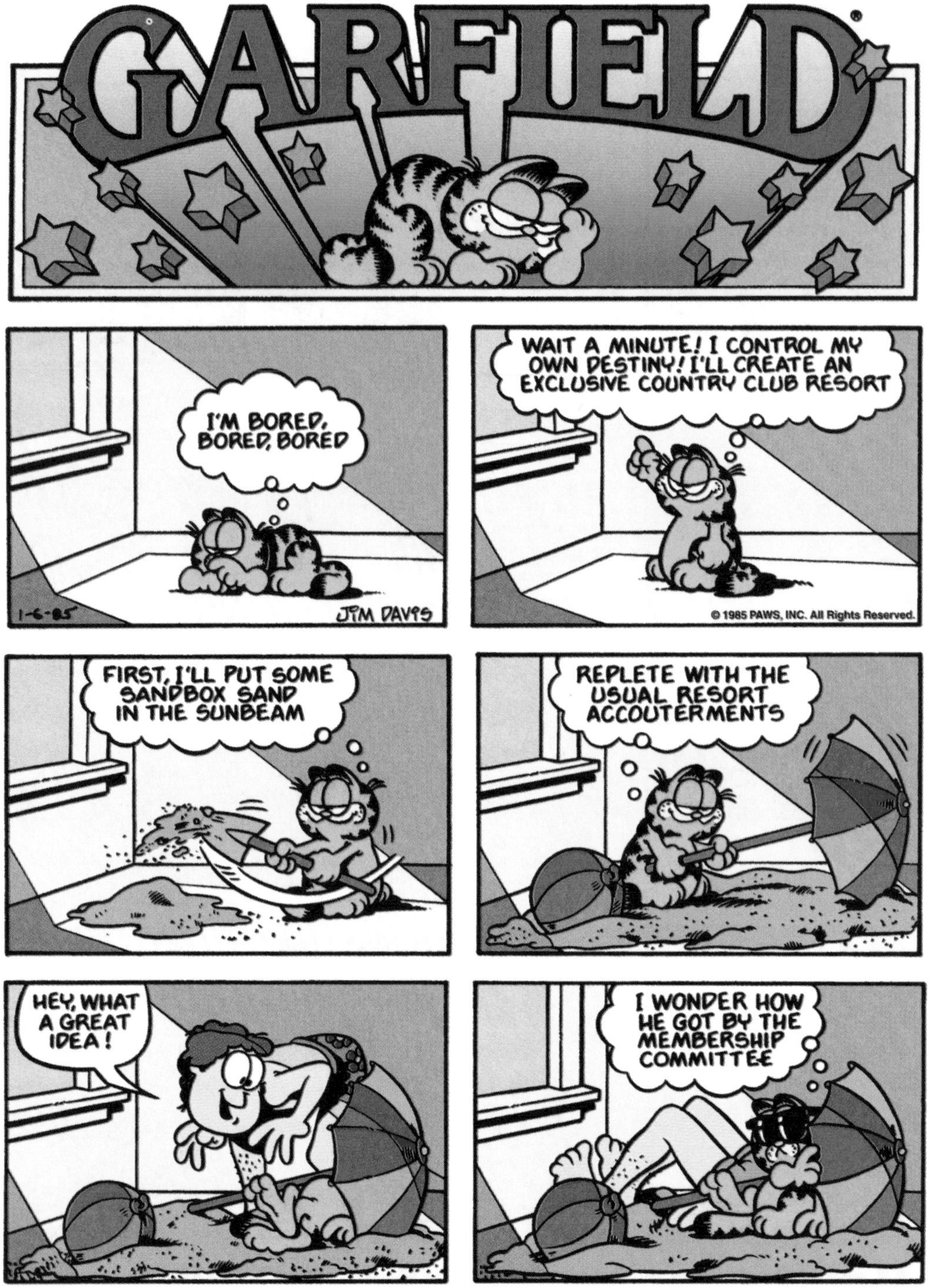
GARFIELD
I'M BORED, BORED, BORED
1-6-85
JIM DAVIS
WAIT A MINUTE! I CONTROL MY OWN DESTINY! I'LL CREATE AN EXCLUSIVE COUNTRY CLUB RESORT
© 1985 PAWS, INC. All Rights Reserved.
FIRST, I'LL PUT SOME SANDBOX SAND IN THE SUNBEAM
REPLETE WITH THE USUAL RESORT ACCOUTERMENTS
HEY, WHAT A GREAT IDEA!
I WONDER HOW HE GOT BY THE MEMBERSHIP COMMITTEE

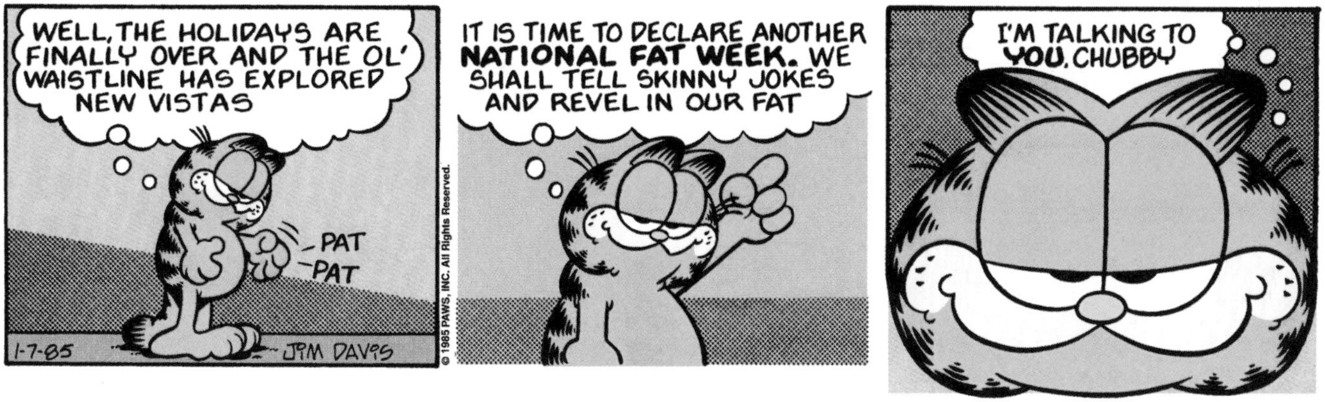
WELL, THE HOLIDAYS ARE FINALLY OVER AND THE OL' WAISTLINE HAS EXPLORED NEW VISTAS
PAT
PAT
1-7-85
JIM DAVIS
© 1985 PAWS, INC. All Rights Reserved.
IT IS TIME TO DECLARE ANOTHER **NATIONAL FAT WEEK.** WE SHALL TELL SKINNY JOKES AND REVEL IN OUR FAT
I'M TALKING TO **YOU**, CHUBBY

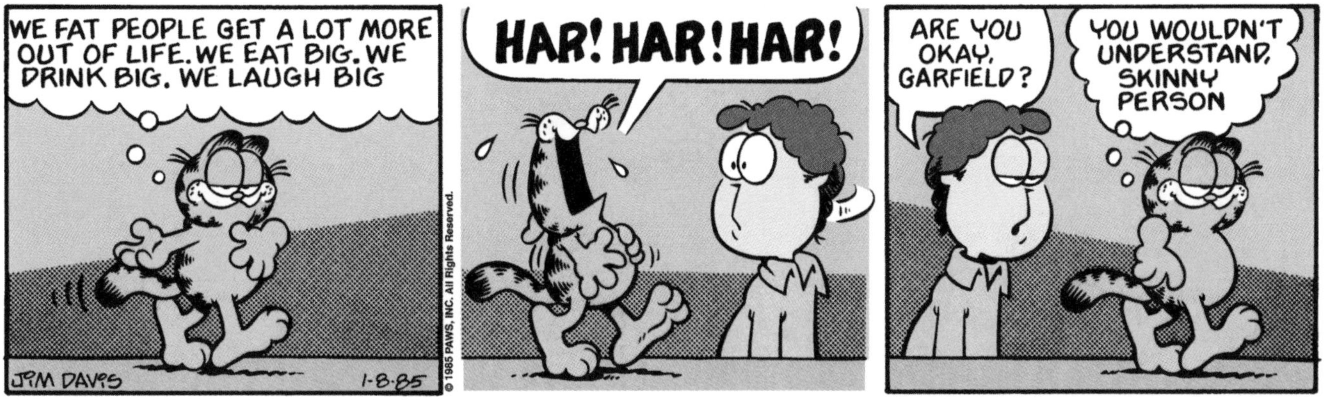
WE FAT PEOPLE GET A LOT MORE OUT OF LIFE. WE EAT BIG. WE DRINK BIG. WE LAUGH BIG
JIM DAVIS
1-8-85
© 1985 PAWS, INC. All Rights Reserved.
HAR! HAR! HAR!
ARE YOU OKAY, GARFIELD?
YOU WOULDN'T UNDERSTAND, SKINNY PERSON

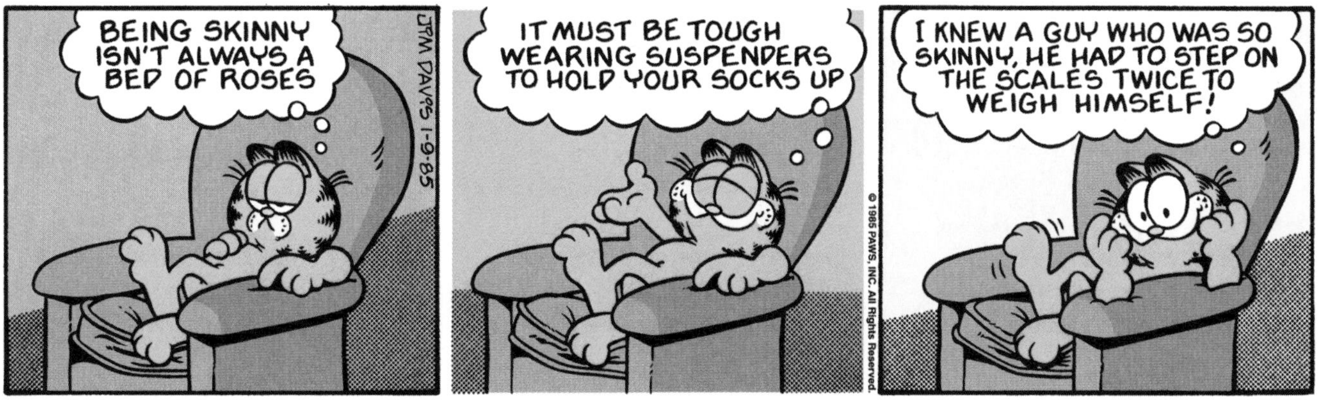
BEING SKINNY ISN'T ALWAYS A BED OF ROSES
JIM DAVIS 1-9-85
IT MUST BE TOUGH WEARING SUSPENDERS TO HOLD YOUR SOCKS UP
© 1985 PAWS, INC. All Rights Reserved.
I KNEW A GUY WHO WAS SO SKINNY, HE HAD TO STEP ON THE SCALES TWICE TO WEIGH HIMSELF!

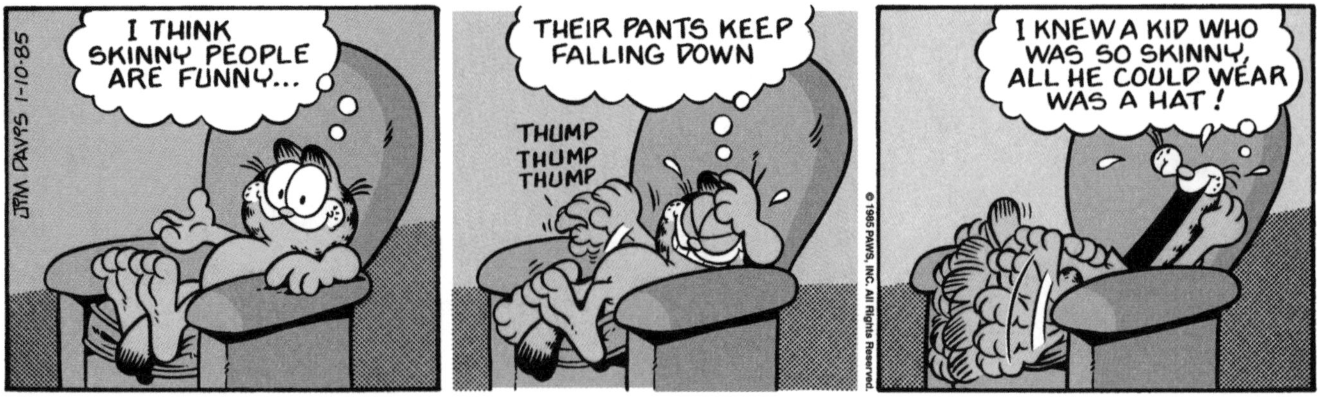
JIM DAVIS 1-10-85
I THINK SKINNY PEOPLE ARE FUNNY...
THEIR PANTS KEEP FALLING DOWN
THUMP THUMP THUMP
I KNEW A KID WHO WAS SO SKINNY, ALL HE COULD WEAR WAS A HAT!
© 1985 PAWS, INC. All Rights Reserved.

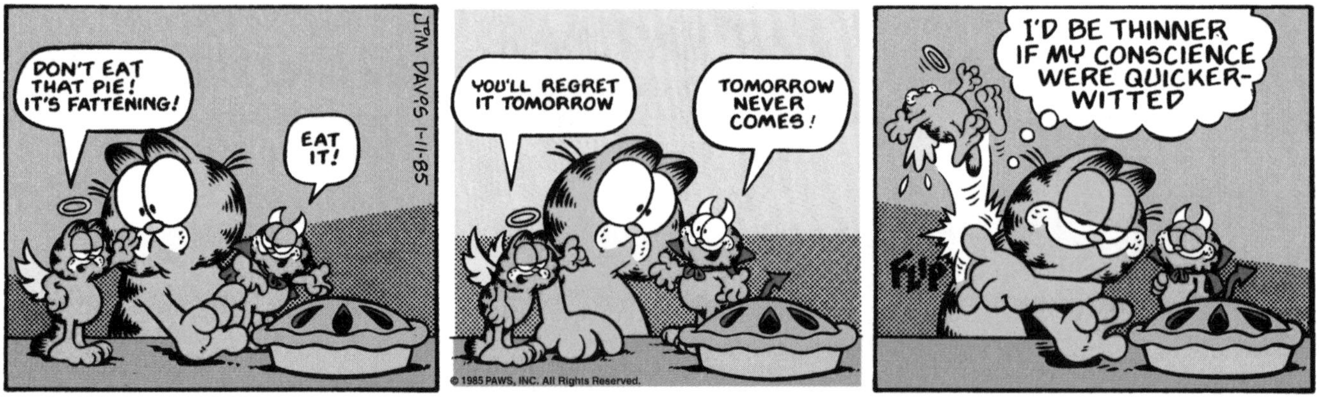
JIM DAVIS 1-11-85
DON'T EAT THAT PIE! IT'S FATTENING!
EAT IT!
YOU'LL REGRET IT TOMORROW
TOMORROW NEVER COMES!
© 1985 PAWS, INC. All Rights Reserved.
FLIP
I'D BE THINNER IF MY CONSCIENCE WERE QUICKER-WITTED

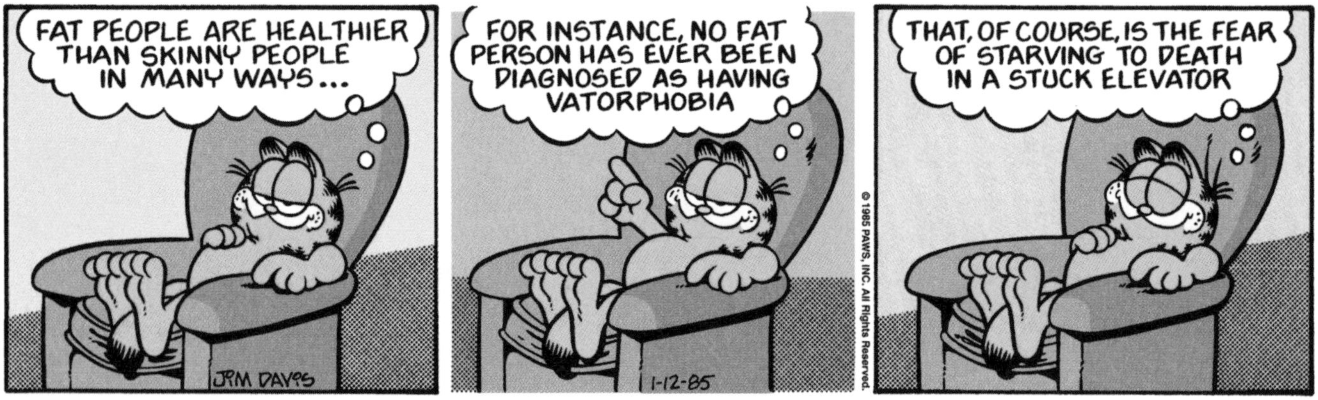
FAT PEOPLE ARE HEALTHIER THAN SKINNY PEOPLE IN MANY WAYS...
JIM DAVIS
FOR INSTANCE, NO FAT PERSON HAS EVER BEEN DIAGNOSED AS HAVING VATORPHOBIA
1-12-85
THAT, OF COURSE, IS THE FEAR OF STARVING TO DEATH IN A STUCK ELEVATOR
© 1985 PAWS, INC. All Rights Reserved.

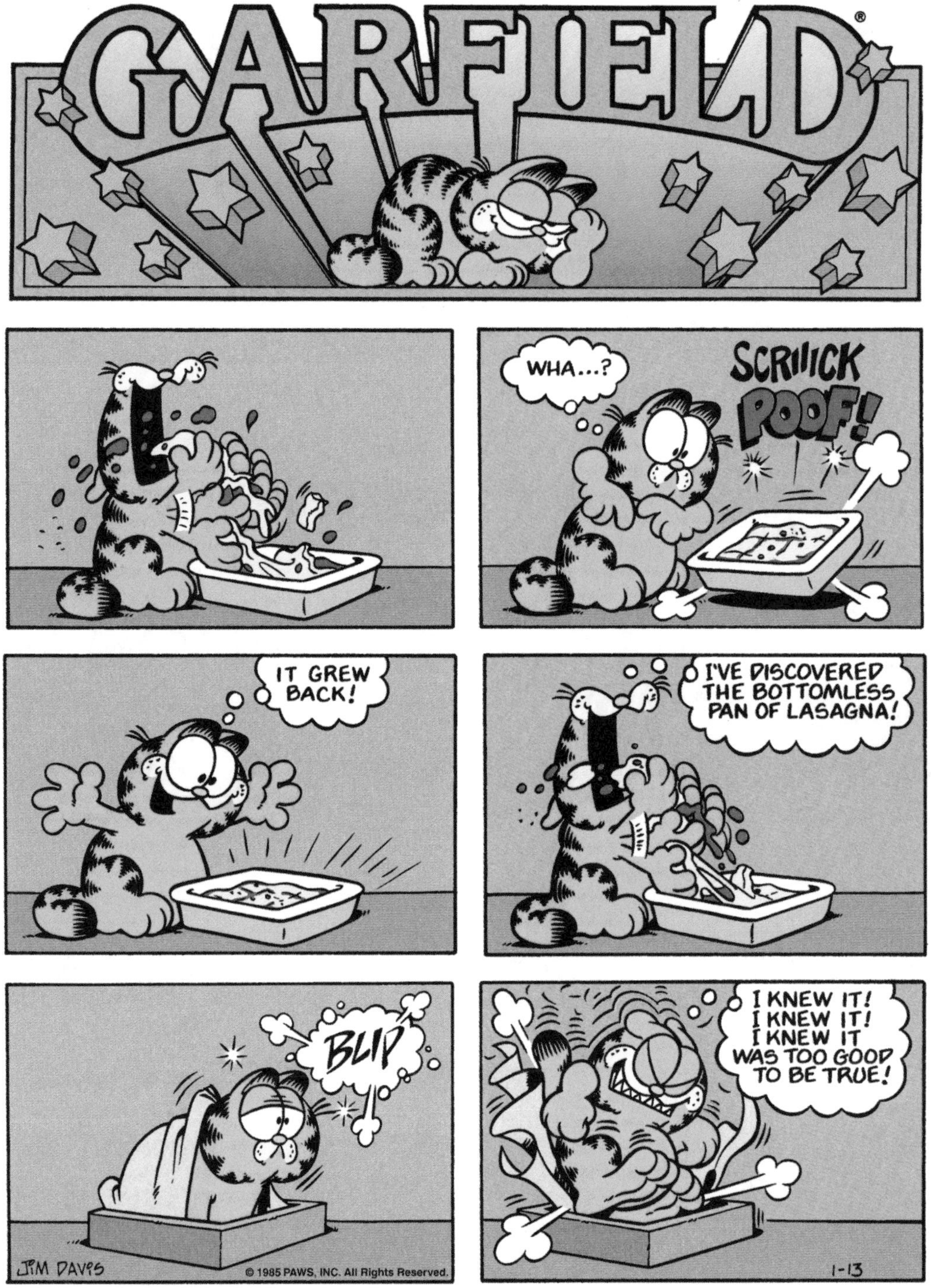
GARFIELD
WHA...?
SCRIIICK
POOF!
IT GREW BACK!
I'VE DISCOVERED THE BOTTOMLESS PAN OF LASAGNA!
BLIP
I KNEW IT! I KNEW IT! I KNEW IT WAS TOO GOOD TO BE TRUE!
JIM DAVIS
© 1985 PAWS, INC. All Rights Reserved.
1-13

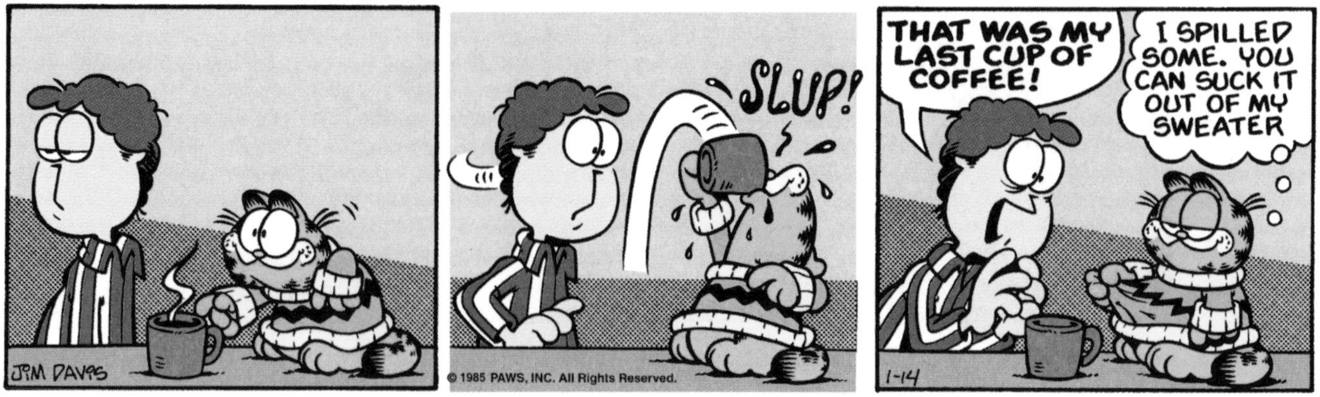
JIM DAVIS
SLUP!
© 1985 PAWS, INC. All Rights Reserved.
THAT WAS MY LAST CUP OF COFFEE!
I SPILLED SOME. YOU CAN SUCK IT OUT OF MY SWEATER
1-14

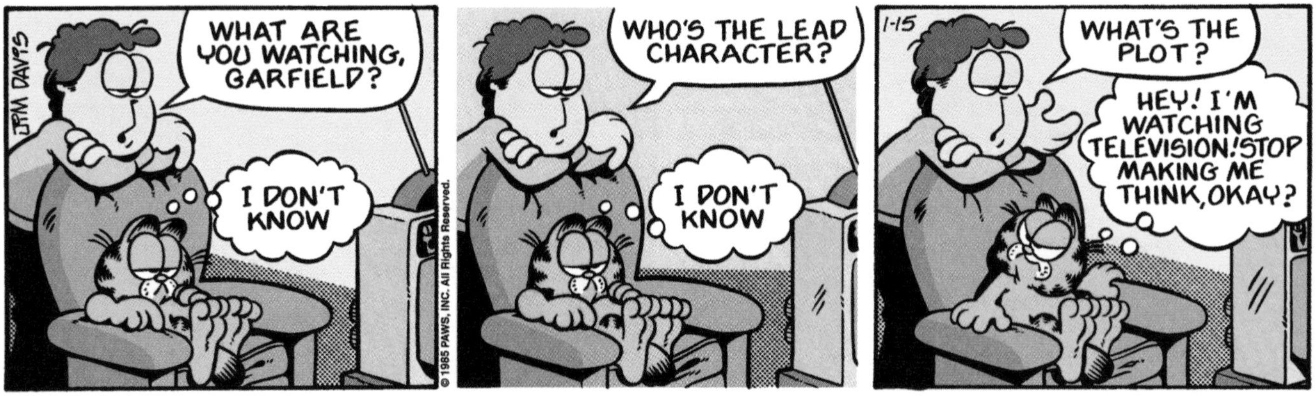
JIM DAVIS
WHAT ARE YOU WATCHING, GARFIELD?
I DON'T KNOW
© 1985 PAWS, INC. All Rights Reserved.
WHO'S THE LEAD CHARACTER?
I DON'T KNOW
1-15
WHAT'S THE PLOT?
HEY! I'M WATCHING TELEVISION! STOP MAKING ME THINK, OKAY?

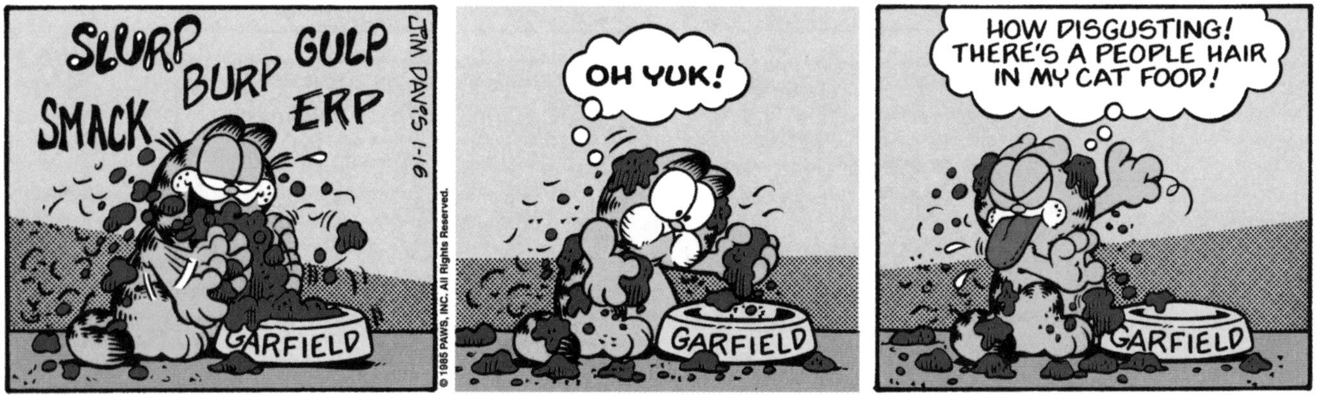
SLURP
BURP
GULP
SMACK
ERP
JIM DAVIS 1-16
GARFIELD
© 1985 PAWS, INC. All Rights Reserved.
OH YUK!
GARFIELD
HOW DISGUSTING! THERE'S A PEOPLE HAIR IN MY CAT FOOD!
GARFIELD

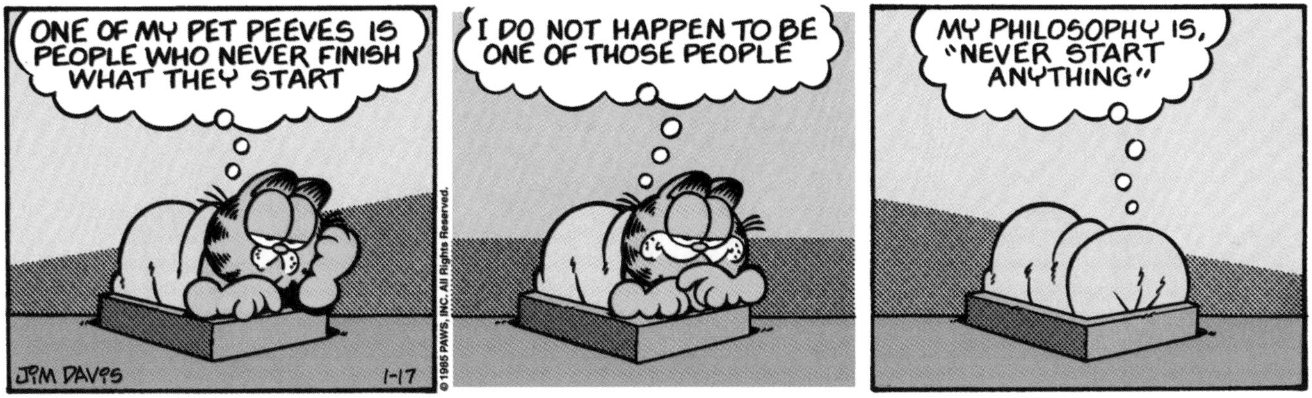
ONE OF MY PET PEEVES IS PEOPLE WHO NEVER FINISH WHAT THEY START
JIM DAVIS
1-17
© 1985 PAWS, INC. All Rights Reserved.
I DO NOT HAPPEN TO BE ONE OF THOSE PEOPLE
MY PHILOSOPHY IS, "NEVER START ANYTHING"

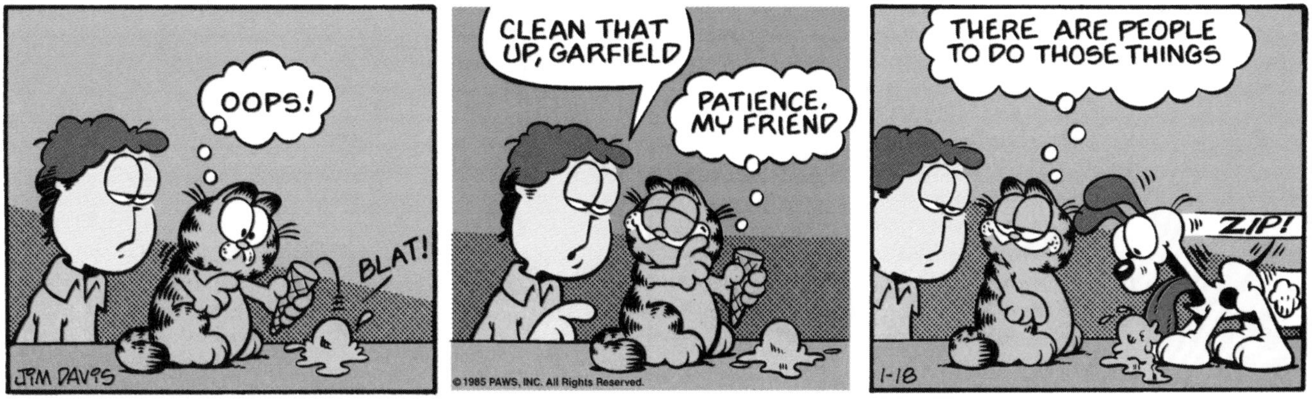
OOPS!
BLAT!
JIM DAVIS
CLEAN THAT UP, GARFIELD
PATIENCE, MY FRIEND
© 1985 PAWS, INC. All Rights Reserved.
THERE ARE PEOPLE TO DO THOSE THINGS
ZIP!
1-18

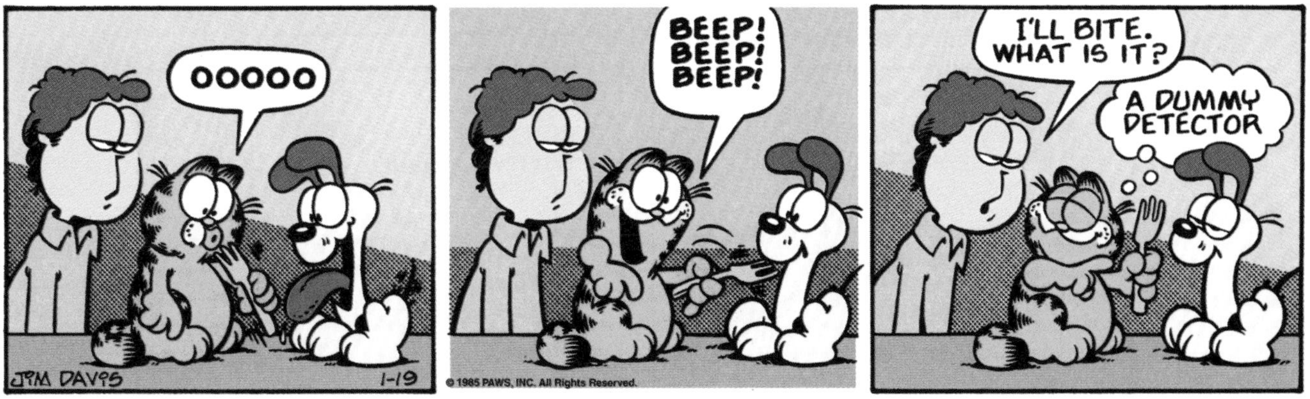
OOOOO
JIM DAVIS
1-19
BEEP! BEEP! BEEP!
© 1985 PAWS, INC. All Rights Reserved.
I'LL BITE. WHAT IS IT?
A DUMMY DETECTOR

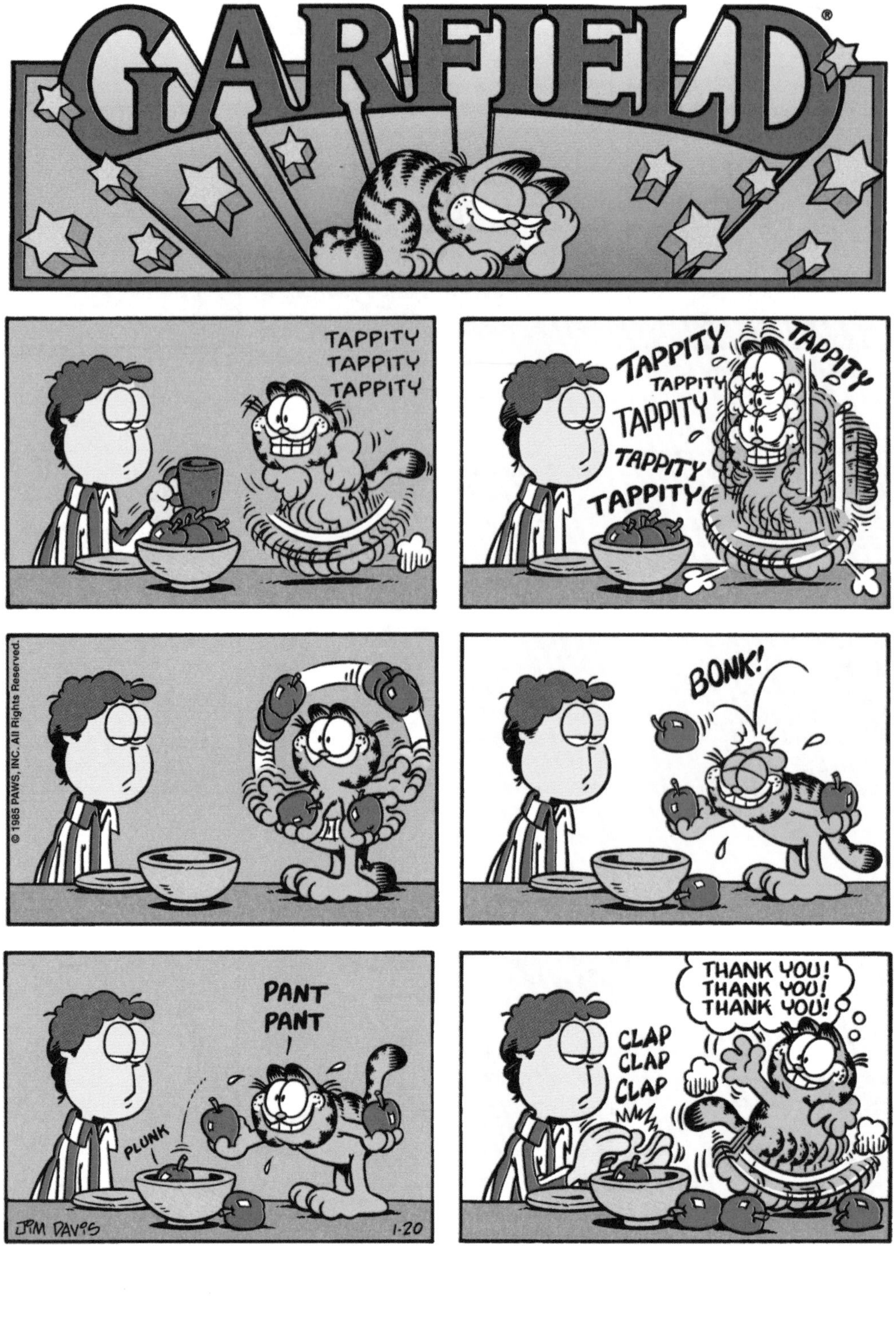

GARFIELD®
TAPPITY
TAPPITY
TAPPITY
TAPPITY
TAPPITY
TAPPITY
TAPPITY
TAPPITY
TAPPITY
© 1985 PAWS, INC. All Rights Reserved.
BONK!
PANT
PANT
PLUNK
JIM DAVIS
1-20
THANK YOU!
THANK YOU!
THANK YOU!
CLAP
CLAP
CLAP

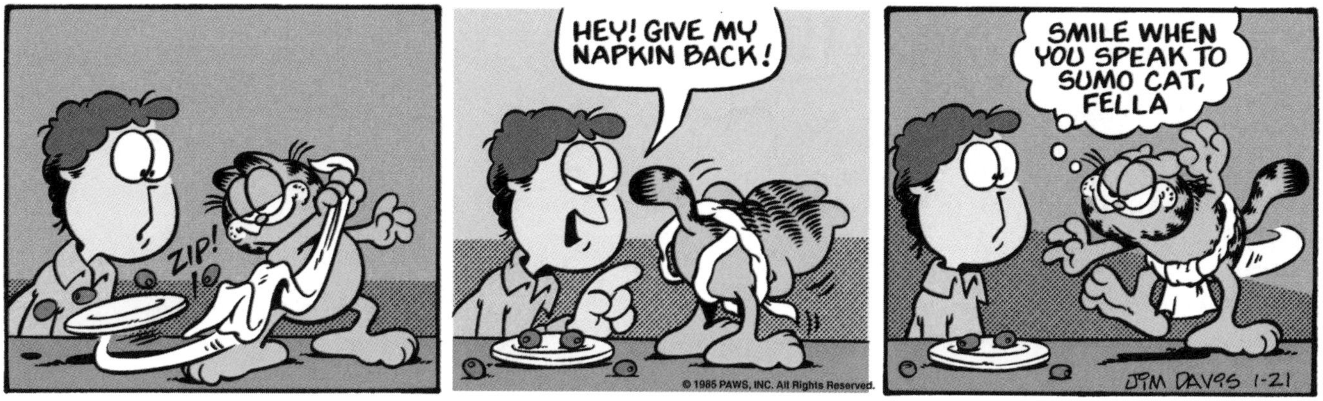
ZIP!
HEY! GIVE MY NAPKIN BACK!
SMILE WHEN YOU SPEAK TO SUMO CAT, FELLA
JIM DAVIS 1-21

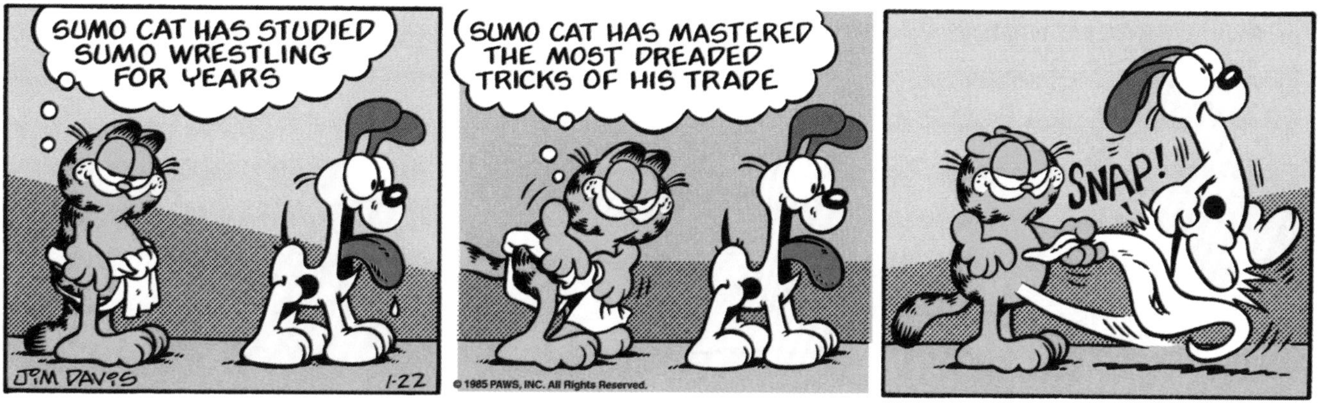
SUMO CAT HAS STUDIED SUMO WRESTLING FOR YEARS
JIM DAVIS 1-22
SUMO CAT HAS MASTERED THE MOST DREADED TRICKS OF HIS TRADE
SNAP!

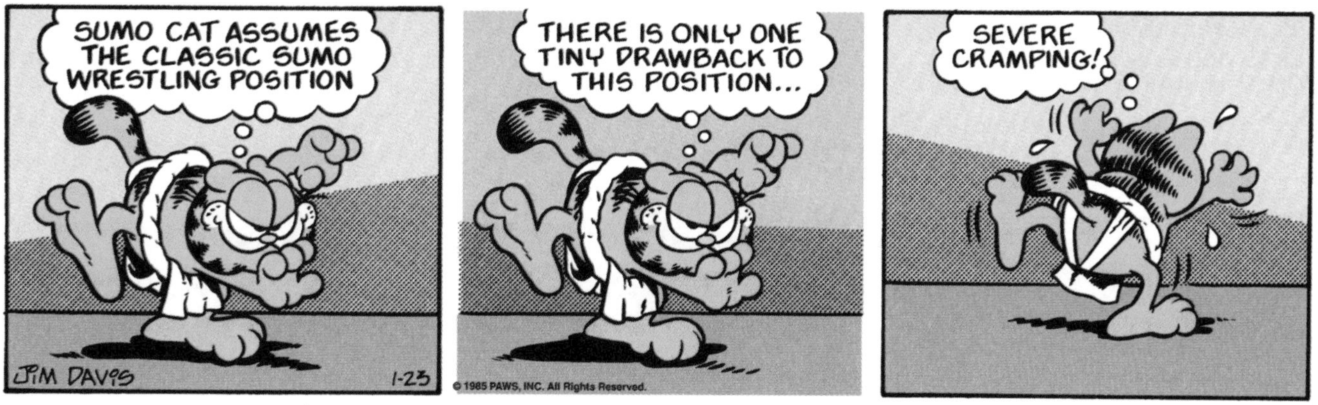
SUMO CAT ASSUMES THE CLASSIC SUMO WRESTLING POSITION
JIM DAVIS 1-23
THERE IS ONLY ONE TINY DRAWBACK TO THIS POSITION...
SEVERE CRAMPING!

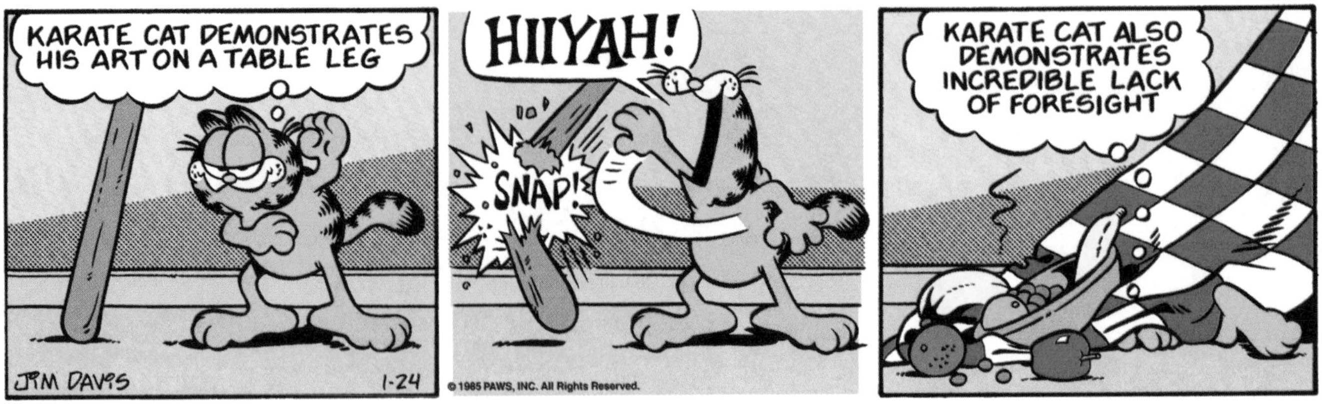
KARATE CAT DEMONSTRATES HIS ART ON A TABLE LEG
JIM DAVIS
1-24
HIIYAH!
SNAP!
© 1985 PAWS, INC. All Rights Reserved.
KARATE CAT ALSO DEMONSTRATES INCREDIBLE LACK OF FORESIGHT

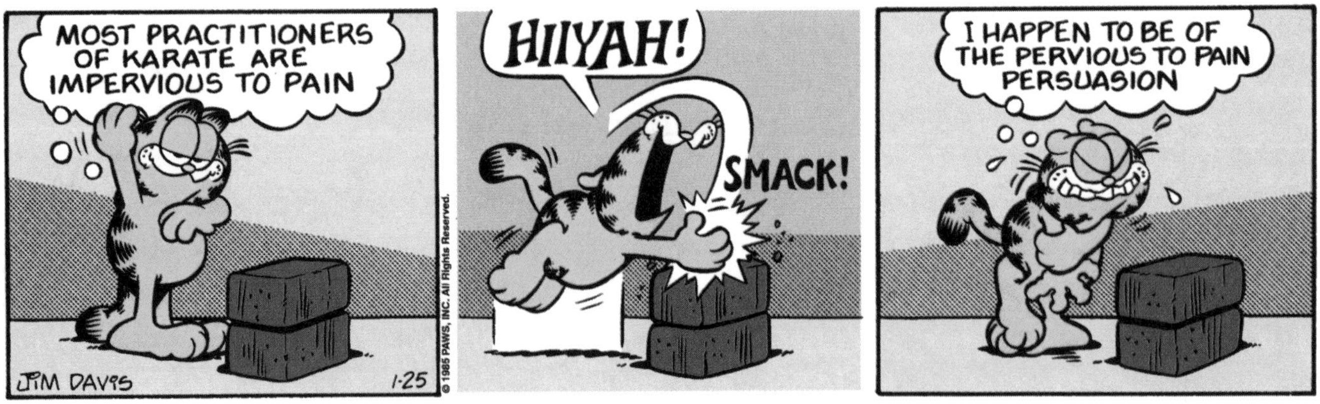
MOST PRACTITIONERS OF KARATE ARE IMPERVIOUS TO PAIN
JIM DAVIS
1-25
© 1985 PAWS, INC. All Rights Reserved.
HIIYAH!
SMACK!
I HAPPEN TO BE OF THE PERVIOUS TO PAIN PERSUASION

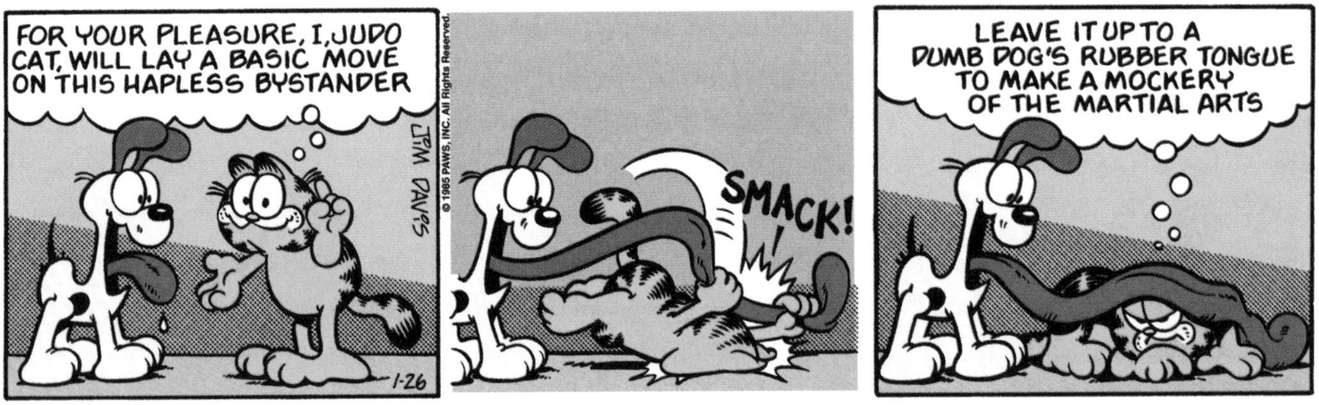
FOR YOUR PLEASURE, I, JUDO CAT, WILL LAY A BASIC MOVE ON THIS HAPLESS BYSTANDER
JIM DAVIS
1-26
© 1985 PAWS, INC. All Rights Reserved.
SMACK!
LEAVE IT UP TO A DUMB DOG'S RUBBER TONGUE TO MAKE A MOCKERY OF THE MARTIAL ARTS

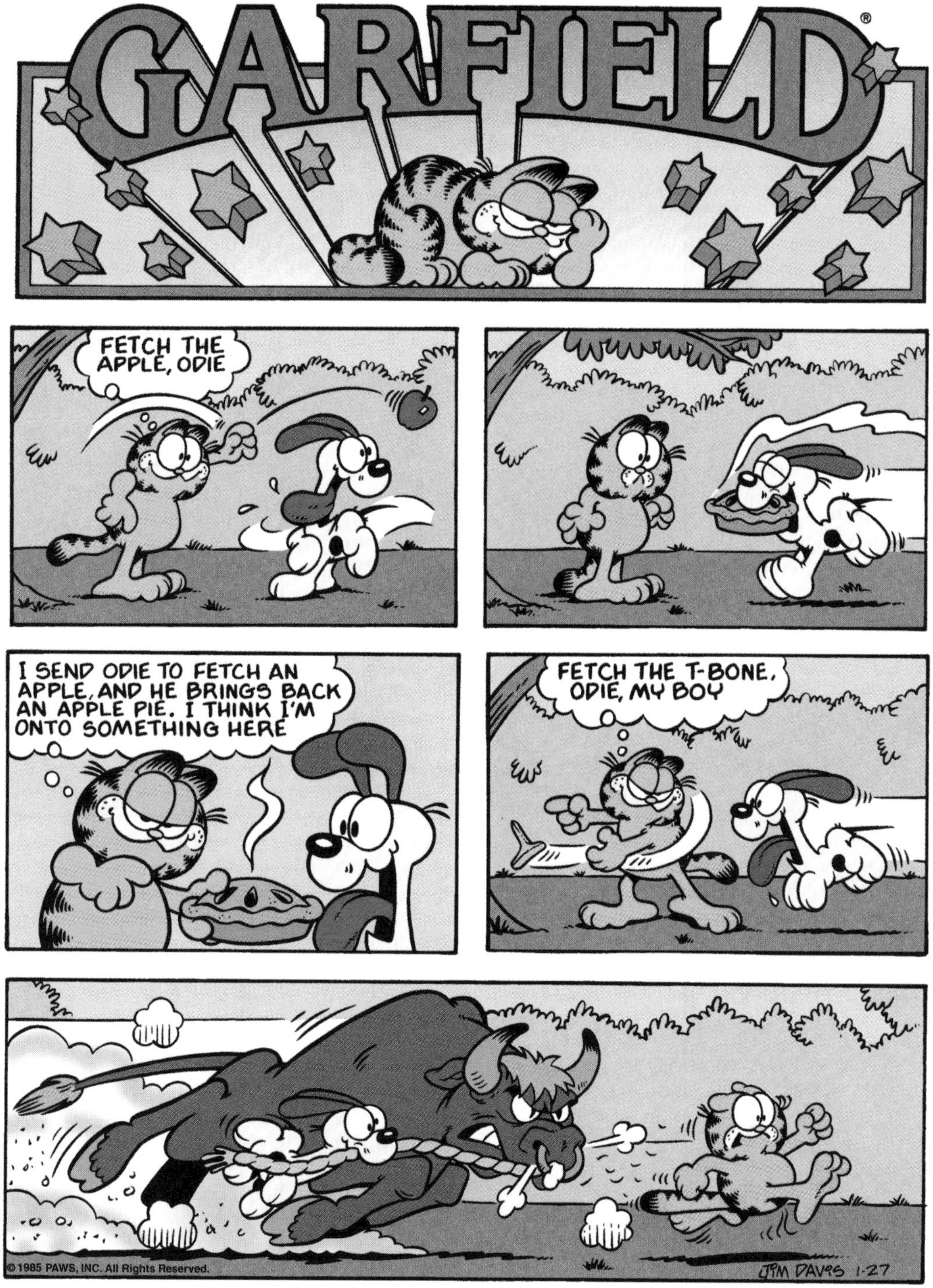
GARFIELD®
FETCH THE APPLE, ODIE
I SEND ODIE TO FETCH AN APPLE, AND HE BRINGS BACK AN APPLE PIE. I THINK I'M ONTO SOMETHING HERE
FETCH THE T-BONE, ODIE, MY BOY
© 1985 PAWS, INC. All Rights Reserved.
JIM DAVIS 1-27

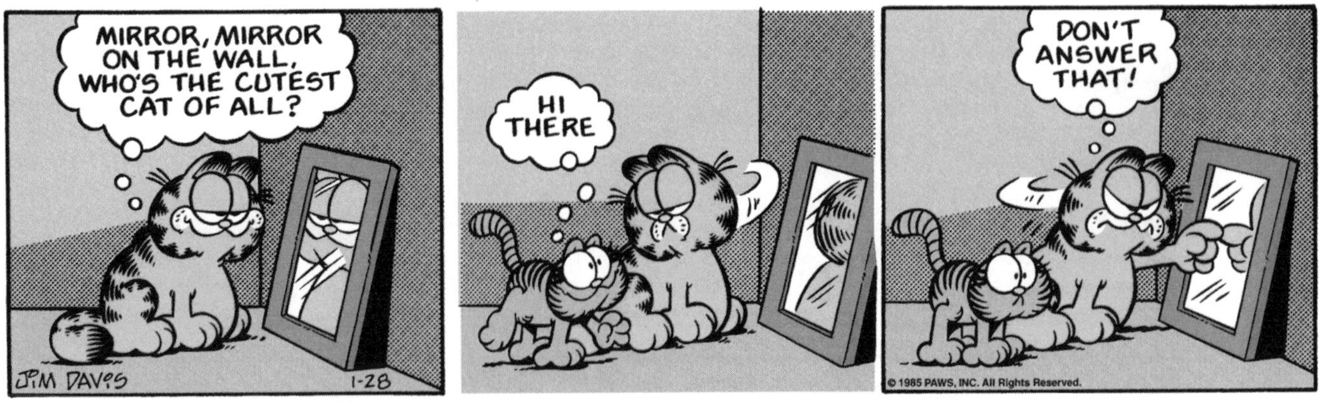
MIRROR, MIRROR ON THE WALL, WHO'S THE CUTEST CAT OF ALL?
JIM DAVIS
1-28
HI THERE
DON'T ANSWER THAT!
© 1985 PAWS, INC. All Rights Reserved.

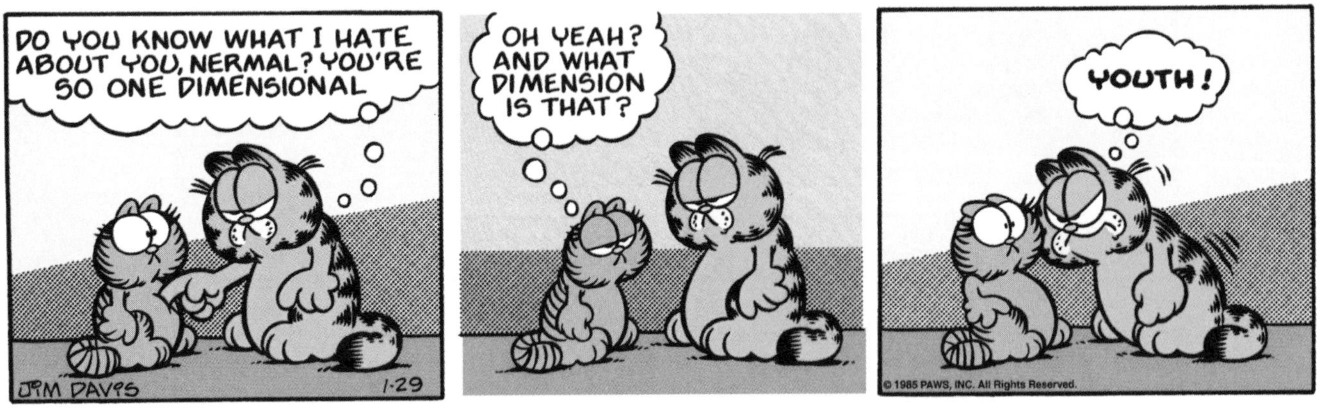
DO YOU KNOW WHAT I HATE ABOUT YOU, NERMAL? YOU'RE SO ONE DIMENSIONAL
JIM DAVIS
1-29
OH YEAH? AND WHAT DIMENSION IS THAT?
YOUTH!
© 1985 PAWS, INC. All Rights Reserved.

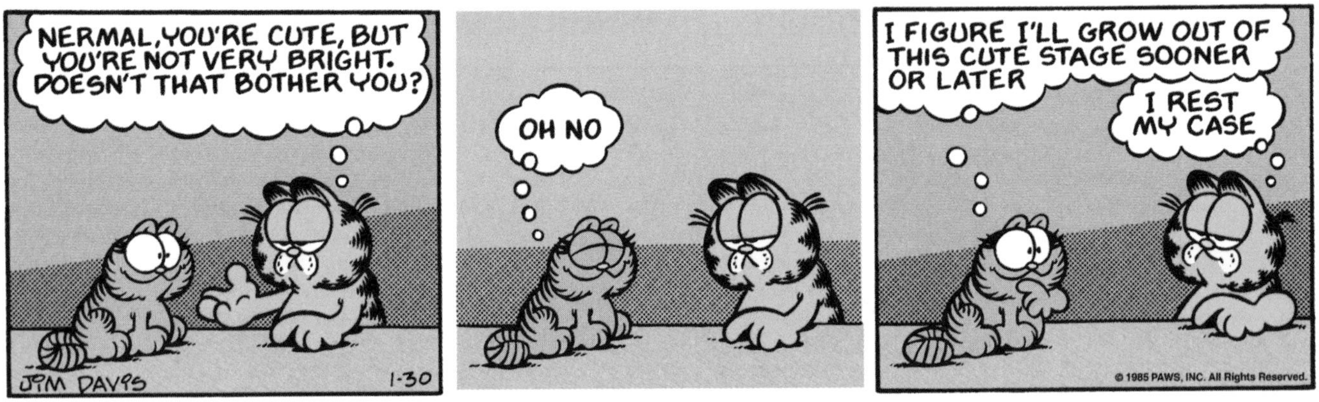
NERMAL, YOU'RE CUTE, BUT YOU'RE NOT VERY BRIGHT. DOESN'T THAT BOTHER YOU?
JIM DAVIS
1-30
OH NO
I FIGURE I'LL GROW OUT OF THIS CUTE STAGE SOONER OR LATER
I REST MY CASE
© 1985 PAWS, INC. All Rights Reserved.

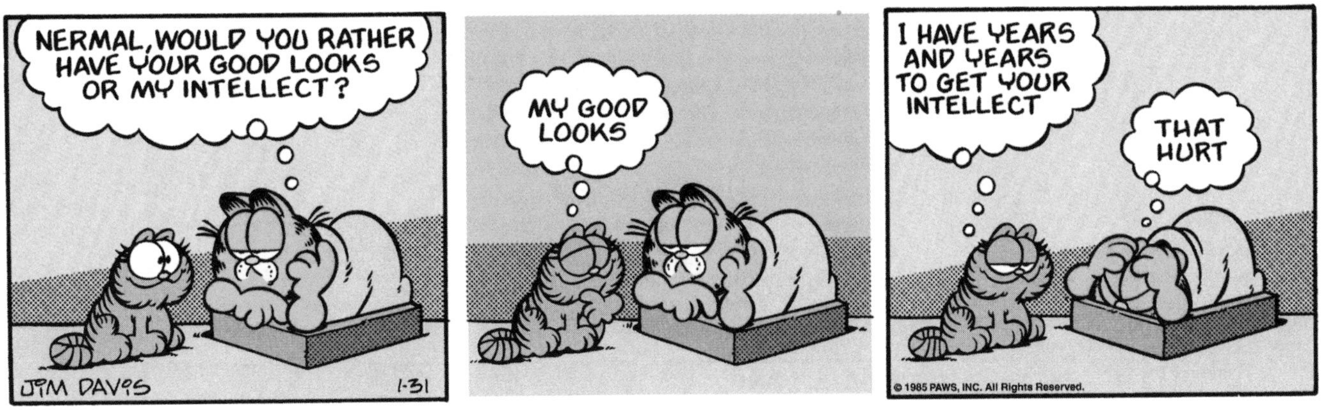
NERMAL, WOULD YOU RATHER HAVE YOUR GOOD LOOKS OR MY INTELLECT?
JIM DAVIS
1-31
MY GOOD LOOKS
I HAVE YEARS AND YEARS TO GET YOUR INTELLECT
THAT HURT
© 1985 PAWS, INC. All Rights Reserved.

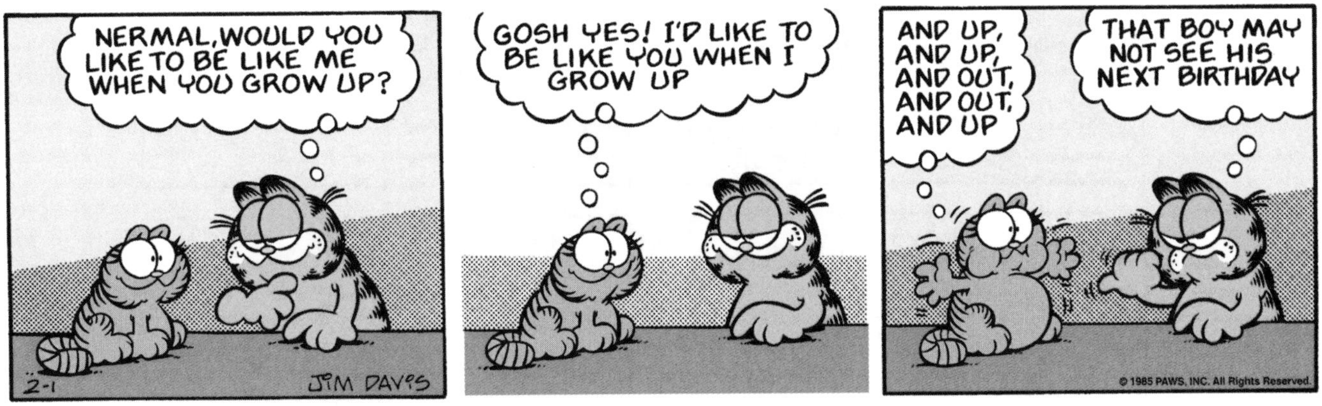
NERMAL, WOULD YOU LIKE TO BE LIKE ME WHEN YOU GROW UP?
2-1
JIM DAVIS
GOSH YES! I'D LIKE TO BE LIKE YOU WHEN I GROW UP
AND UP, AND UP, AND OUT, AND OUT, AND UP
THAT BOY MAY NOT SEE HIS NEXT BIRTHDAY
© 1985 PAWS, INC. All Rights Reserved.

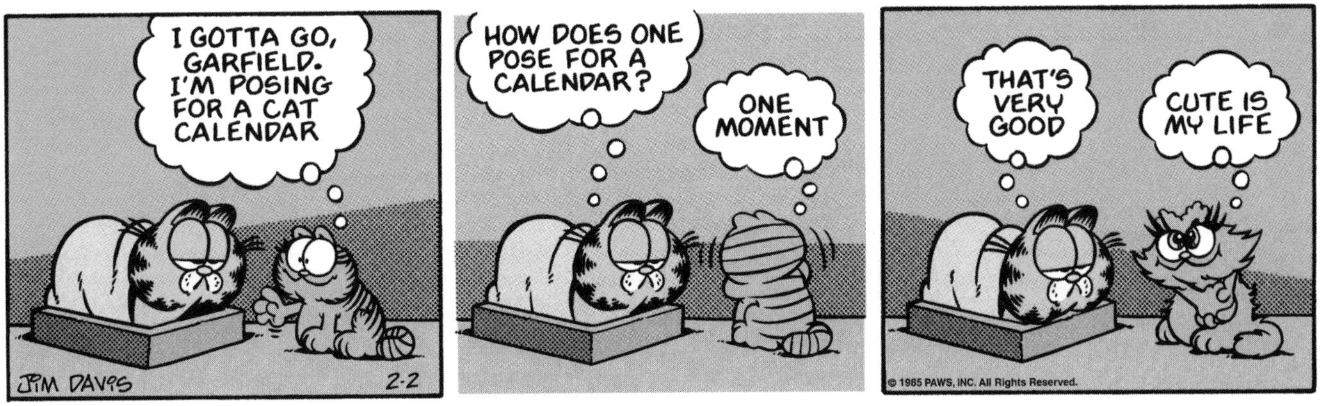
I GOTTA GO, GARFIELD. I'M POSING FOR A CAT CALENDAR
JIM DAVIS
2-2
HOW DOES ONE POSE FOR A CALENDAR?
ONE MOMENT
THAT'S VERY GOOD
CUTE IS MY LIFE
© 1985 PAWS, INC. All Rights Reserved.

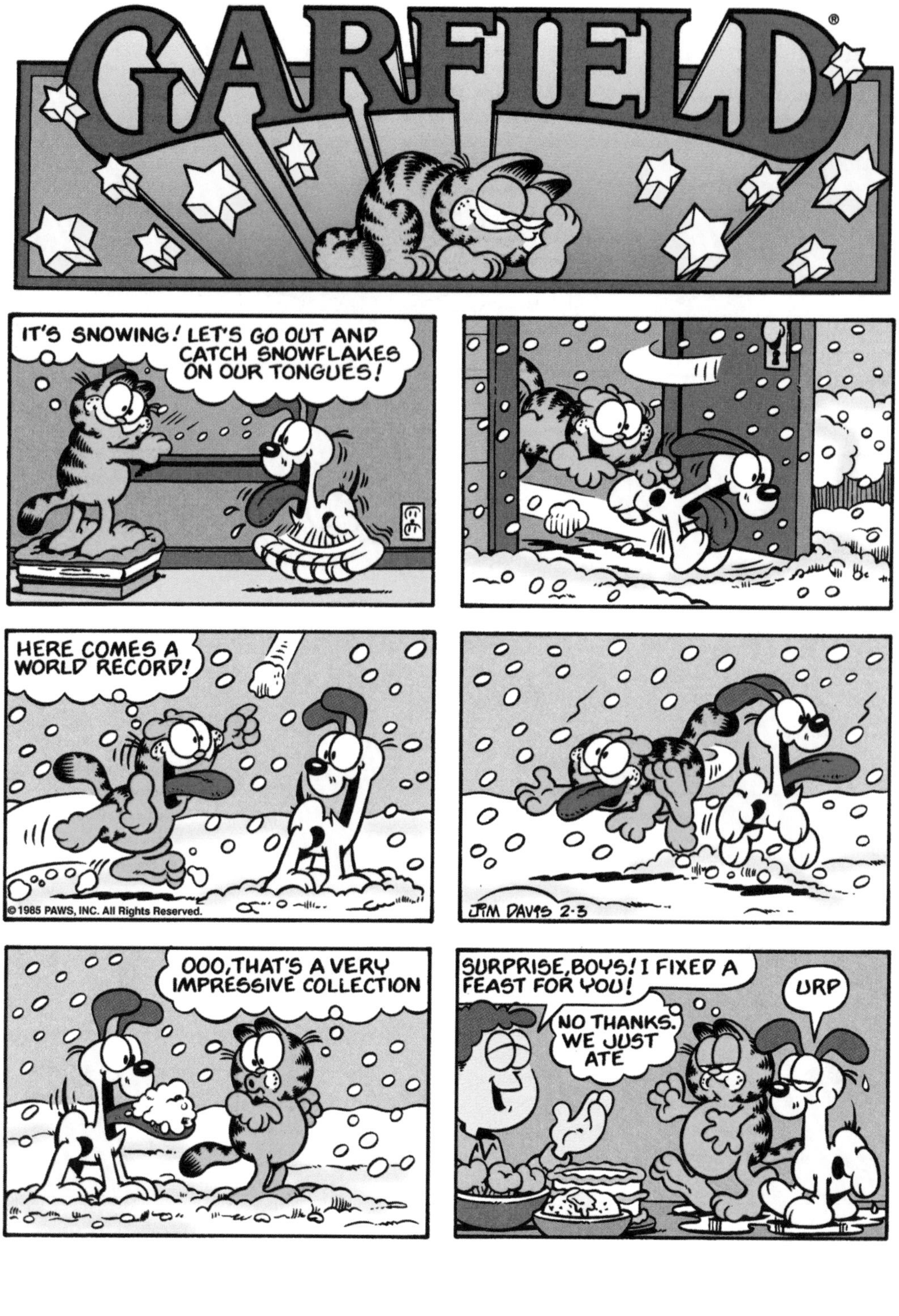
GARFIELD®
IT'S SNOWING! LET'S GO OUT AND CATCH SNOWFLAKES ON OUR TONGUES!
HERE COMES A WORLD RECORD!
© 1985 PAWS, INC. All Rights Reserved.
JIM DAVIS 2-3
OOO, THAT'S A VERY IMPRESSIVE COLLECTION
SURPRISE, BOYS! I FIXED A FEAST FOR YOU!
NO THANKS. WE JUST ATE
URP

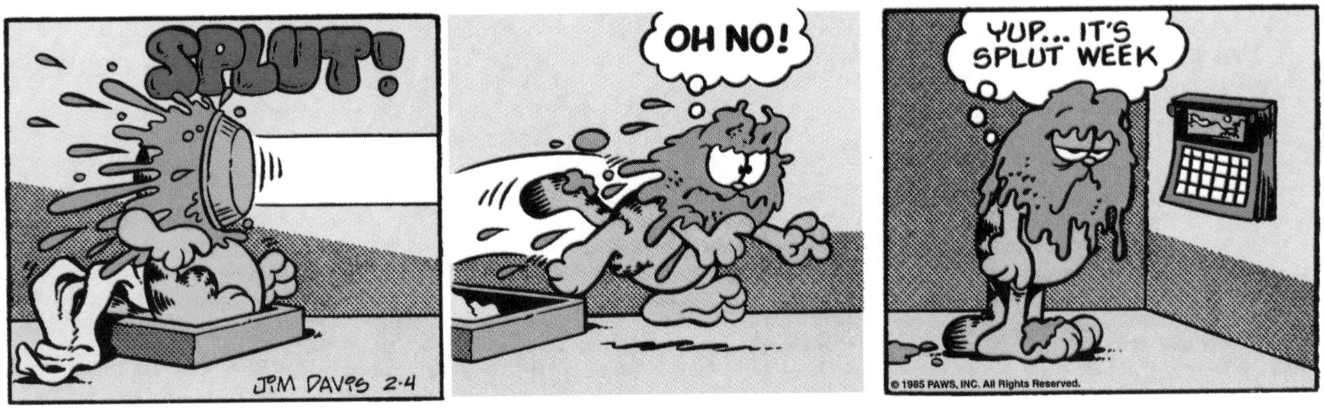
SPLUT!
JIM DAVIS 2-4
OH NO!
YUP... IT'S SPLUT WEEK
© 1985 PAWS, INC. All Rights Reserved.

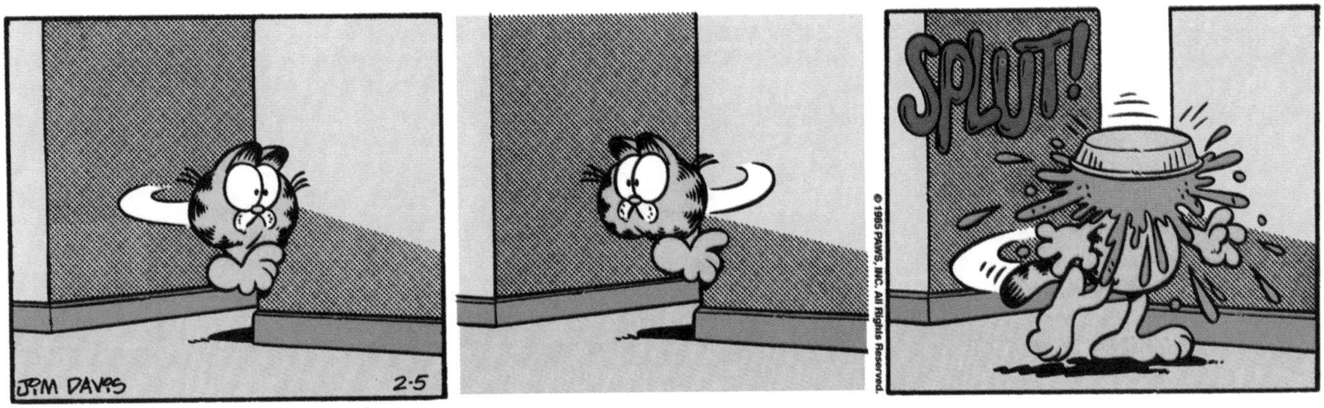
JIM DAVIS 2-5
© 1985 PAWS, INC. All Rights Reserved.
SPLUT!

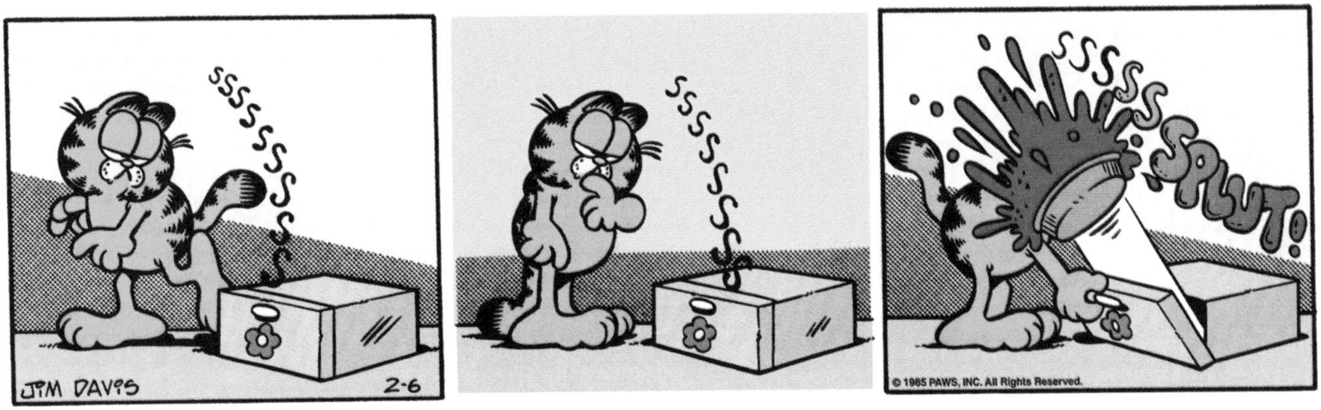
SSSSSSSS
JIM DAVIS 2-6
SSSSSSS
SSSSS
SPLUT!
© 1985 PAWS, INC. All Rights Reserved.

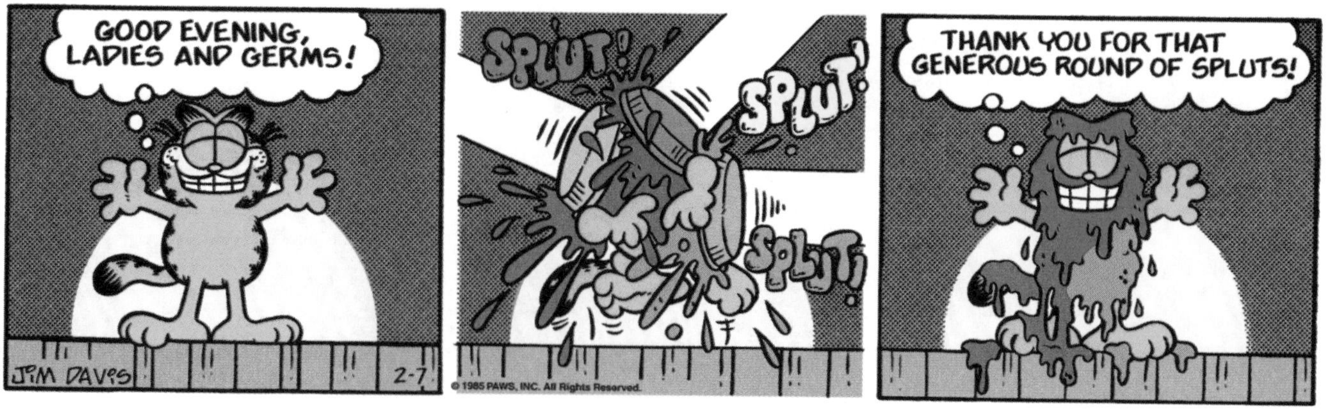
GOOD EVENING, LADIES AND GERMS!
JIM DAVIS
2-7
SPLUT!
SPLUT!
SPLUT!
© 1985 PAWS, INC. All Rights Reserved.
THANK YOU FOR THAT GENEROUS ROUND OF SPLUTS!

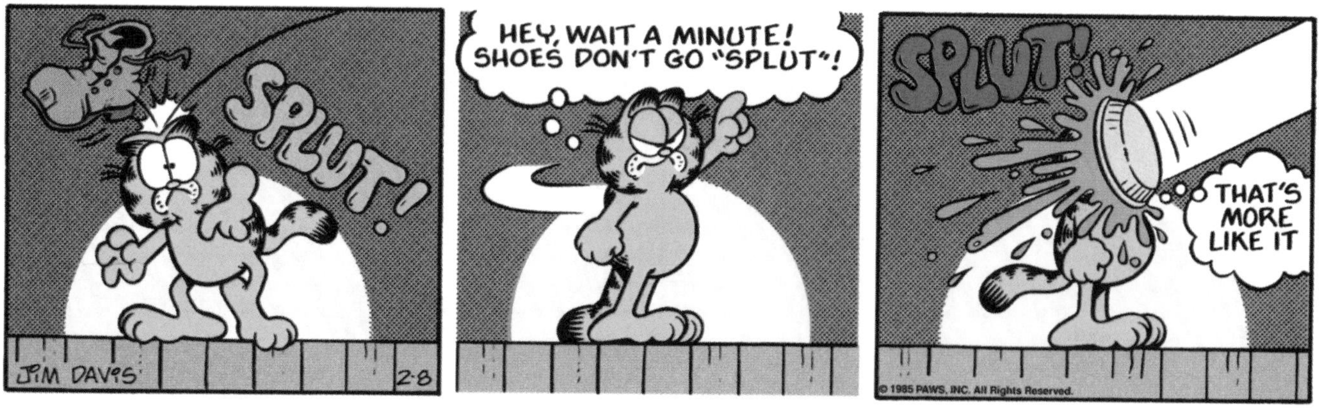
SPLUT!
JIM DAVIS
2-8
HEY, WAIT A MINUTE! SHOES DON'T GO "SPLUT"!
SPLUT!
THAT'S MORE LIKE IT
© 1985 PAWS, INC. All Rights Reserved.

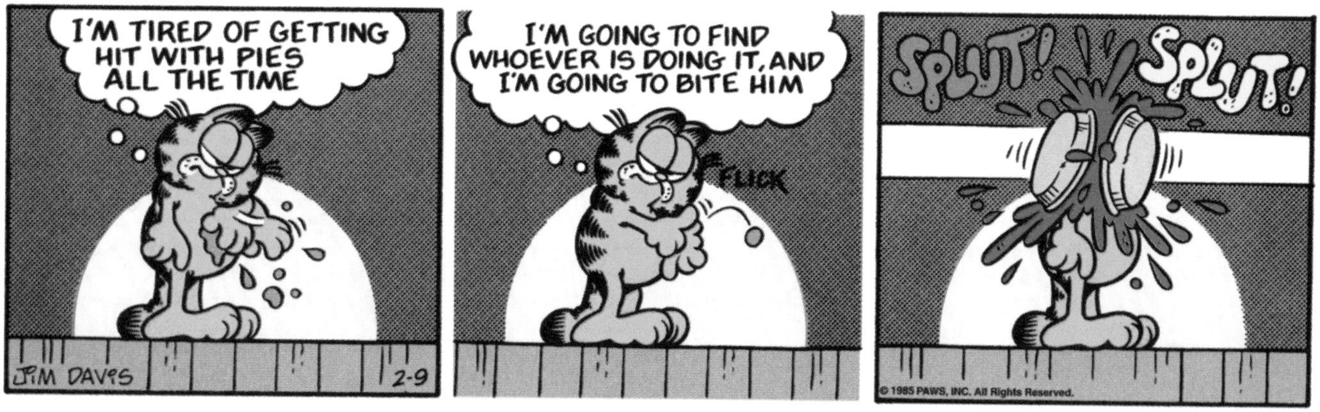
I'M TIRED OF GETTING HIT WITH PIES ALL THE TIME
JIM DAVIS
2-9
I'M GOING TO FIND WHOEVER IS DOING IT, AND I'M GOING TO BITE HIM
FLICK
SPLUT!
SPLUT!
© 1985 PAWS, INC. All Rights Reserved.

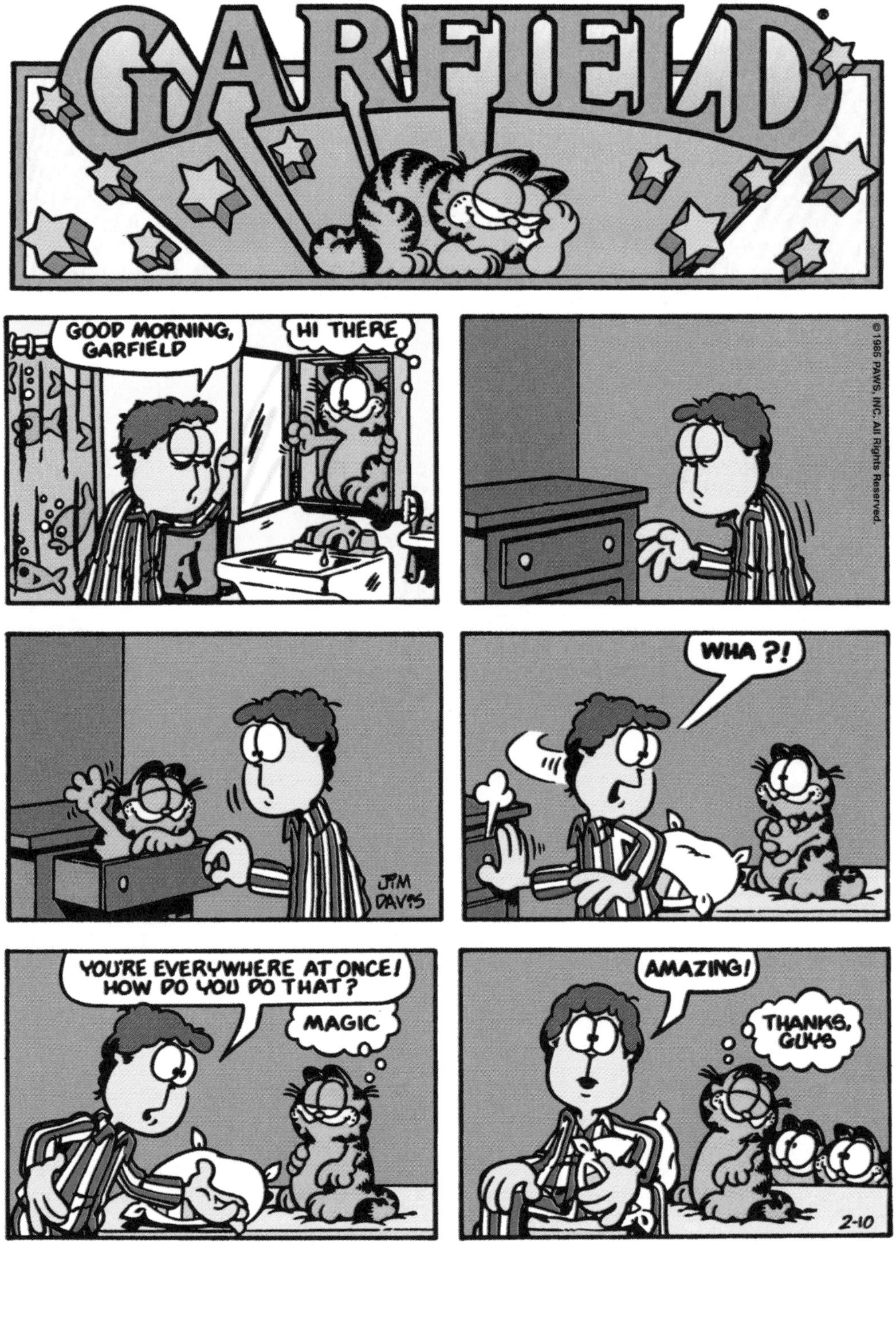
GARFIELD
GOOD MORNING, GARFIELD
HI THERE
© 1985 PAWS, INC. All Rights Reserved.
JIM DAVIS
WHA ?!
YOU'RE EVERYWHERE AT ONCE! HOW DO YOU DO THAT?
MAGIC
AMAZING!
THANKS, GUYS
2-10

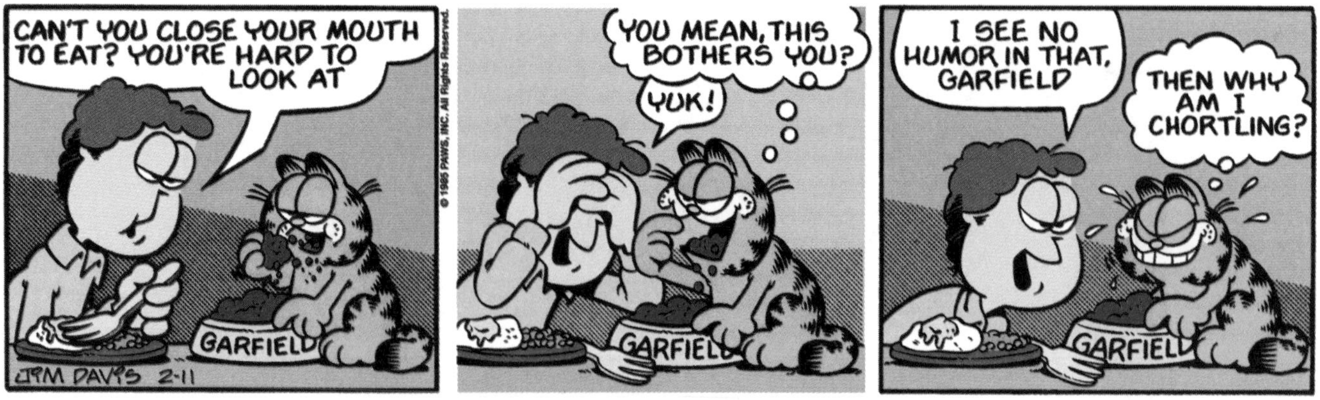
CAN'T YOU CLOSE YOUR MOUTH TO EAT? YOU'RE HARD TO LOOK AT
GARFIELD
JIM DAVIS 2-11
© 1985 PAWS, INC. All Rights Reserved.
YOU MEAN, THIS BOTHERS YOU?
YUK!
GARFIELD
I SEE NO HUMOR IN THAT, GARFIELD
THEN WHY AM I CHORTLING?
GARFIELD

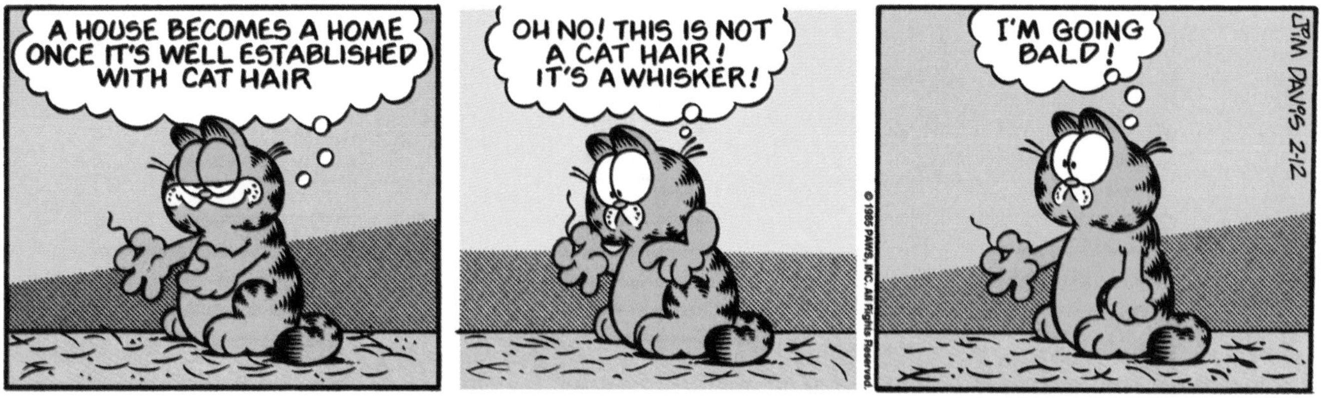
A HOUSE BECOMES A HOME ONCE IT'S WELL ESTABLISHED WITH CAT HAIR
OH NO! THIS IS NOT A CAT HAIR! IT'S A WHISKER!
© 1985 PAWS, INC. All Rights Reserved.
I'M GOING BALD!
JIM DAVIS 2-12

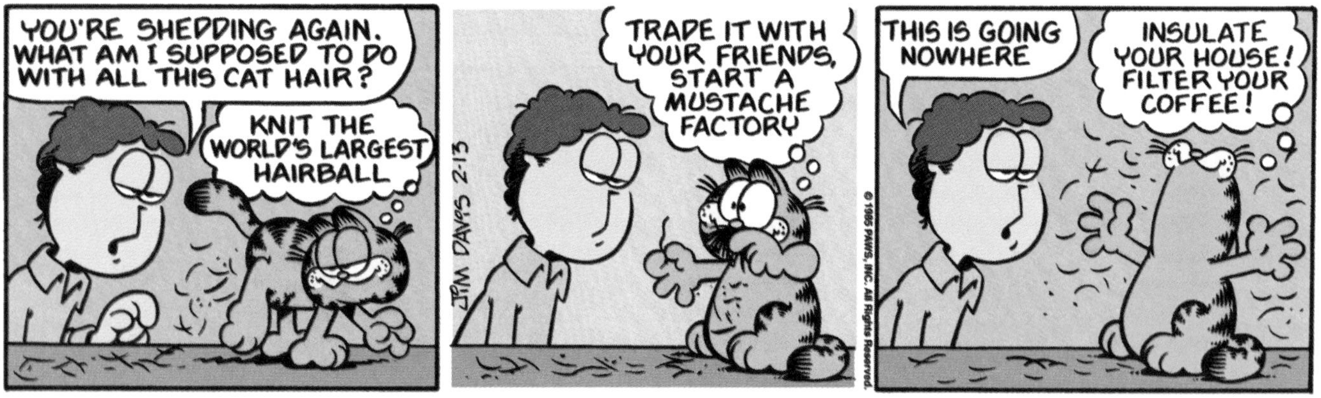
YOU'RE SHEDDING AGAIN. WHAT AM I SUPPOSED TO DO WITH ALL THIS CAT HAIR?
KNIT THE WORLD'S LARGEST HAIRBALL
JIM DAVIS 2-13
TRADE IT WITH YOUR FRIENDS, START A MUSTACHE FACTORY
© 1985 PAWS, INC. All Rights Reserved.
THIS IS GOING NOWHERE
INSULATE YOUR HOUSE! FILTER YOUR COFFEE!

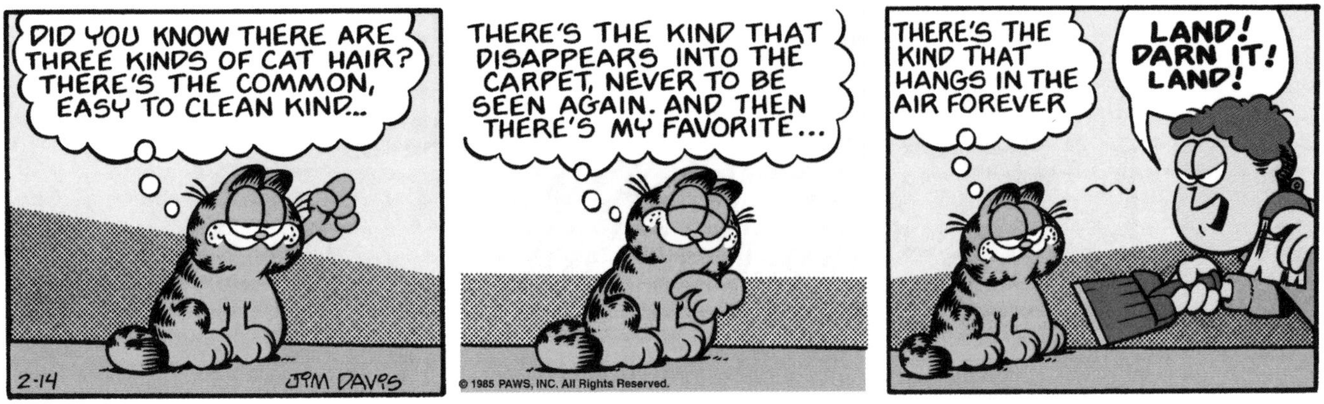
DID YOU KNOW THERE ARE THREE KINDS OF CAT HAIR? THERE'S THE COMMON, EASY TO CLEAN KIND...
2-14
JIM DAVIS
THERE'S THE KIND THAT DISAPPEARS INTO THE CARPET, NEVER TO BE SEEN AGAIN. AND THEN THERE'S MY FAVORITE...
© 1985 PAWS, INC. All Rights Reserved.
THERE'S THE KIND THAT HANGS IN THE AIR FOREVER
LAND! DARN IT! LAND!

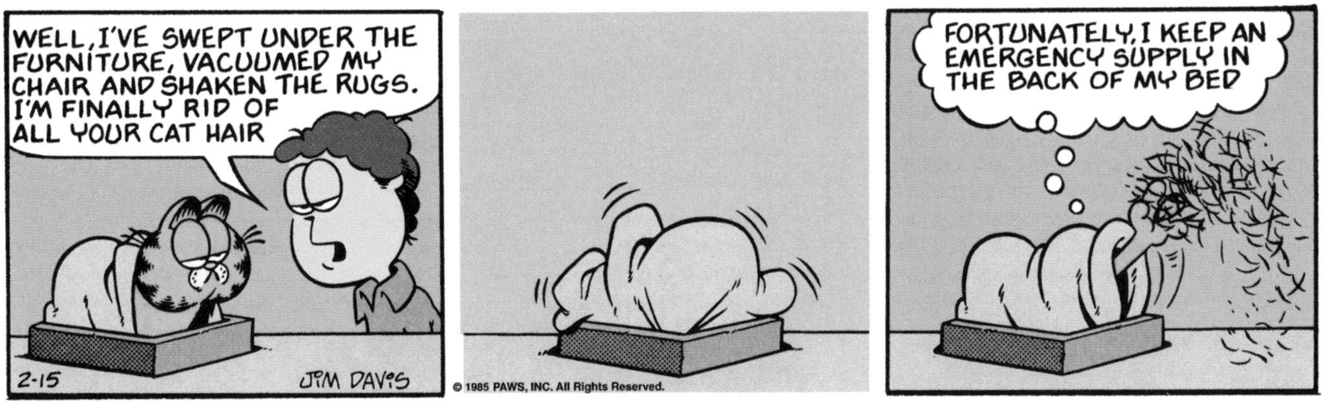
WELL, I'VE SWEPT UNDER THE FURNITURE, VACUUMED MY CHAIR AND SHAKEN THE RUGS. I'M FINALLY RID OF ALL YOUR CAT HAIR
2-15
JIM DAVIS
© 1985 PAWS, INC. All Rights Reserved.
FORTUNATELY, I KEEP AN EMERGENCY SUPPLY IN THE BACK OF MY BED

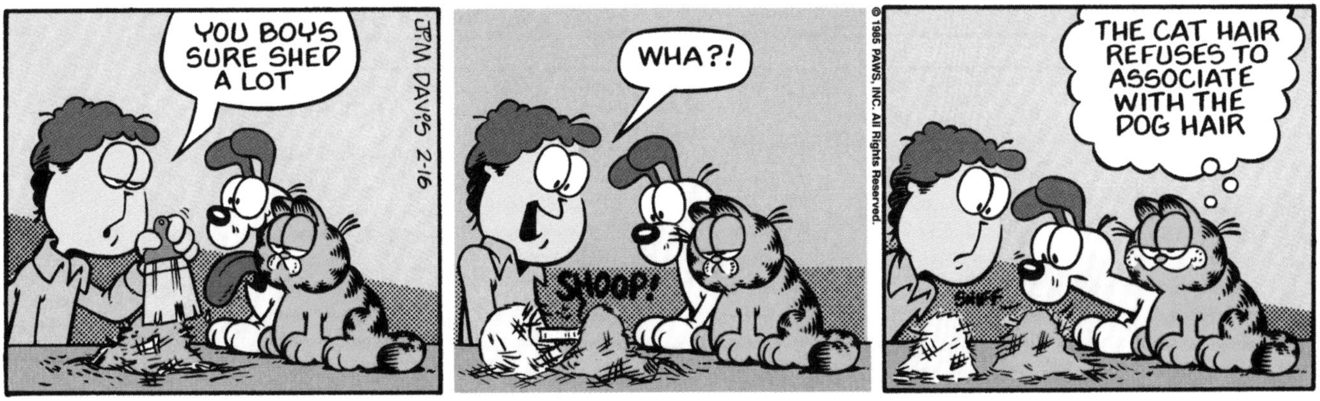
YOU BOYS SURE SHED A LOT
JIM DAVIS 2-16
WHA?!
SHOOP!
© 1985 PAWS, INC. All Rights Reserved.
THE CAT HAIR REFUSES TO ASSOCIATE WITH THE DOG HAIR

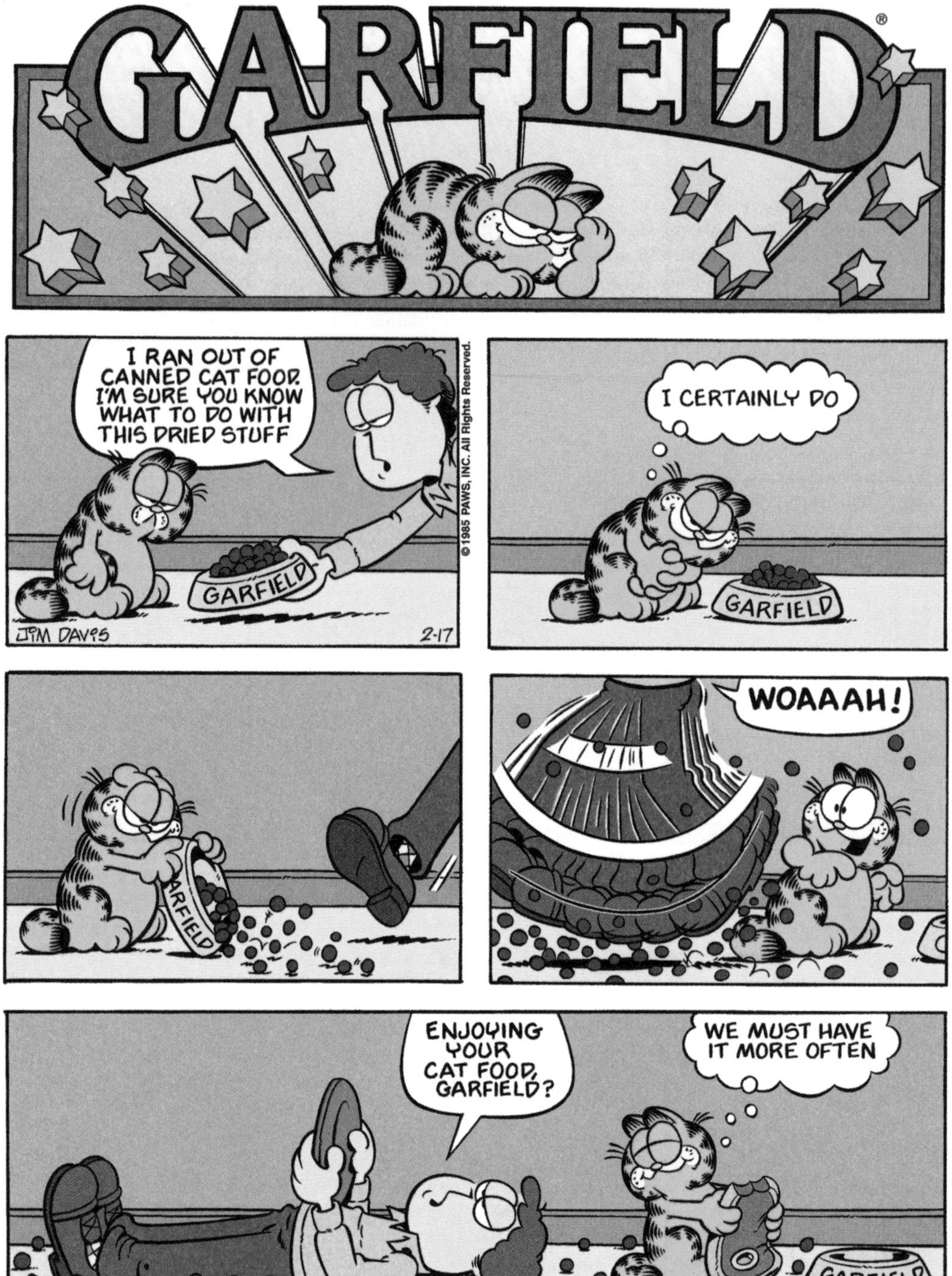
GARFIELD
I RAN OUT OF CANNED CAT FOOD. I'M SURE YOU KNOW WHAT TO DO WITH THIS DRIED STUFF
GARFIELD
JIM DAVIS
2-17
I CERTAINLY DO
GARFIELD
GARFIELD
WOAAAH!
ENJOYING YOUR CAT FOOD, GARFIELD?
WE MUST HAVE IT MORE OFTEN
GARFIELD

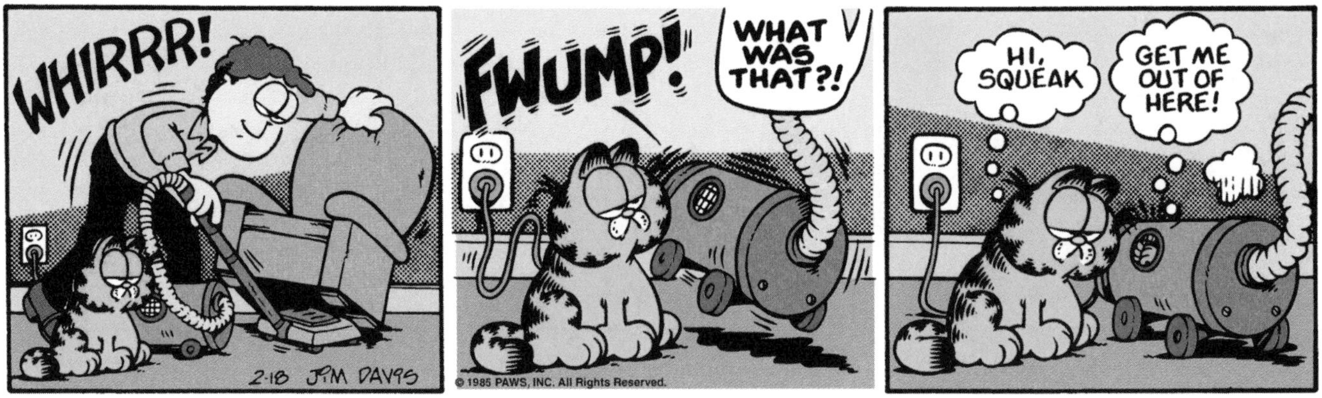
WHIRRR!
2-18 JIM DAVIS
FWUMP!
WHAT WAS THAT?!
© 1985 PAWS, INC. All Rights Reserved.
HI, SQUEAK
GET ME OUT OF HERE!

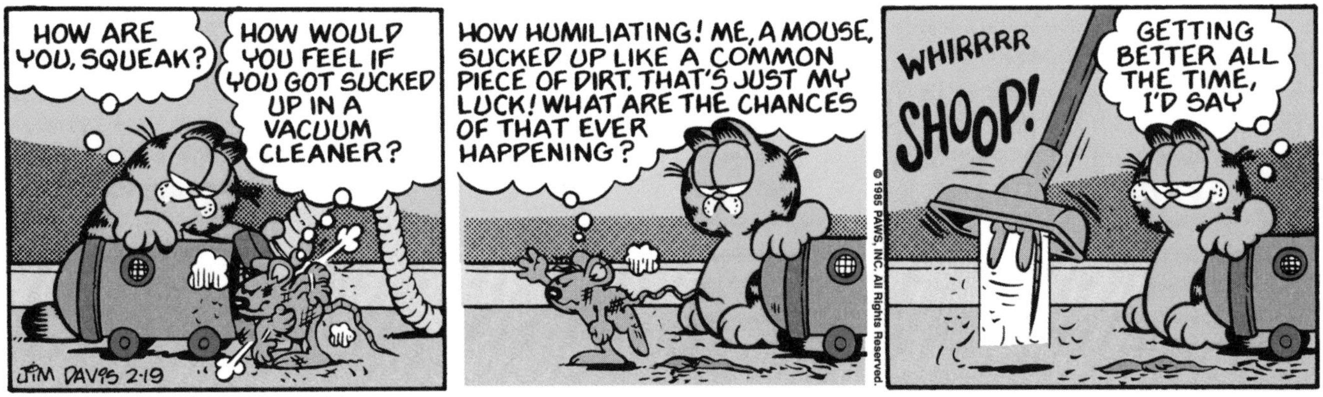
HOW ARE YOU, SQUEAK?
HOW WOULD YOU FEEL IF YOU GOT SUCKED UP IN A VACUUM CLEANER?
JIM DAVIS 2-19
HOW HUMILIATING! ME, A MOUSE, SUCKED UP LIKE A COMMON PIECE OF DIRT. THAT'S JUST MY LUCK! WHAT ARE THE CHANCES OF THAT EVER HAPPENING?
© 1985 PAWS, INC. All Rights Reserved.
WHIRRRR
SHOOP!
GETTING BETTER ALL THE TIME, I'D SAY

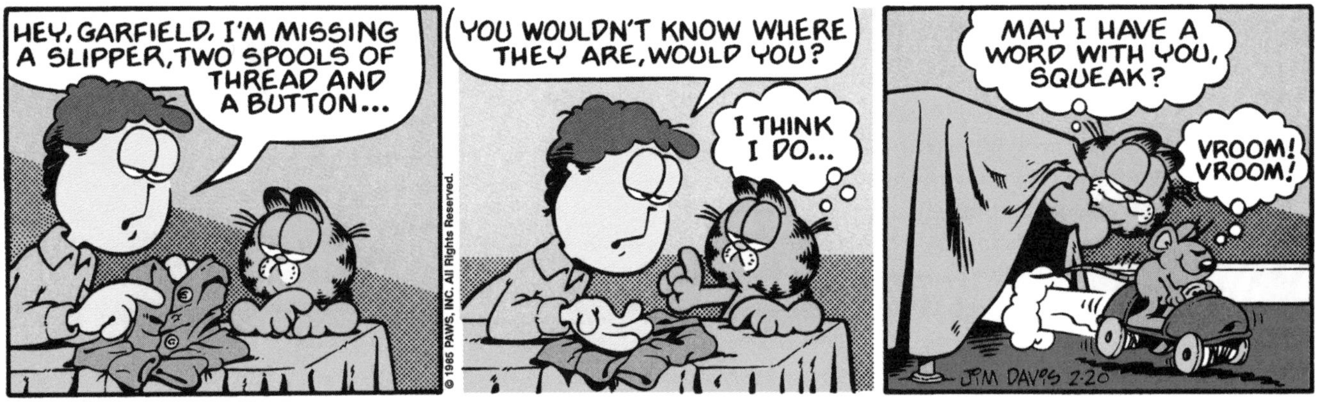
HEY, GARFIELD, I'M MISSING A SLIPPER, TWO SPOOLS OF THREAD AND A BUTTON...
© 1985 PAWS, INC. All Rights Reserved.
YOU WOULDN'T KNOW WHERE THEY ARE, WOULD YOU?
I THINK I DO...
MAY I HAVE A WORD WITH YOU, SQUEAK?
VROOM! VROOM!
JIM DAVIS 2-20

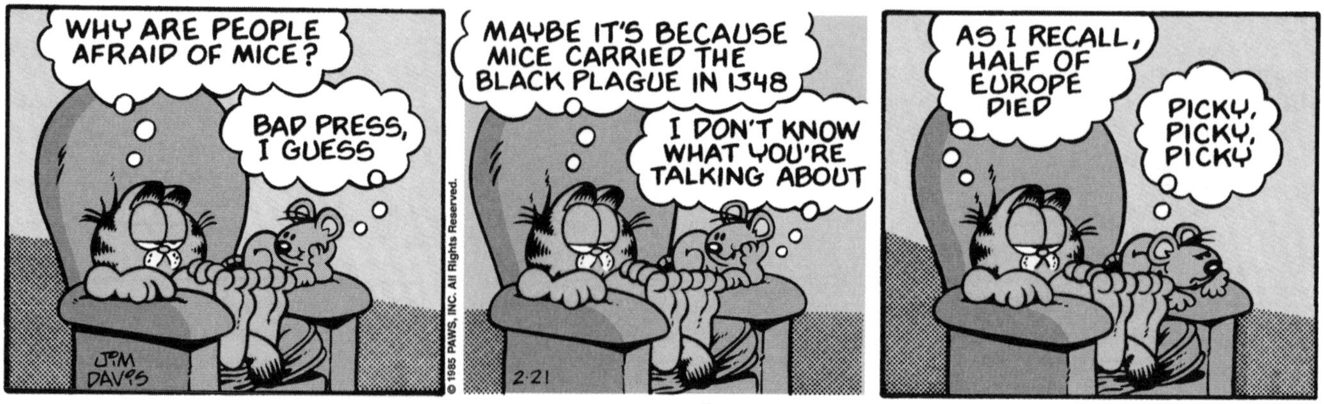
WHY ARE PEOPLE AFRAID OF MICE?
BAD PRESS, I GUESS
JIM DAVIS
© 1985 PAWS, INC. All Rights Reserved.
MAYBE IT'S BECAUSE MICE CARRIED THE BLACK PLAGUE IN 1348
I DON'T KNOW WHAT YOU'RE TALKING ABOUT
2-21
AS I RECALL, HALF OF EUROPE DIED
PICKY, PICKY, PICKY

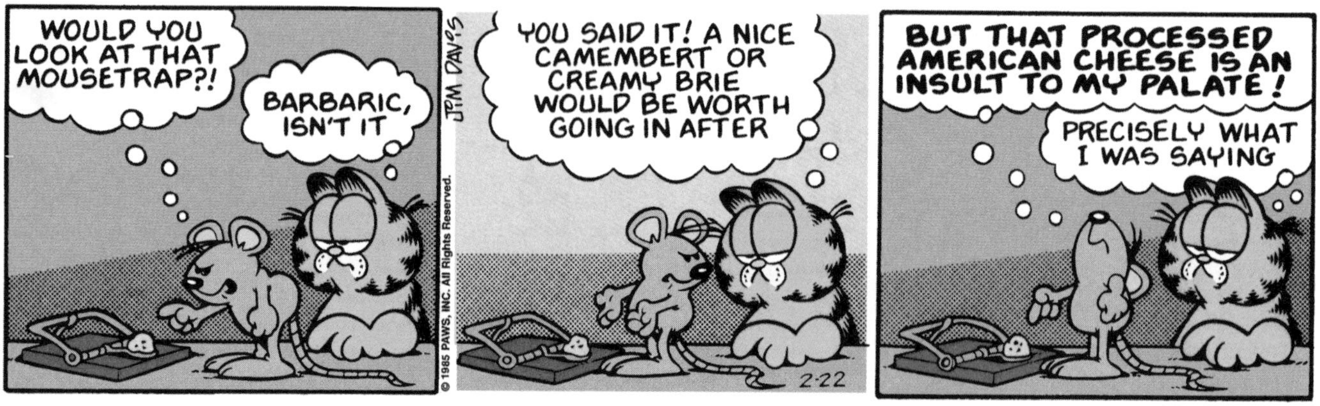
WOULD YOU LOOK AT THAT MOUSETRAP?!
BARBARIC, ISN'T IT
JIM DAVIS
© 1985 PAWS, INC. All Rights Reserved.
YOU SAID IT! A NICE CAMEMBERT OR CREAMY BRIE WOULD BE WORTH GOING IN AFTER
2-22
BUT THAT PROCESSED AMERICAN CHEESE IS AN INSULT TO MY PALATE!
PRECISELY WHAT I WAS SAYING

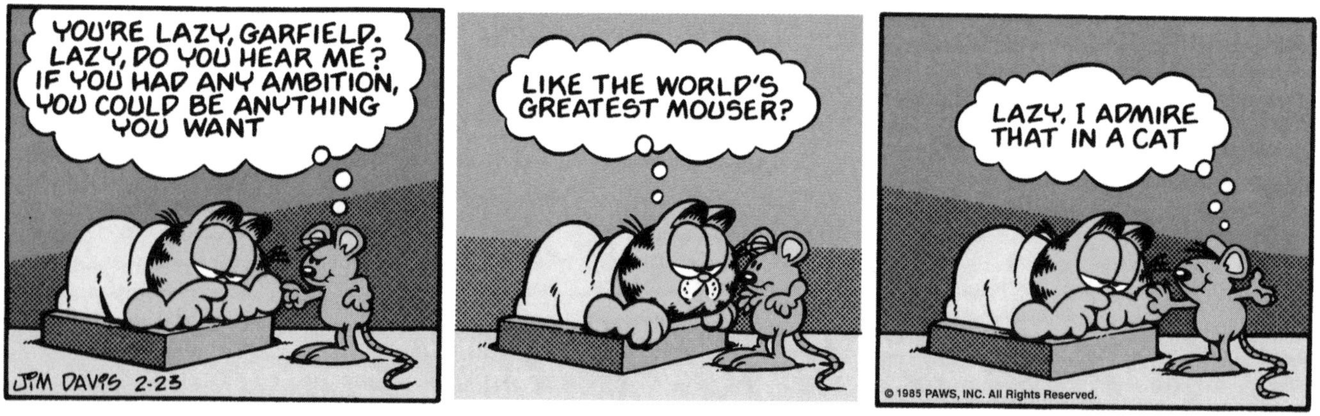
YOU'RE LAZY, GARFIELD. LAZY, DO YOU HEAR ME? IF YOU HAD ANY AMBITION, YOU COULD BE ANYTHING YOU WANT
JIM DAVIS 2-23
LIKE THE WORLD'S GREATEST MOUSER?
LAZY, I ADMIRE THAT IN A CAT
© 1985 PAWS, INC. All Rights Reserved.

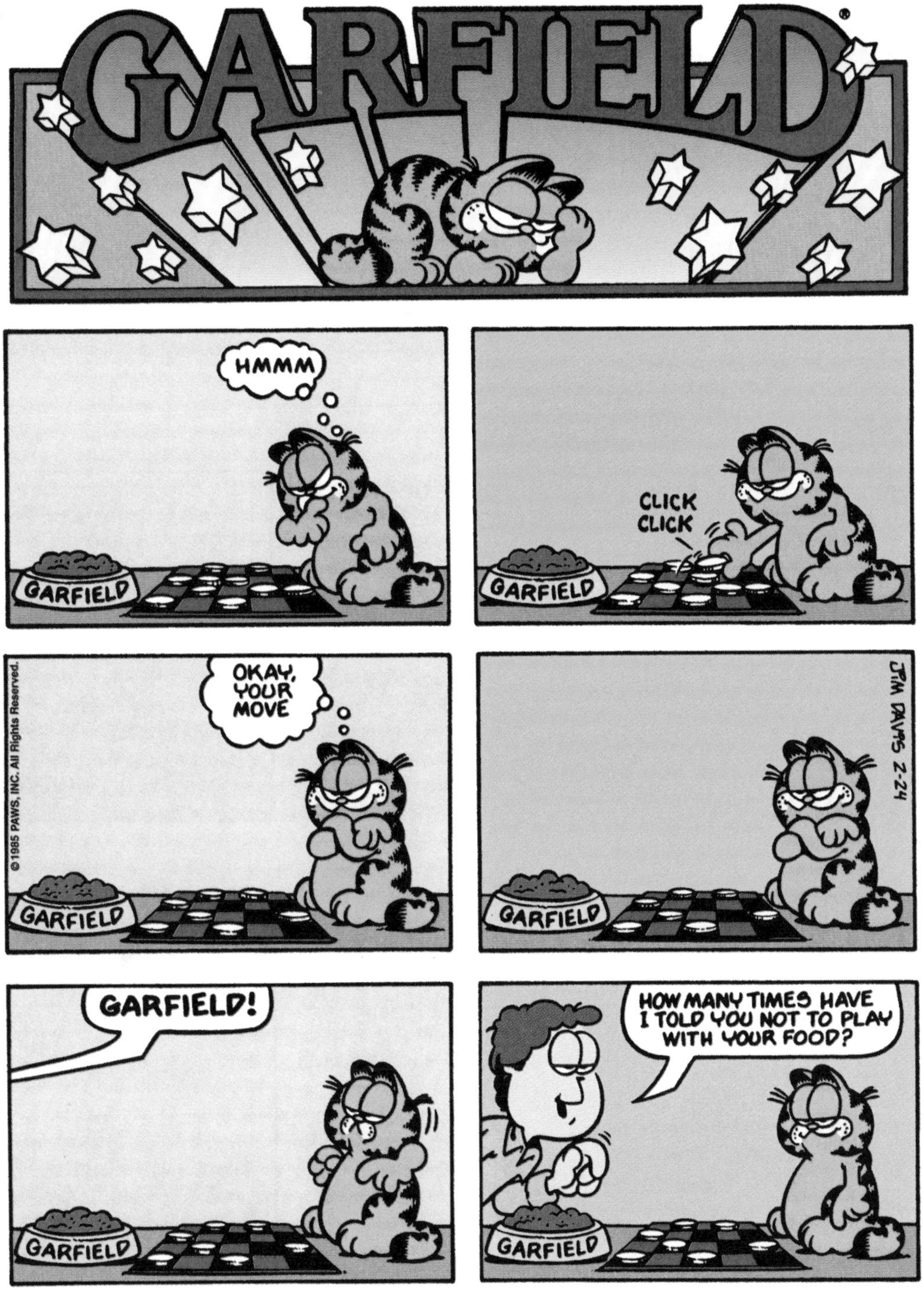
GARFIELD
HMMM
GARFIELD
CLICK CLICK
GARFIELD
OKAY, YOUR MOVE
GARFIELD
© 1985 PAWS, INC. All Rights Reserved.
JIM DAVIS 2-24
GARFIELD
GARFIELD!
GARFIELD
HOW MANY TIMES HAVE I TOLD YOU NOT TO PLAY WITH YOUR FOOD?
GARFIELD

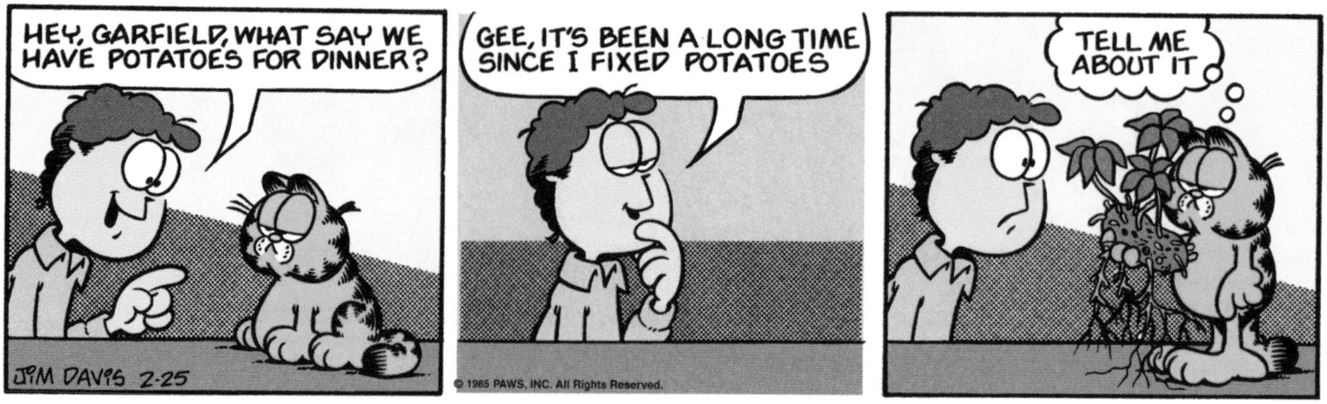
HEY, GARFIELD, WHAT SAY WE HAVE POTATOES FOR DINNER?
JIM DAVIS 2-25
GEE, IT'S BEEN A LONG TIME SINCE I FIXED POTATOES
© 1985 PAWS, INC. All Rights Reserved.
TELL ME ABOUT IT

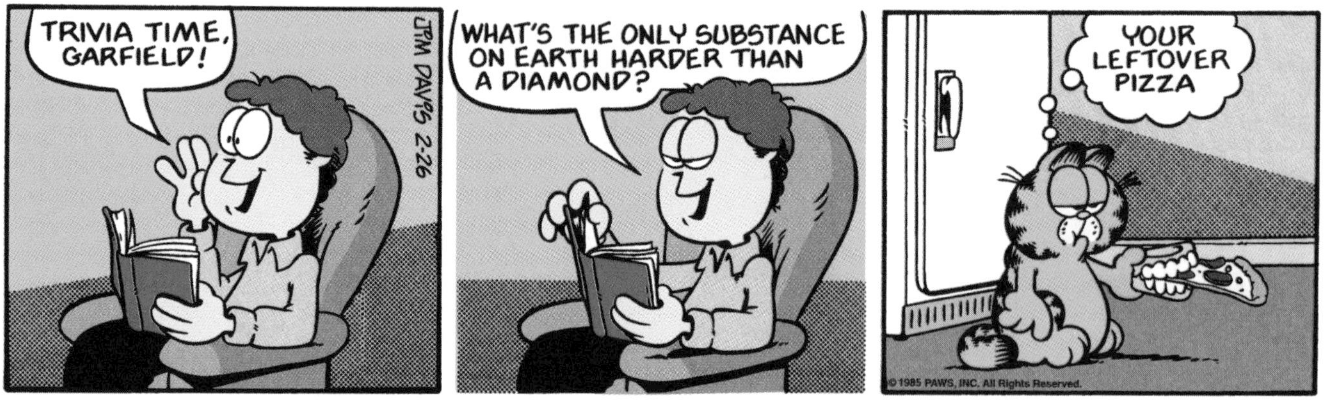
TRIVIA TIME, GARFIELD!
JIM DAVIS 2-26
WHAT'S THE ONLY SUBSTANCE ON EARTH HARDER THAN A DIAMOND?
YOUR LEFTOVER PIZZA
© 1985 PAWS, INC. All Rights Reserved.

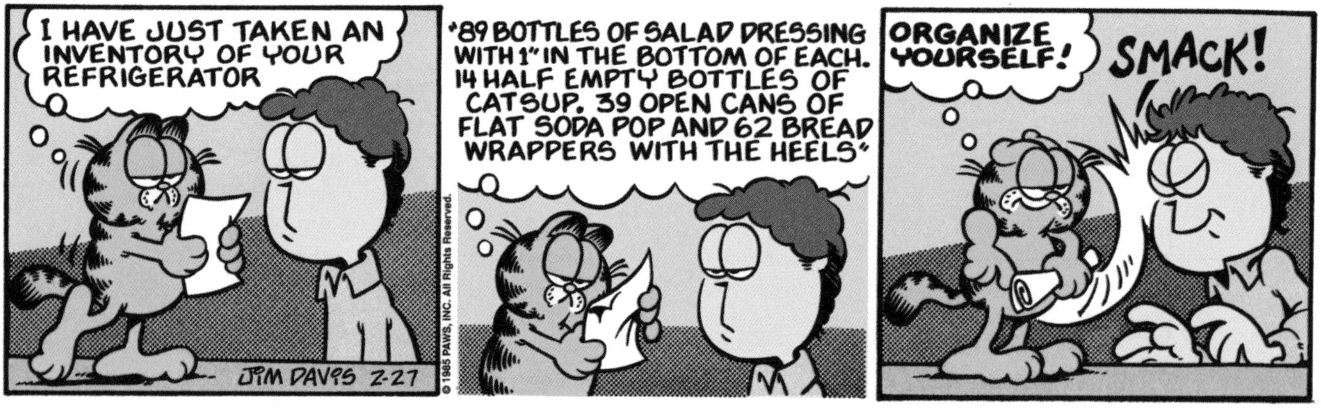
I HAVE JUST TAKEN AN INVENTORY OF YOUR REFRIGERATOR
JIM DAVIS 2-27
"89 BOTTLES OF SALAD DRESSING WITH 1" IN THE BOTTOM OF EACH. 14 HALF EMPTY BOTTLES OF CATSUP. 39 OPEN CANS OF FLAT SODA POP AND 62 BREAD WRAPPERS WITH THE HEELS"
© 1985 PAWS, INC. All Rights Reserved.
ORGANIZE YOURSELF!
SMACK!

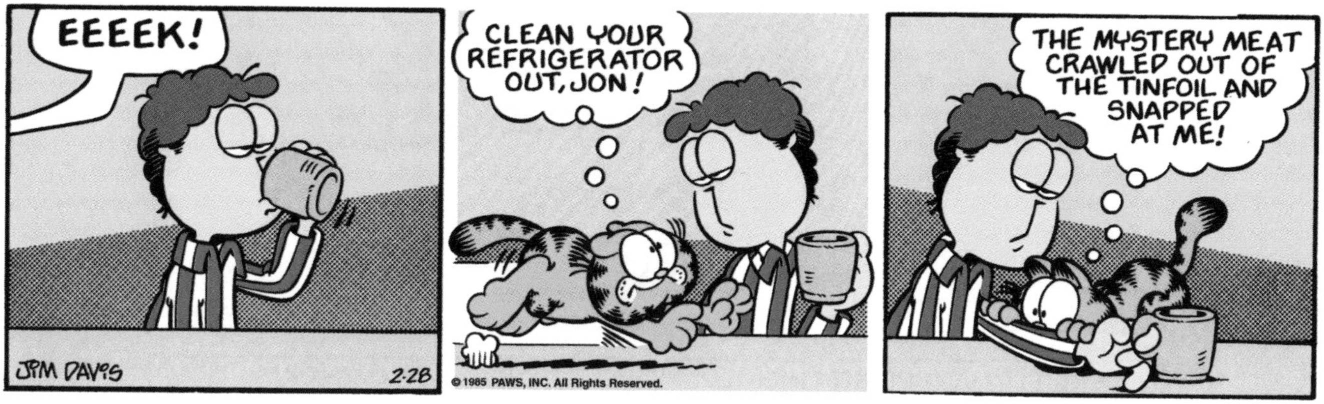
EEEEK!
CLEAN YOUR REFRIGERATOR OUT, JON!
THE MYSTERY MEAT CRAWLED OUT OF THE TINFOIL AND SNAPPED AT ME!
JIM DAVIS
2-28
© 1985 PAWS, INC. All Rights Reserved.

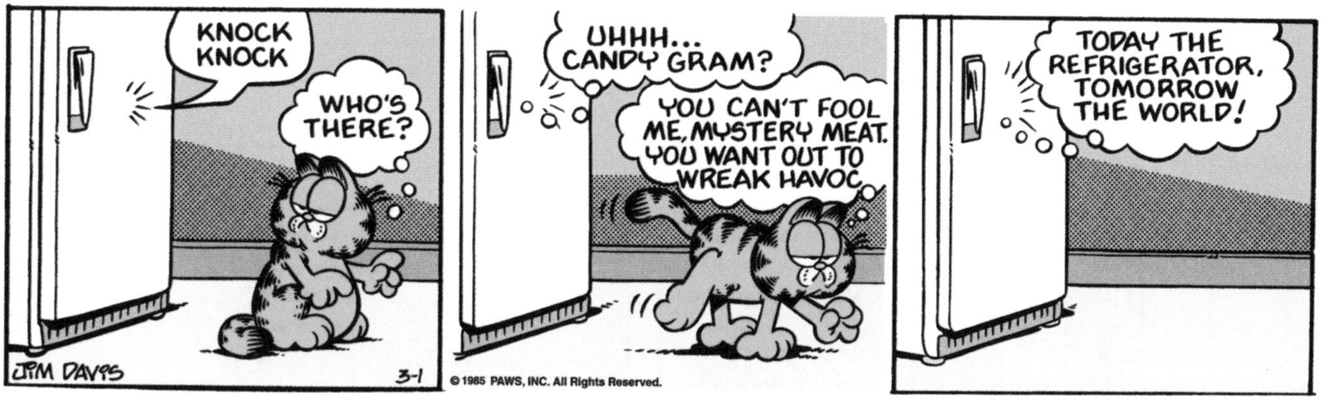
KNOCK KNOCK
WHO'S THERE?
UHHH... CANDY GRAM?
YOU CAN'T FOOL ME, MYSTERY MEAT. YOU WANT OUT TO WREAK HAVOC
TODAY THE REFRIGERATOR, TOMORROW THE WORLD!
JIM DAVIS
3-1
© 1985 PAWS, INC. All Rights Reserved.

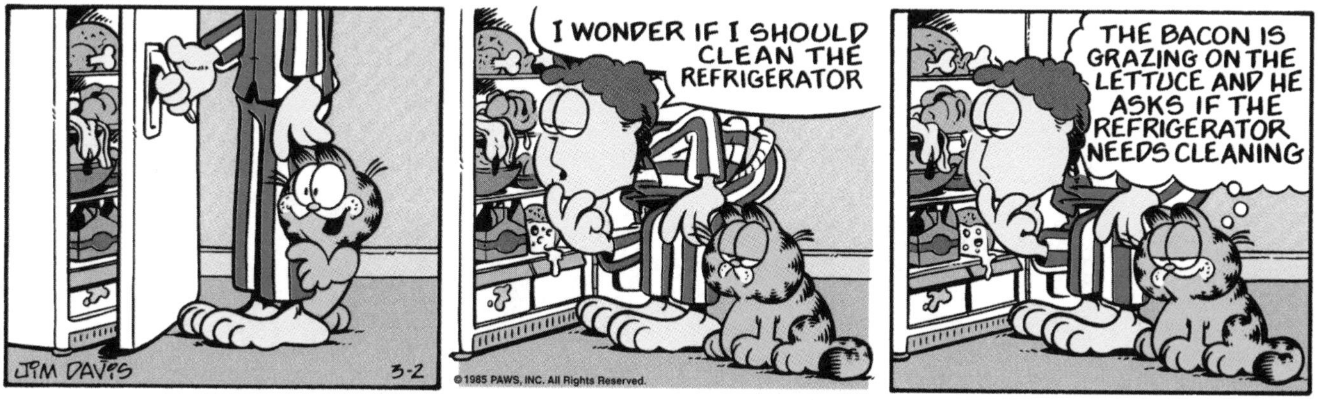
I WONDER IF I SHOULD CLEAN THE REFRIGERATOR
THE BACON IS GRAZING ON THE LETTUCE AND HE ASKS IF THE REFRIGERATOR NEEDS CLEANING
JIM DAVIS
3-2
© 1985 PAWS, INC. All Rights Reserved.

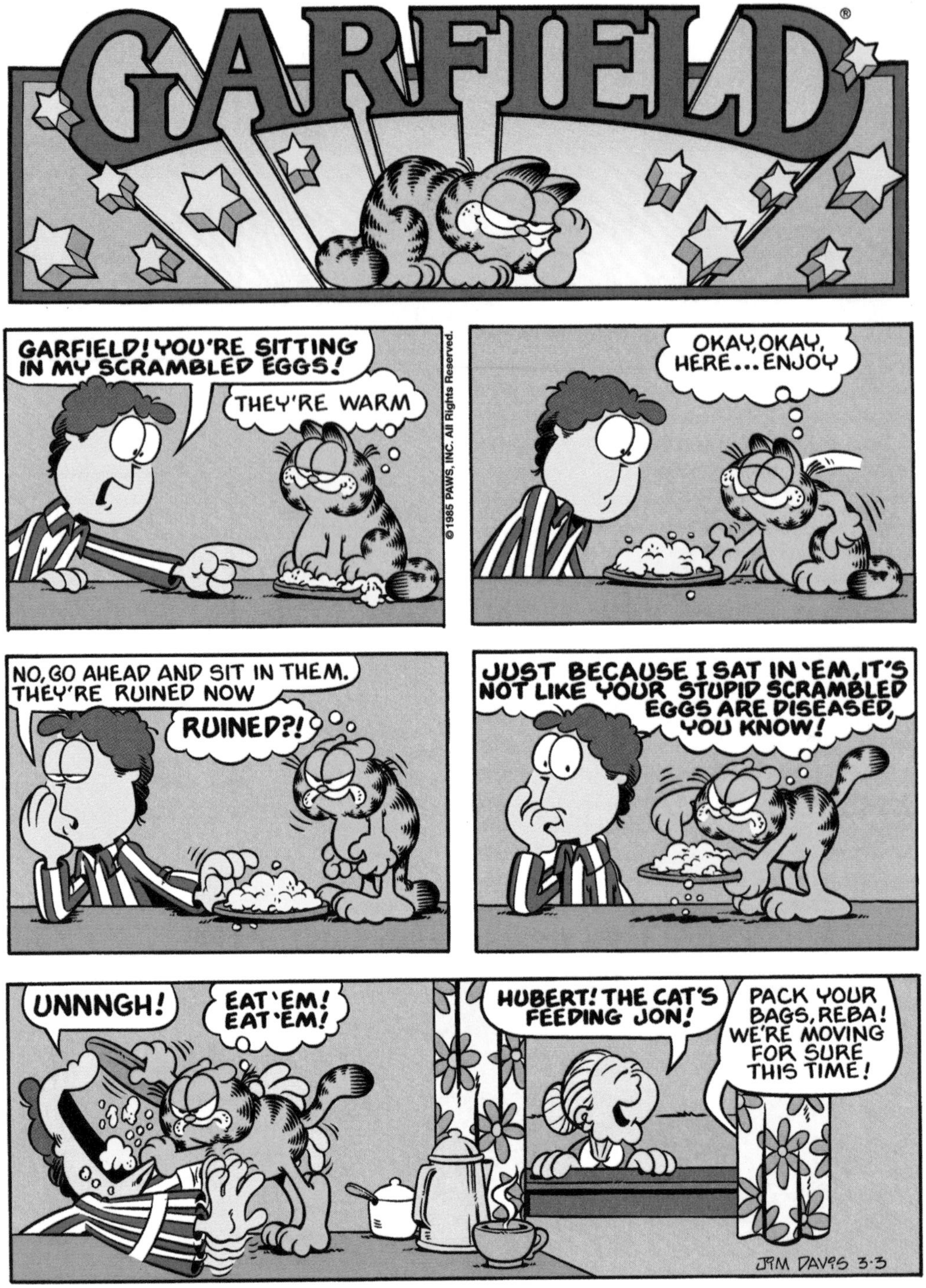
GARFIELD®
GARFIELD! YOU'RE SITTING IN MY SCRAMBLED EGGS!
THEY'RE WARM
©1985 PAWS, INC. All Rights Reserved.
OKAY, OKAY, HERE... ENJOY
NO, GO AHEAD AND SIT IN THEM. THEY'RE RUINED NOW
RUINED?!
JUST BECAUSE I SAT IN 'EM, IT'S NOT LIKE YOUR STUPID SCRAMBLED EGGS ARE DISEASED, YOU KNOW!
UNNNGH!
EAT 'EM! EAT 'EM!
HUBERT! THE CAT'S FEEDING JON!
PACK YOUR BAGS, REBA! WE'RE MOVING FOR SURE THIS TIME!
JIM DAVIS 3-3

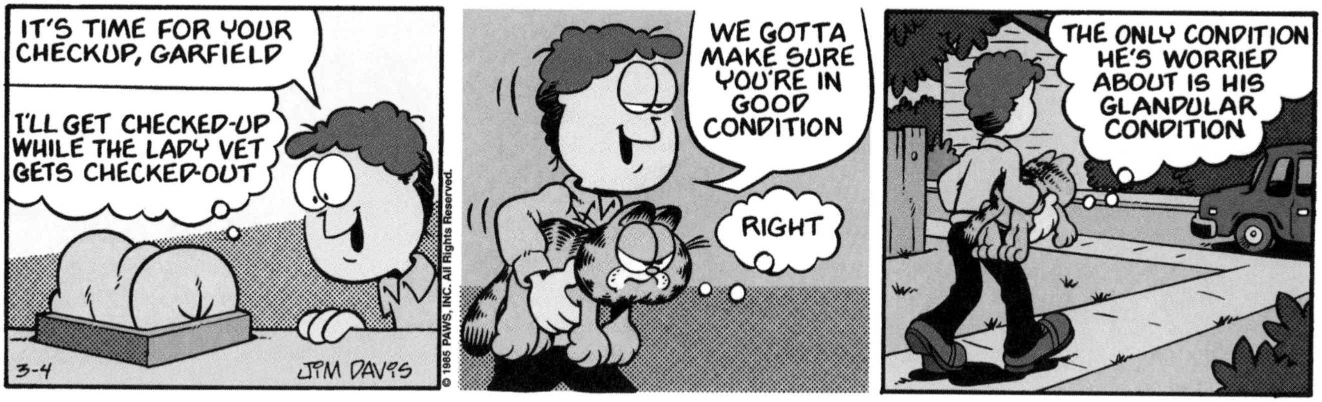
IT'S TIME FOR YOUR CHECKUP, GARFIELD
I'LL GET CHECKED-UP WHILE THE LADY VET GETS CHECKED-OUT
3-4
JIM DAVIS
© 1985 PAWS, INC. All Rights Reserved.
WE GOTTA MAKE SURE YOU'RE IN GOOD CONDITION
RIGHT
THE ONLY CONDITION HE'S WORRIED ABOUT IS HIS GLANDULAR CONDITION

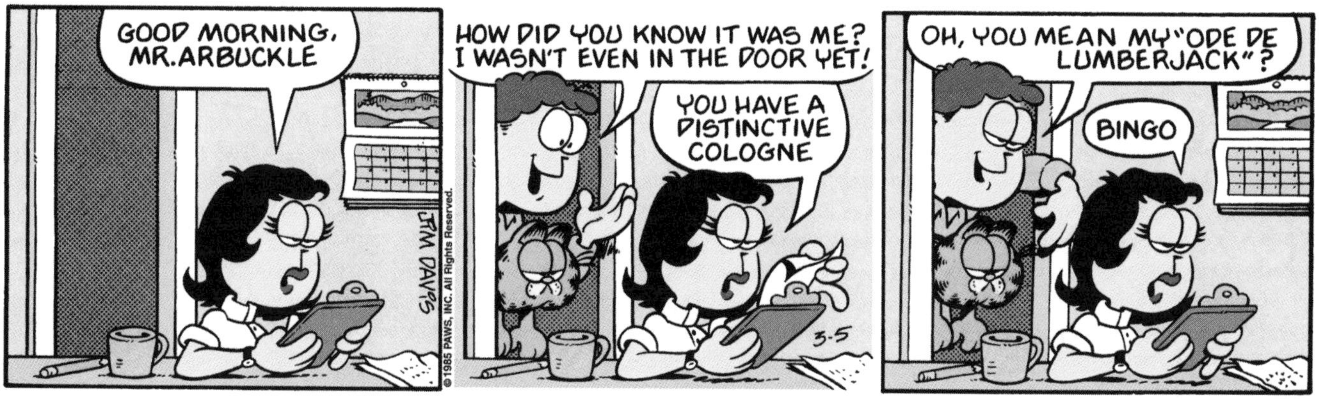
GOOD MORNING, MR. ARBUCKLE
JIM DAVIS
© 1985 PAWS, INC. All Rights Reserved.
HOW DID YOU KNOW IT WAS ME? I WASN'T EVEN IN THE DOOR YET!
YOU HAVE A DISTINCTIVE COLOGNE
3-5
OH, YOU MEAN MY "ODE DE LUMBERJACK"?
BINGO

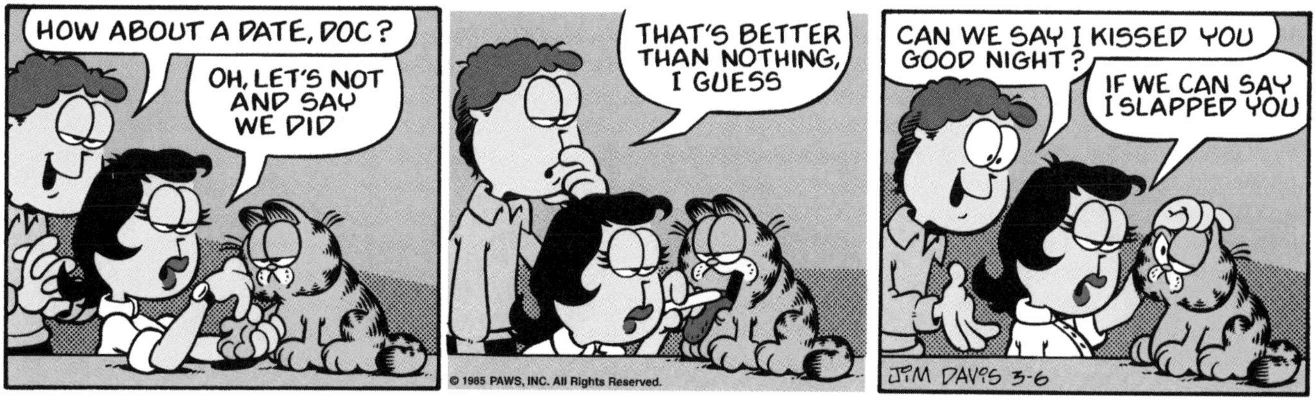
HOW ABOUT A DATE, DOC?
OH, LET'S NOT AND SAY WE DID
THAT'S BETTER THAN NOTHING, I GUESS
© 1985 PAWS, INC. All Rights Reserved.
CAN WE SAY I KISSED YOU GOOD NIGHT?
IF WE CAN SAY I SLAPPED YOU
JIM DAVIS 3-6

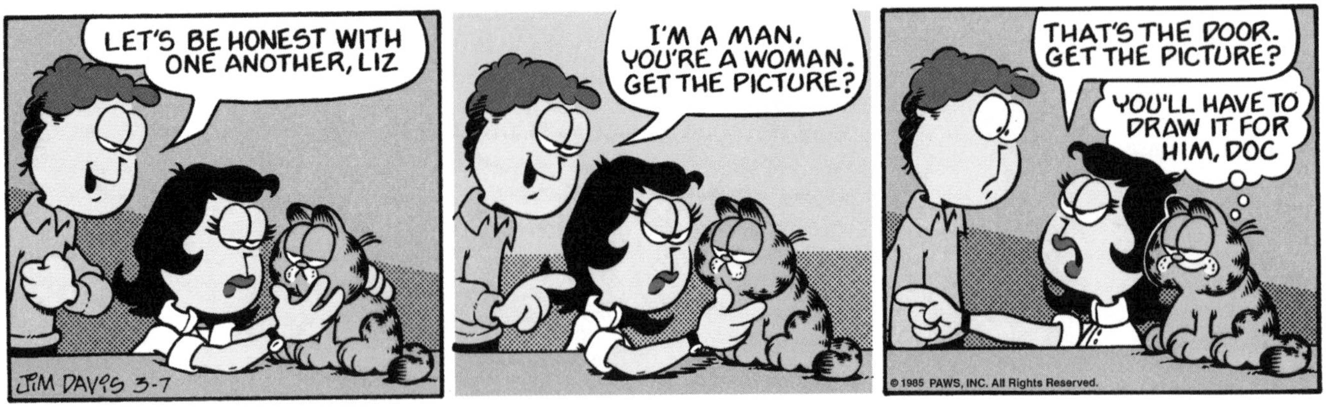
LET'S BE HONEST WITH ONE ANOTHER, LIZ
JIM DAVIS 3-7
I'M A MAN. YOU'RE A WOMAN. GET THE PICTURE?
THAT'S THE DOOR. GET THE PICTURE?
YOU'LL HAVE TO DRAW IT FOR HIM, DOC
© 1985 PAWS, INC. All Rights Reserved.

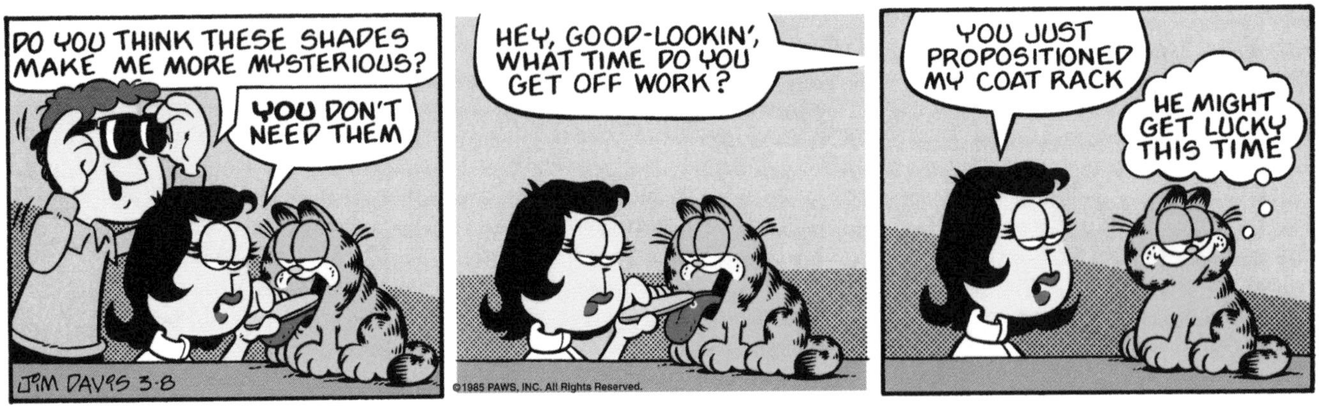
DO YOU THINK THESE SHADES MAKE ME MORE MYSTERIOUS?
YOU DON'T NEED THEM
JIM DAVIS 3-8
HEY, GOOD-LOOKIN', WHAT TIME DO YOU GET OFF WORK?
©1985 PAWS, INC. All Rights Reserved.
YOU JUST PROPOSITIONED MY COAT RACK
HE MIGHT GET LUCKY THIS TIME

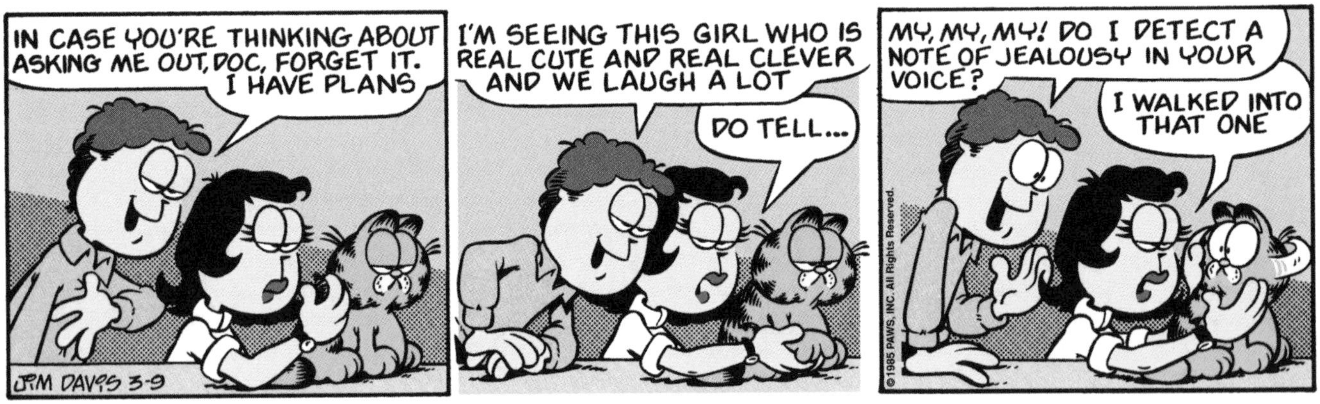
IN CASE YOU'RE THINKING ABOUT ASKING ME OUT, DOC, FORGET IT. I HAVE PLANS
JIM DAVIS 3-9
I'M SEEING THIS GIRL WHO IS REAL CUTE AND REAL CLEVER AND WE LAUGH A LOT
DO TELL...
MY, MY, MY! DO I DETECT A NOTE OF JEALOUSY IN YOUR VOICE?
I WALKED INTO THAT ONE
© 1985 PAWS, INC. All Rights Reserved.

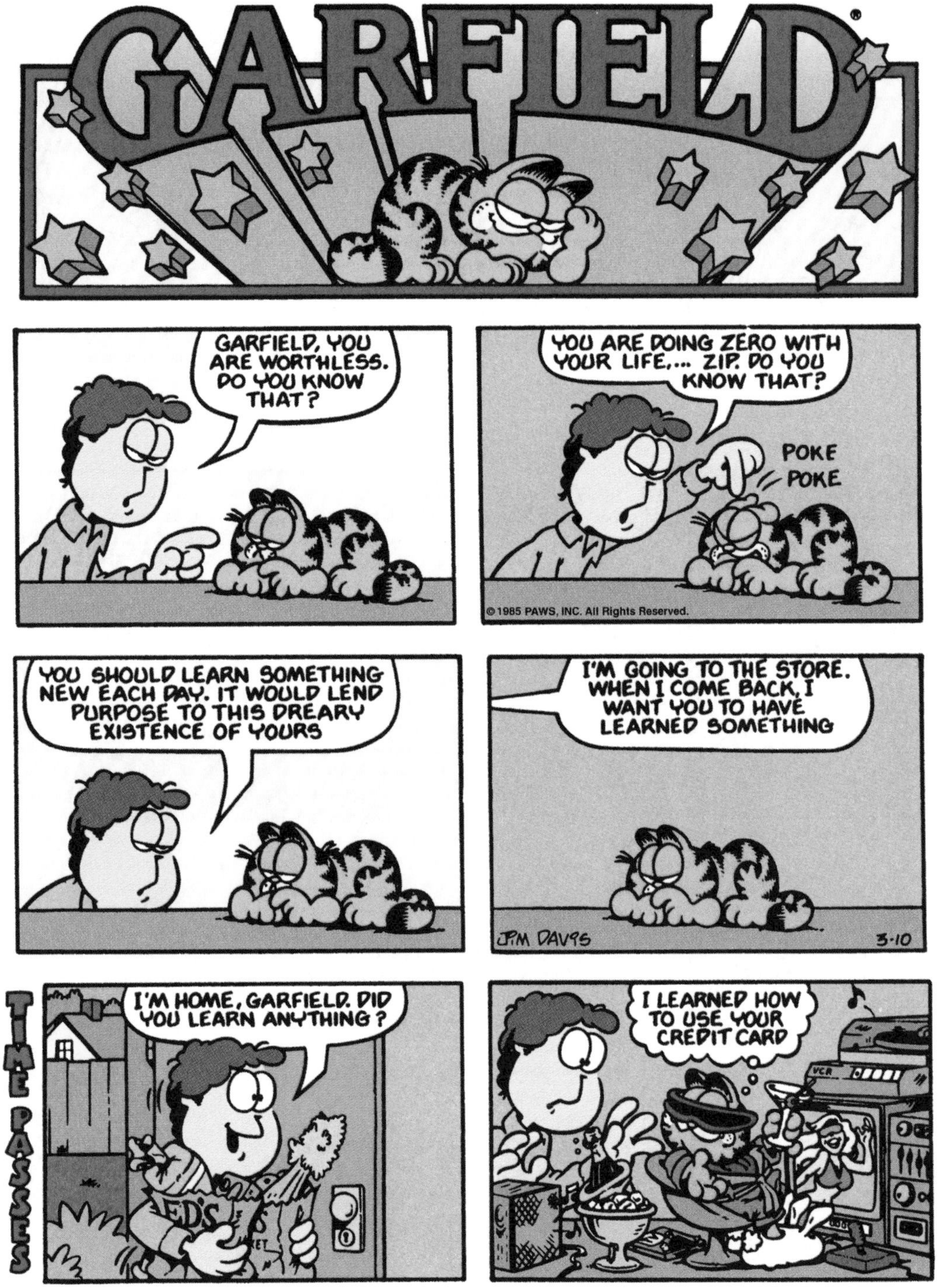
GARFIELD
GARFIELD, YOU ARE WORTHLESS. DO YOU KNOW THAT?
YOU ARE DOING ZERO WITH YOUR LIFE,... ZIP. DO YOU KNOW THAT?
POKE POKE
© 1985 PAWS, INC. All Rights Reserved.
YOU SHOULD LEARN SOMETHING NEW EACH DAY. IT WOULD LEND PURPOSE TO THIS DREARY EXISTENCE OF YOURS
I'M GOING TO THE STORE. WHEN I COME BACK, I WANT YOU TO HAVE LEARNED SOMETHING
JIM DAVIS
3-10
TIME PASSES
I'M HOME, GARFIELD. DID YOU LEARN ANYTHING?
ED'S
I LEARNED HOW TO USE YOUR CREDIT CARD
VCR

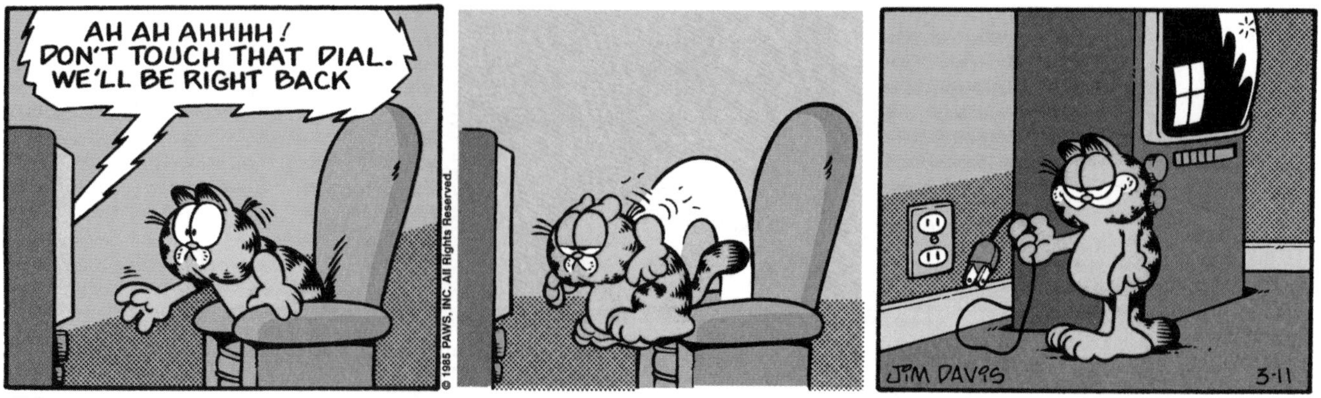
AH AH AHHHH! DON'T TOUCH THAT DIAL. WE'LL BE RIGHT BACK
JIM DAVIS
3-11

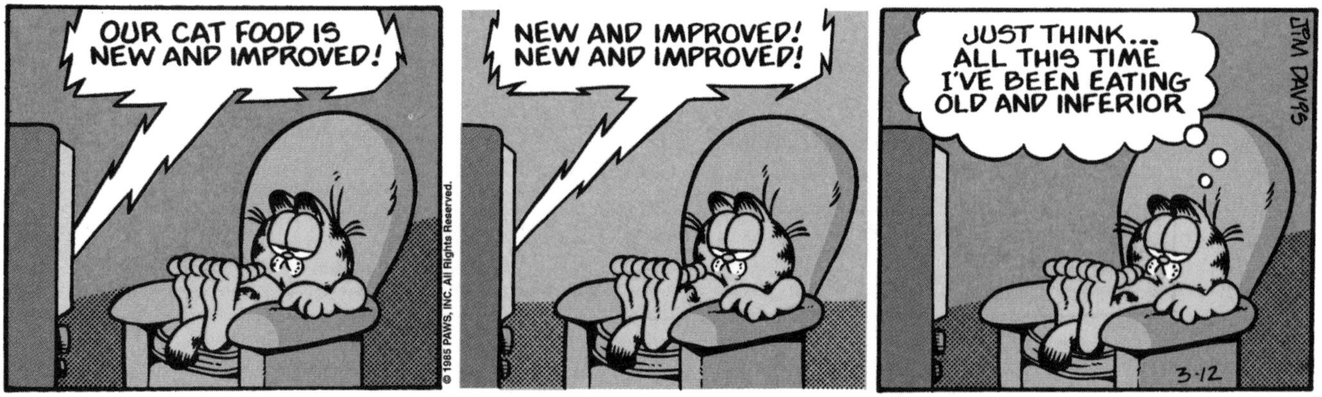
OUR CAT FOOD IS NEW AND IMPROVED!
NEW AND IMPROVED! NEW AND IMPROVED!
JUST THINK... ALL THIS TIME I'VE BEEN EATING OLD AND INFERIOR
JIM DAVIS
3-12

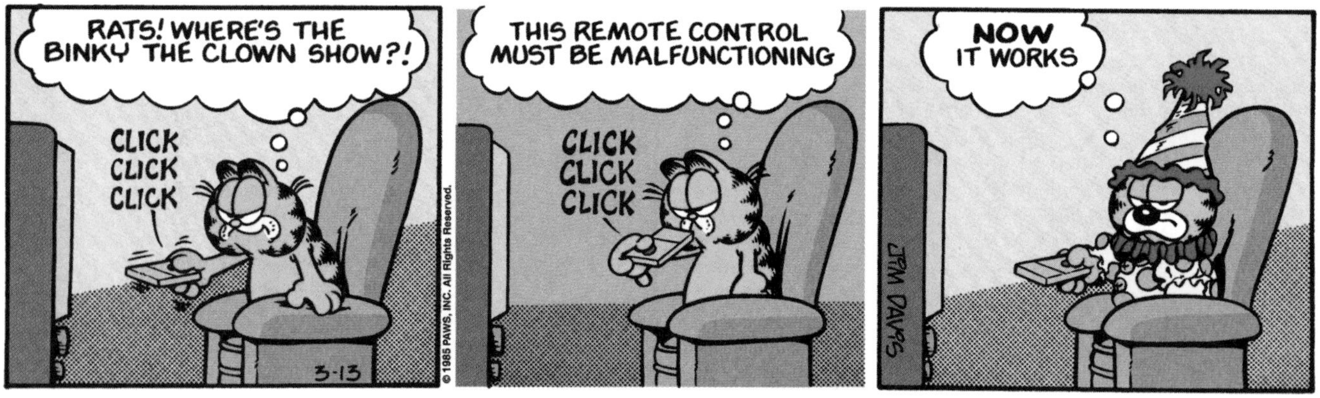
RATS! WHERE'S THE BINKY THE CLOWN SHOW?!
CLICK CLICK CLICK
3-13
THIS REMOTE CONTROL MUST BE MALFUNCTIONING
CLICK CLICK CLICK
NOW IT WORKS
JIM DAVIS

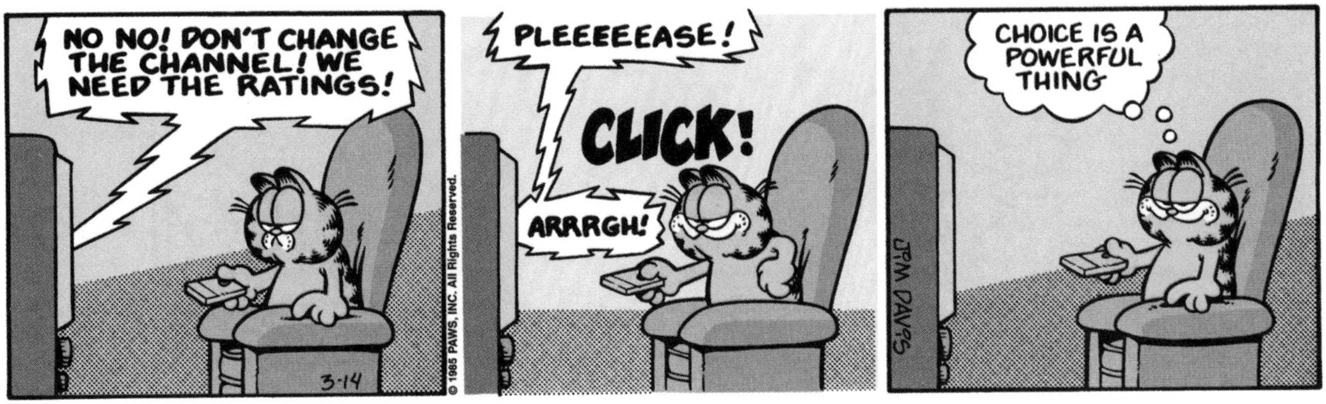
NO NO! DON'T CHANGE THE CHANNEL! WE NEED THE RATINGS!
3-14
© 1985 PAWS, INC. All Rights Reserved.
PLEEEEEEASE!
CLICK!
ARRRGH!
CHOICE IS A POWERFUL THING
JIM DAVIS

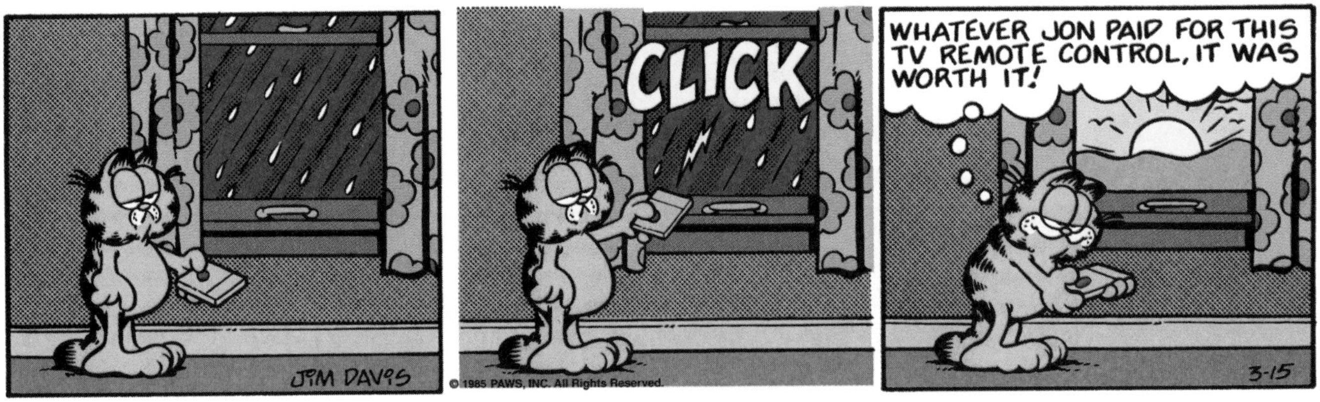
JIM DAVIS
CLICK
© 1985 PAWS, INC. All Rights Reserved.
WHATEVER JON PAID FOR THIS TV REMOTE CONTROL, IT WAS WORTH IT!
3-15

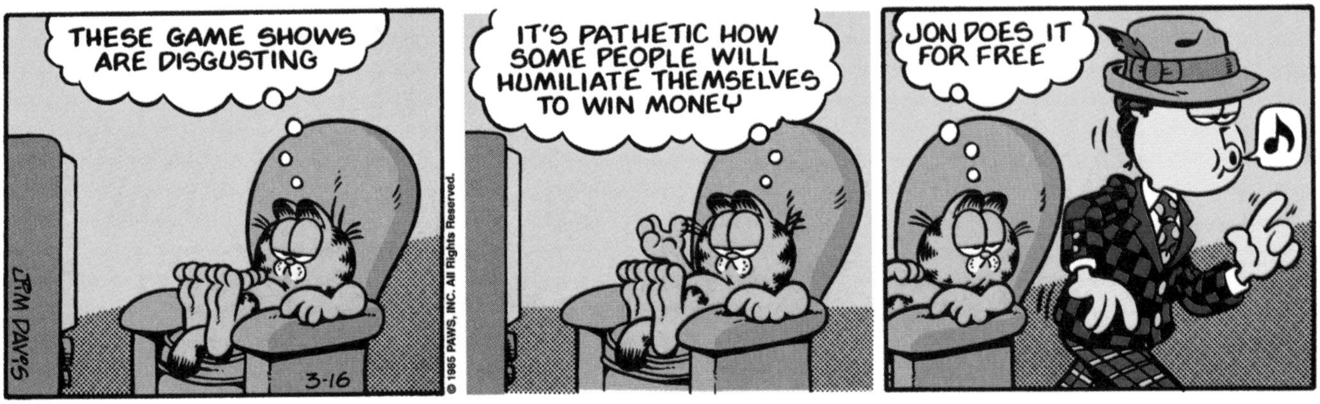
THESE GAME SHOWS ARE DISGUSTING
JIM DAVIS
3-16
© 1985 PAWS, INC. All Rights Reserved.
IT'S PATHETIC HOW SOME PEOPLE WILL HUMILIATE THEMSELVES TO WIN MONEY
JON DOES IT FOR FREE

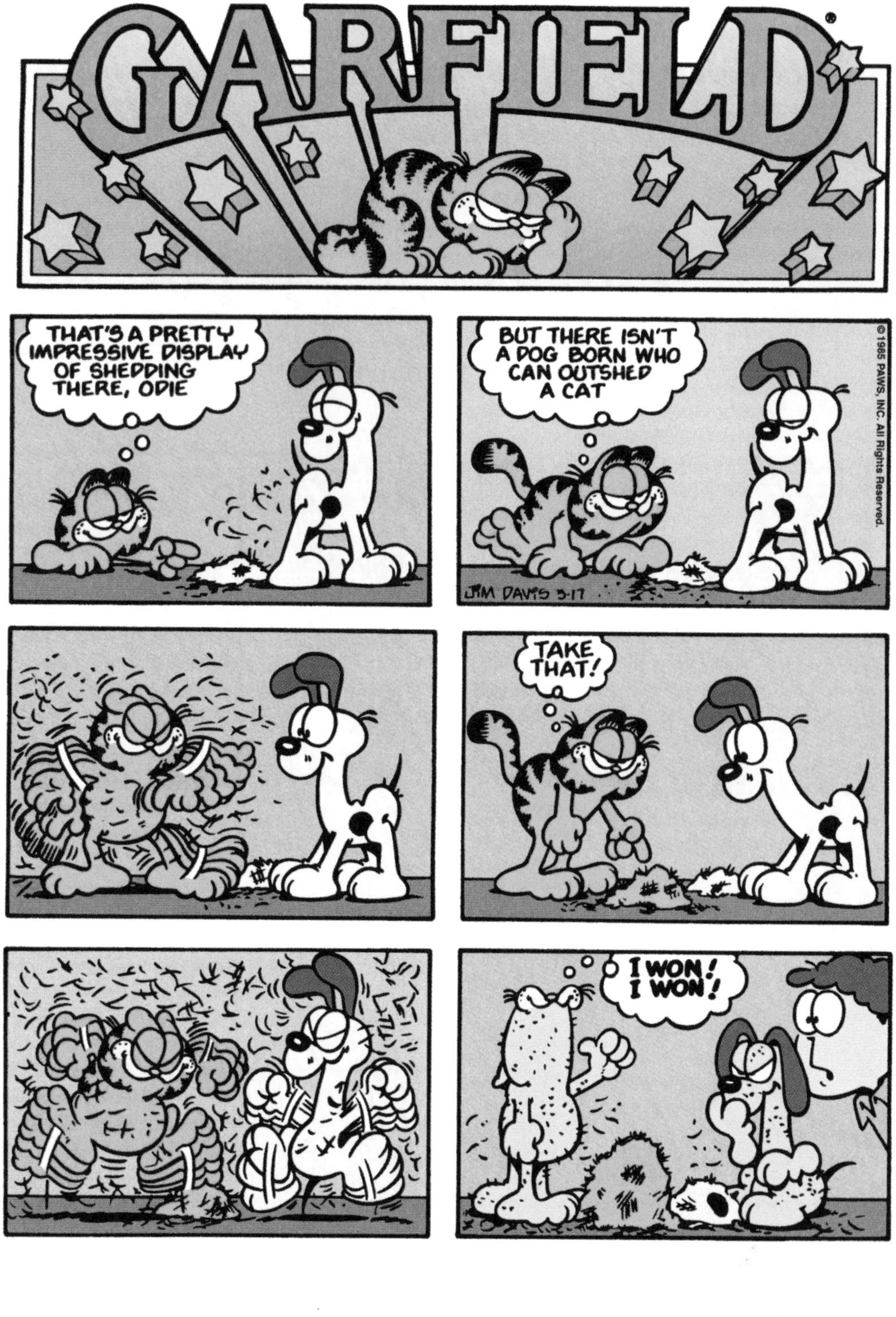
GARFIELD®
THAT'S A PRETTY IMPRESSIVE DISPLAY OF SHEDDING THERE, ODIE
BUT THERE ISN'T A DOG BORN WHO CAN OUTSHED A CAT
© 1985 PAWS, INC. All Rights Reserved.
JIM DAVIS 3-17
TAKE THAT!
I WON! I WON!

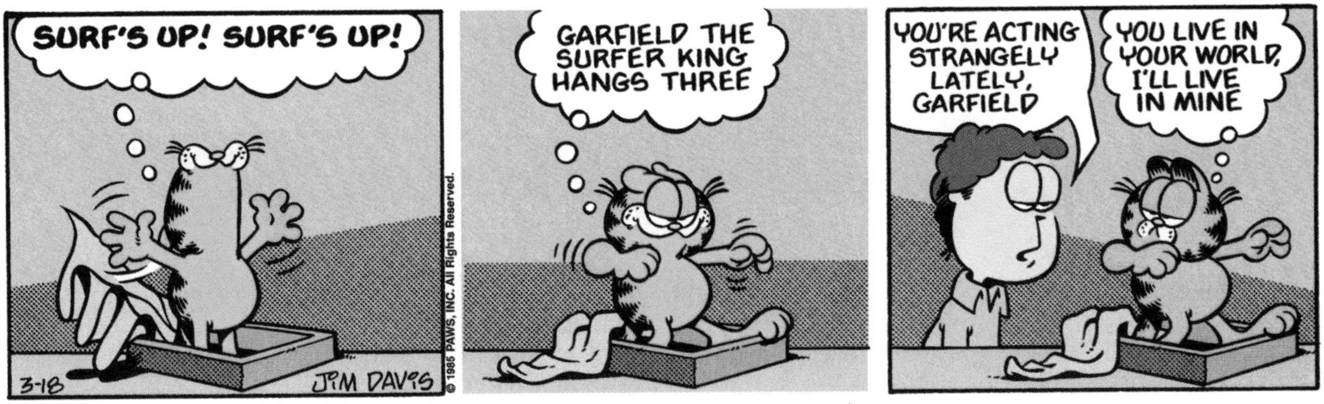
SURF'S UP! SURF'S UP!
3-18
JIM DAVIS
© 1985 PAWS, INC. All Rights Reserved.
GARFIELD THE SURFER KING HANGS THREE
YOU'RE ACTING STRANGELY LATELY, GARFIELD
YOU LIVE IN YOUR WORLD, I'LL LIVE IN MINE

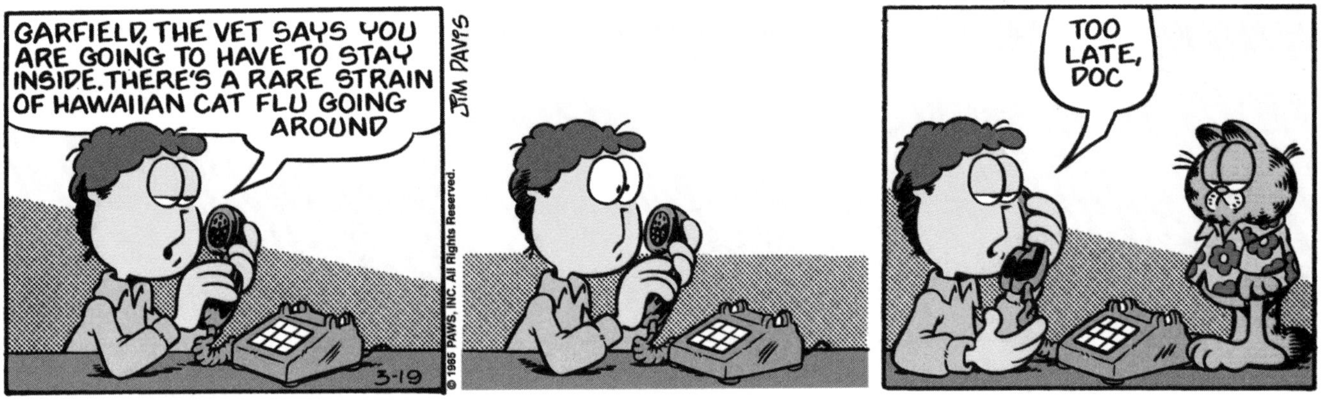
GARFIELD, THE VET SAYS YOU ARE GOING TO HAVE TO STAY INSIDE. THERE'S A RARE STRAIN OF HAWAIIAN CAT FLU GOING AROUND
3-19
JIM DAVIS
© 1985 PAWS, INC. All Rights Reserved.
TOO LATE, DOC

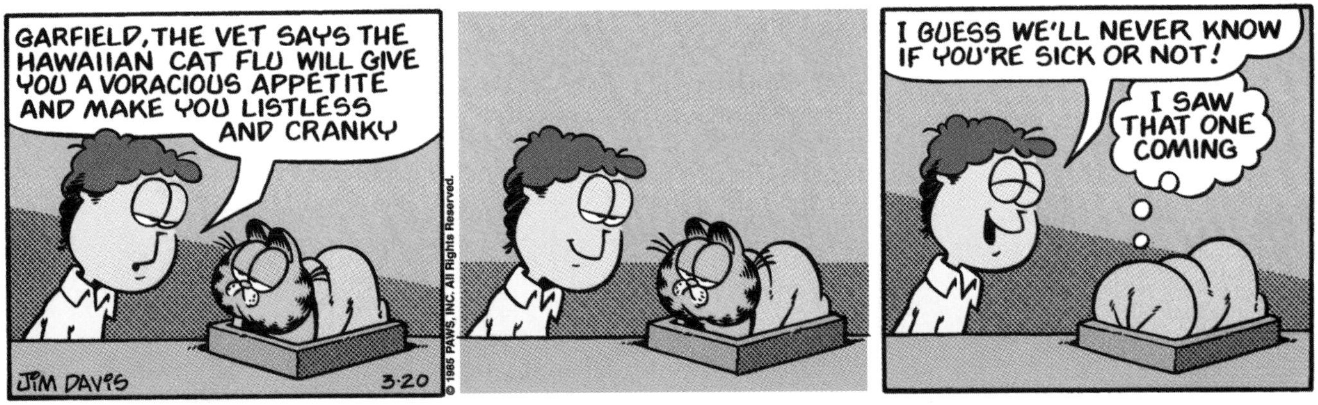
GARFIELD, THE VET SAYS THE HAWAIIAN CAT FLU WILL GIVE YOU A VORACIOUS APPETITE AND MAKE YOU LISTLESS AND CRANKY
JIM DAVIS
3-20
© 1985 PAWS, INC. All Rights Reserved.
I GUESS WE'LL NEVER KNOW IF YOU'RE SICK OR NOT!
I SAW THAT ONE COMING

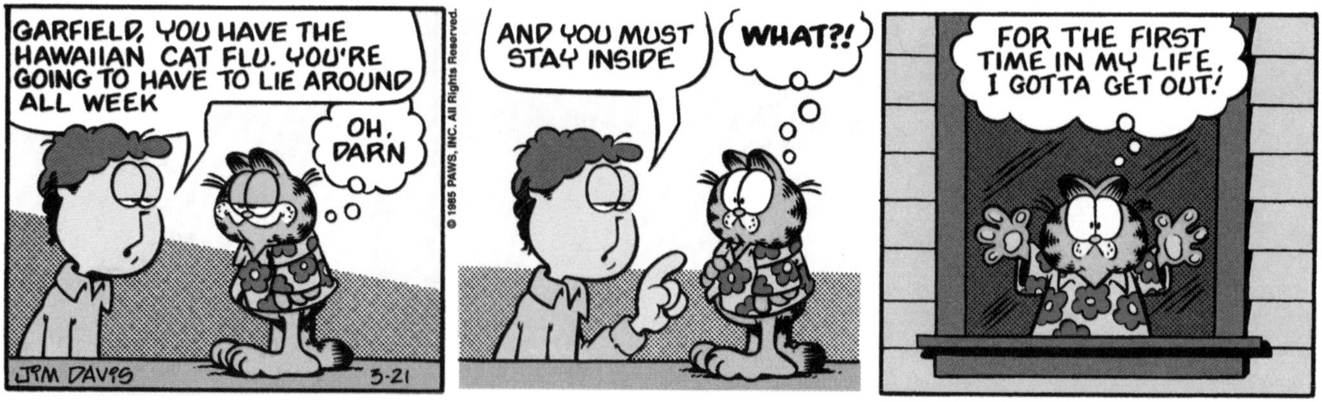
GARFIELD, YOU HAVE THE HAWAIIAN CAT FLU. YOU'RE GOING TO HAVE TO LIE AROUND ALL WEEK
OH, DARN
JIM DAVIS 3-21
© 1985 PAWS, INC. All Rights Reserved.
AND YOU MUST STAY INSIDE
WHAT?!
FOR THE FIRST TIME IN MY LIFE, I GOTTA GET OUT!

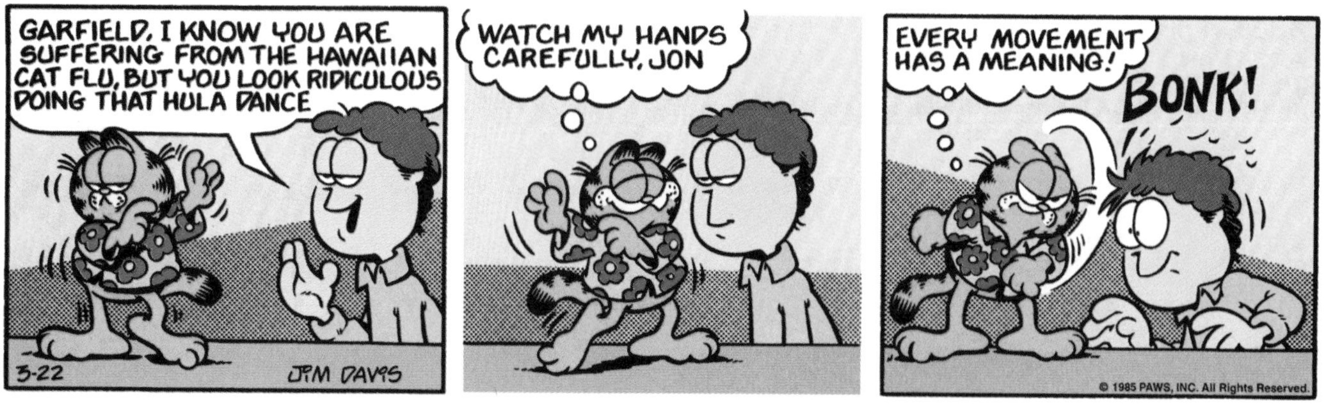
GARFIELD, I KNOW YOU ARE SUFFERING FROM THE HAWAIIAN CAT FLU, BUT YOU LOOK RIDICULOUS DOING THAT HULA DANCE
3-22 JIM DAVIS
WATCH MY HANDS CAREFULLY, JON
EVERY MOVEMENT HAS A MEANING!
BONK!
© 1985 PAWS, INC. All Rights Reserved.

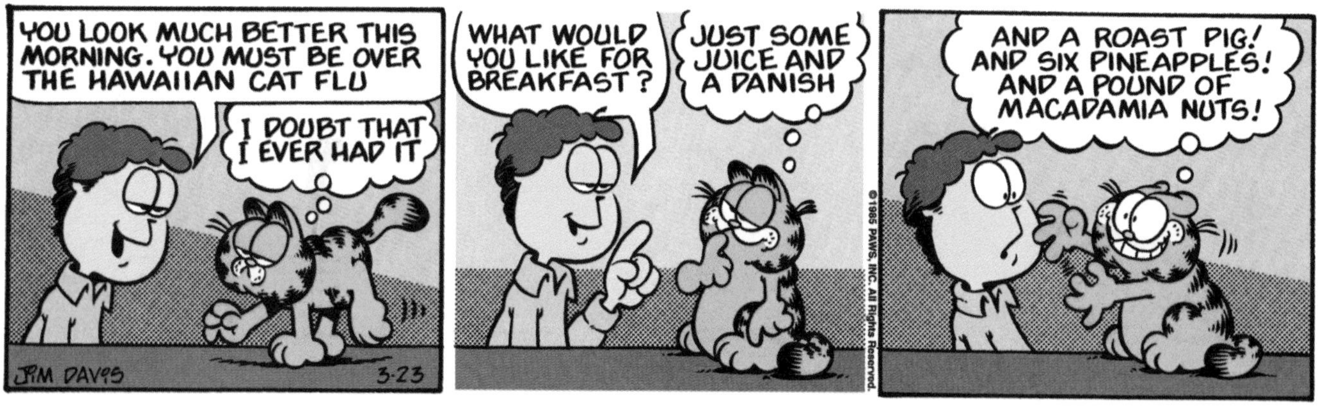
YOU LOOK MUCH BETTER THIS MORNING. YOU MUST BE OVER THE HAWAIIAN CAT FLU
I DOUBT THAT I EVER HAD IT
JIM DAVIS 3-23
WHAT WOULD YOU LIKE FOR BREAKFAST?
JUST SOME JUICE AND A DANISH
© 1985 PAWS, INC. All Rights Reserved.
AND A ROAST PIG! AND SIX PINEAPPLES! AND A POUND OF MACADAMIA NUTS!

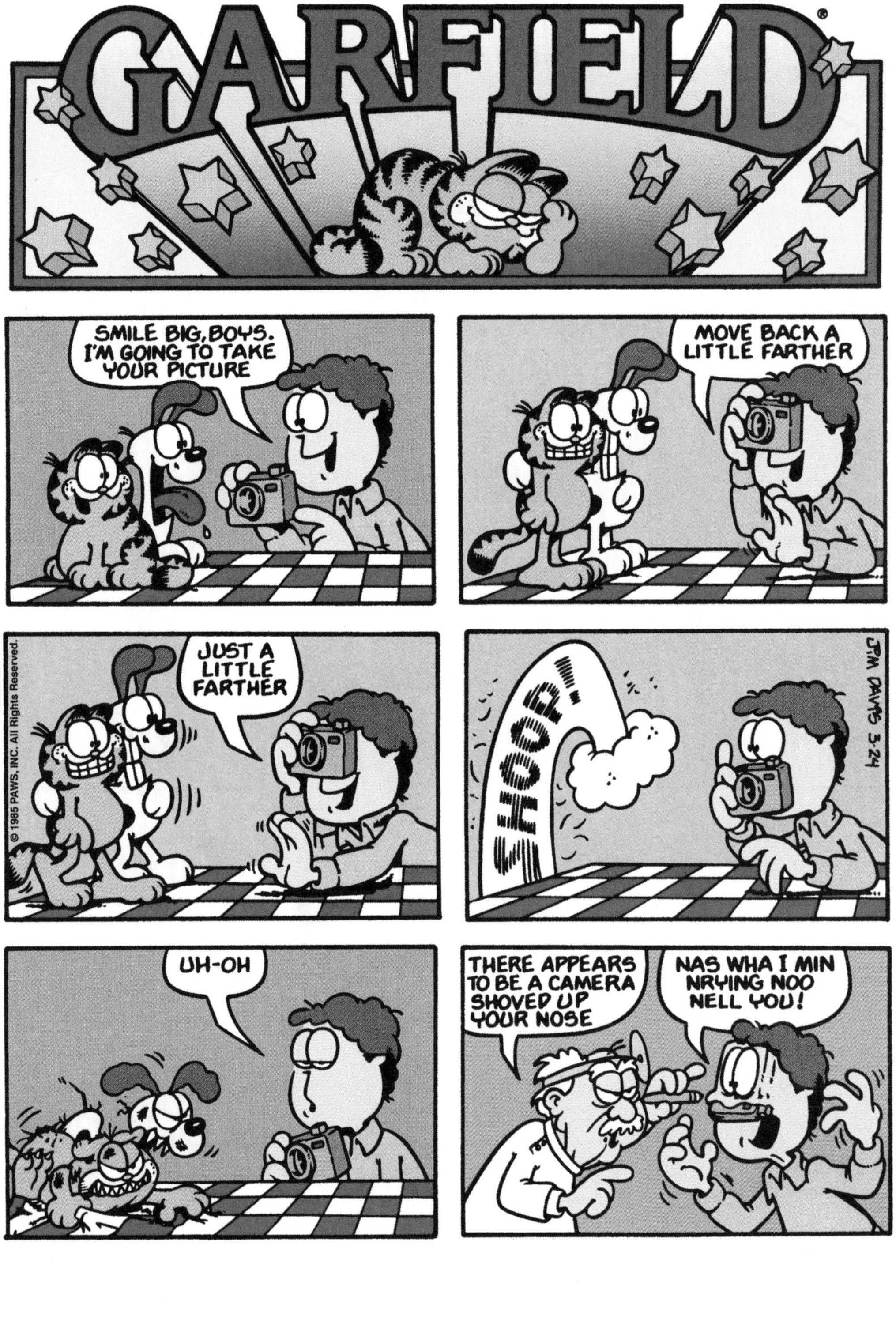
GARFIELD
SMILE BIG, BOYS. I'M GOING TO TAKE YOUR PICTURE
MOVE BACK A LITTLE FARTHER
JUST A LITTLE FARTHER
SHOOP!!!
JIM DAVIS 3-24
UH-OH
THERE APPEARS TO BE A CAMERA SHOVED UP YOUR NOSE
NAS WHA I MIN NRYING NOO NELL YOU!

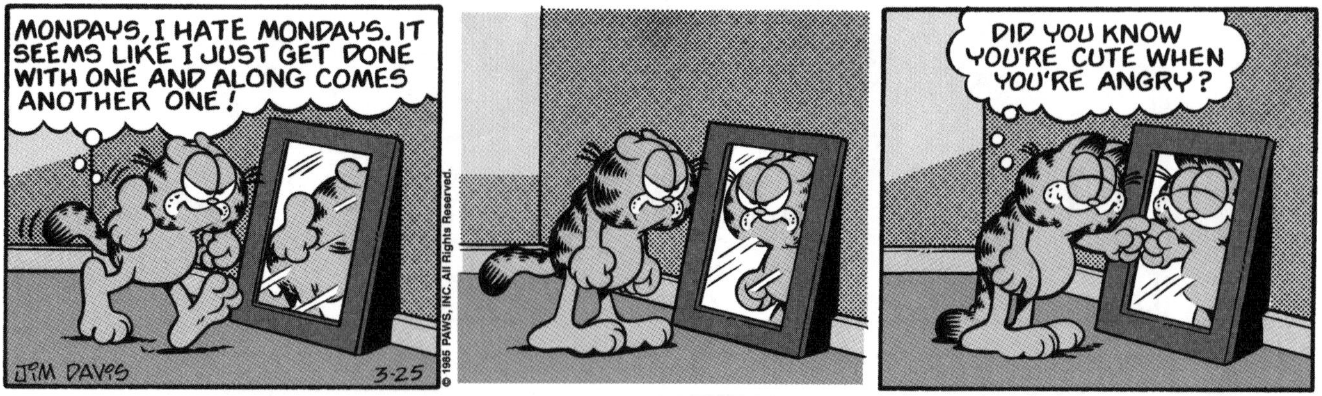
MONDAYS, I HATE MONDAYS. IT SEEMS LIKE I JUST GET DONE WITH ONE AND ALONG COMES ANOTHER ONE!
JIM DAVIS
3-25
© 1985 PAWS, INC. All Rights Reserved.
DID YOU KNOW YOU'RE CUTE WHEN YOU'RE ANGRY?

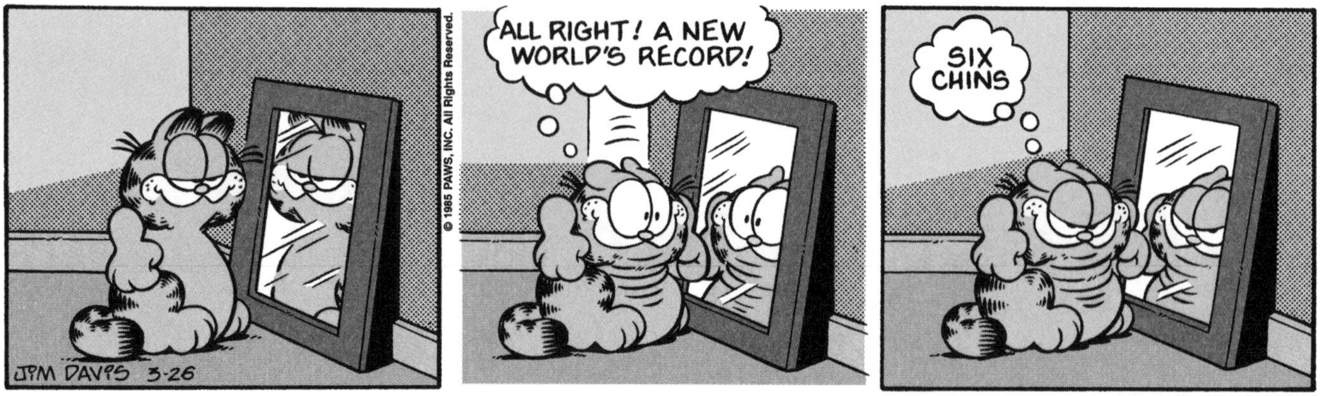
JIM DAVIS 3-26
© 1985 PAWS, INC. All Rights Reserved.
ALL RIGHT! A NEW WORLD'S RECORD!
SIX CHINS

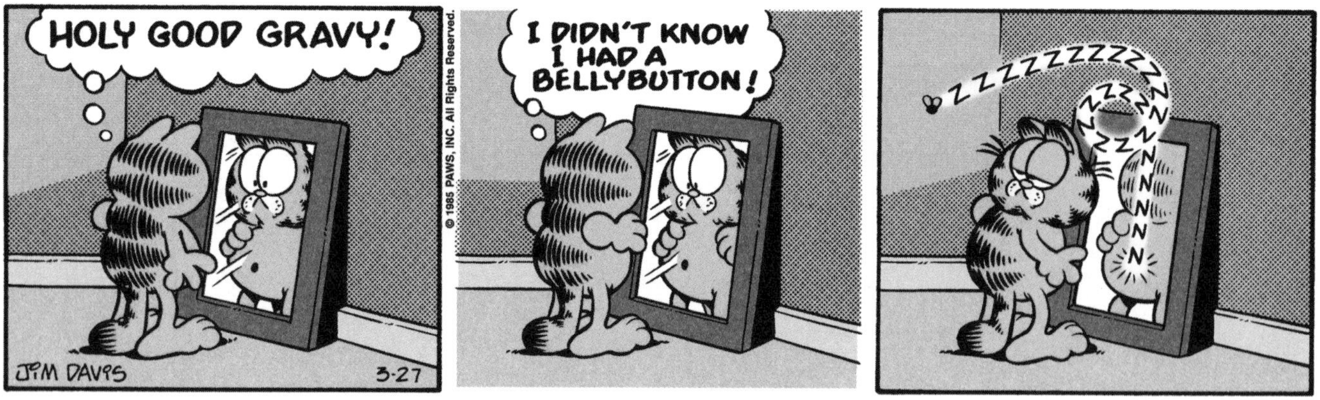
HOLY GOOD GRAVY!
JIM DAVIS
3-27
© 1985 PAWS, INC. All Rights Reserved.
I DIDN'T KNOW I HAD A BELLYBUTTON!

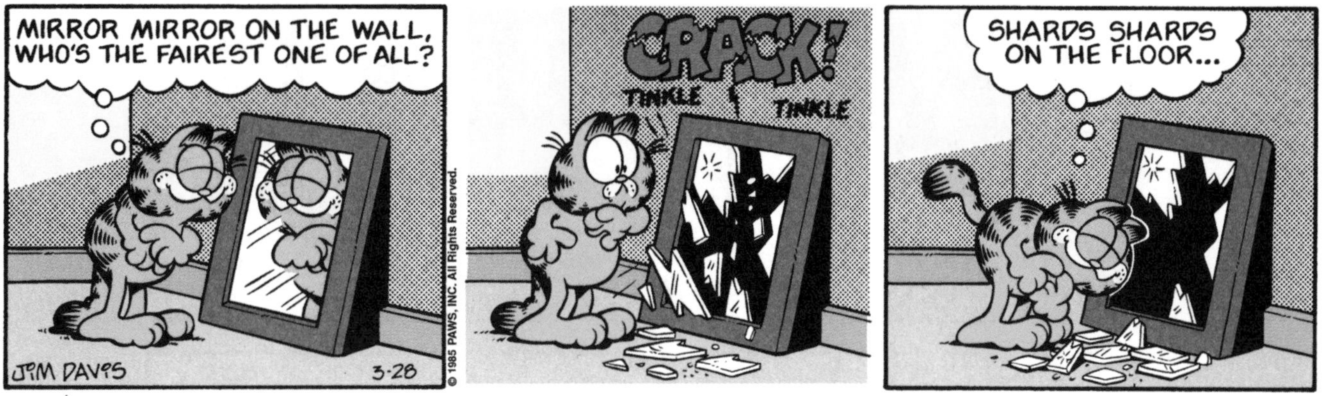
MIRROR MIRROR ON THE WALL, WHO'S THE FAIREST ONE OF ALL?
JIM DAVIS
3-28
© 1985 PAWS, INC. All Rights Reserved.
CRACK!
TINKLE
TINKLE
SHARDS SHARDS ON THE FLOOR...

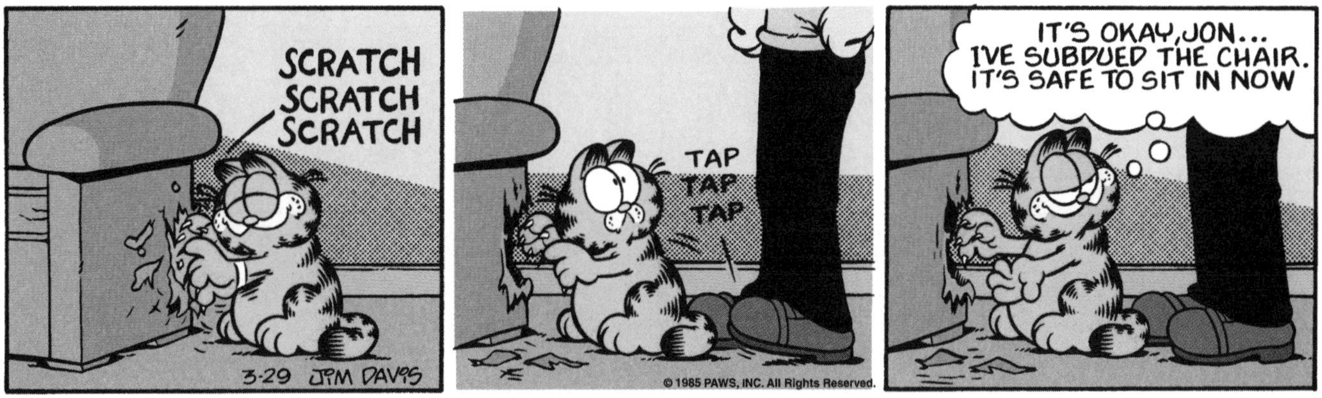
SCRATCH SCRATCH SCRATCH
3-29 JIM DAVIS
TAP TAP TAP
© 1985 PAWS, INC. All Rights Reserved.
IT'S OKAY, JON... I'VE SUBDUED THE CHAIR. IT'S SAFE TO SIT IN NOW

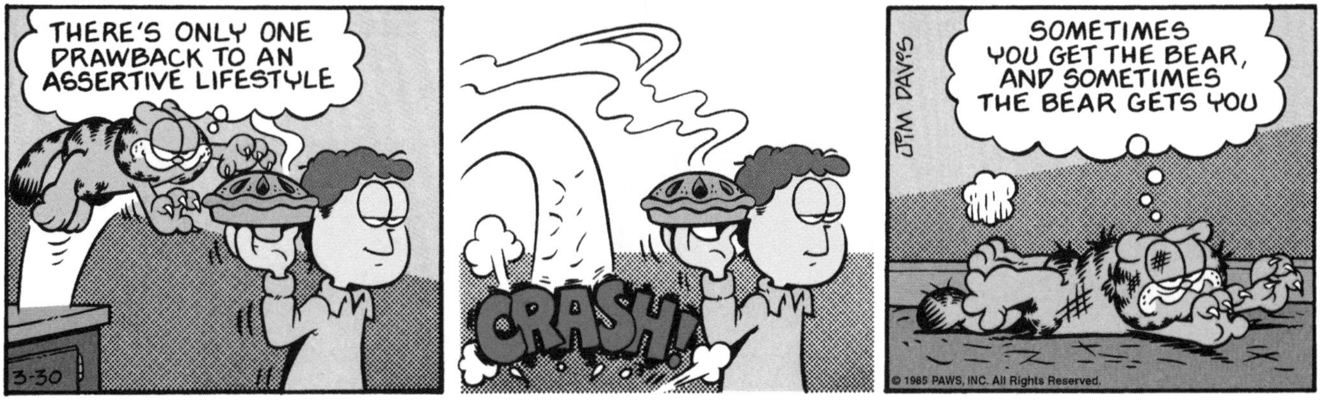
THERE'S ONLY ONE DRAWBACK TO AN ASSERTIVE LIFESTYLE
3-30
CRASH!
JIM DAVIS
SOMETIMES YOU GET THE BEAR, AND SOMETIMES THE BEAR GETS YOU
© 1985 PAWS, INC. All Rights Reserved.

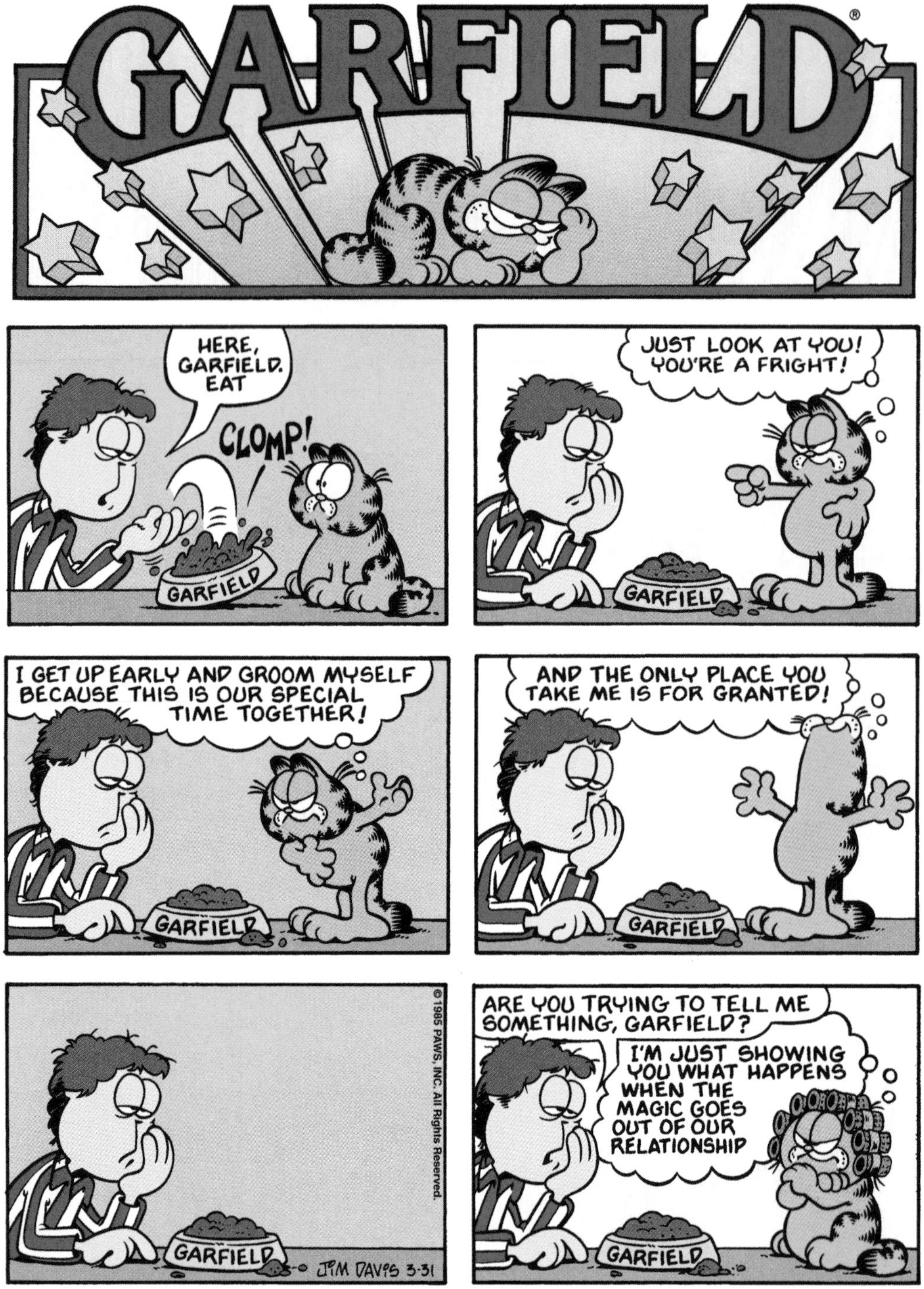
GARFIELD
HERE, GARFIELD. EAT
CLOMP!
GARFIELD
JUST LOOK AT YOU! YOU'RE A FRIGHT!
GARFIELD
I GET UP EARLY AND GROOM MYSELF BECAUSE THIS IS OUR SPECIAL TIME TOGETHER!
GARFIELD
AND THE ONLY PLACE YOU TAKE ME IS FOR GRANTED!
GARFIELD
GARFIELD
JIM DAVIS 3-31
© 1985 PAWS, INC. All Rights Reserved.
ARE YOU TRYING TO TELL ME SOMETHING, GARFIELD?
I'M JUST SHOWING YOU WHAT HAPPENS WHEN THE MAGIC GOES OUT OF OUR RELATIONSHIP
GARFIELD

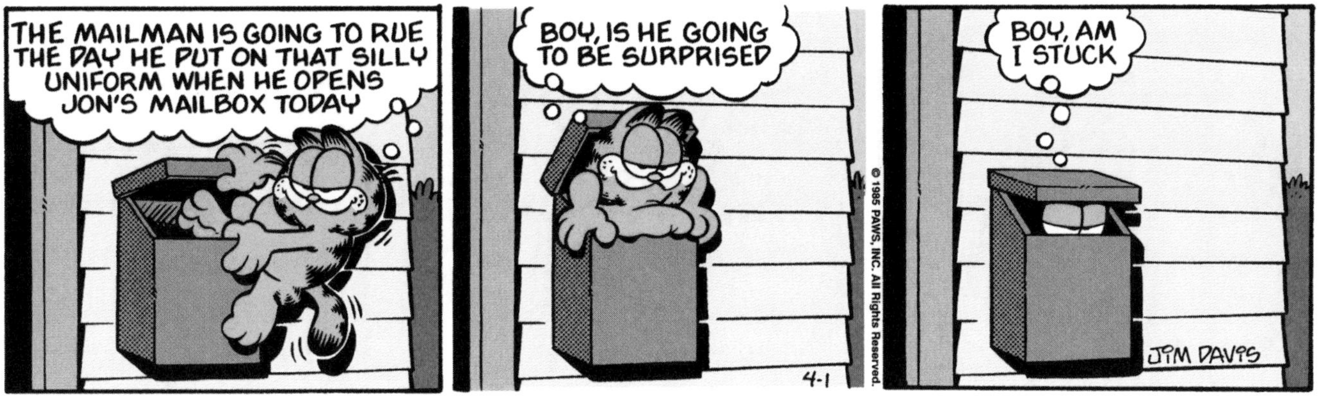
THE MAILMAN IS GOING TO RUE THE DAY HE PUT ON THAT SILLY UNIFORM WHEN HE OPENS JON'S MAILBOX TODAY
BOY, IS HE GOING TO BE SURPRISED
4-1
© 1985 PAWS, INC. All Rights Reserved.
BOY, AM I STUCK
JIM DAVIS

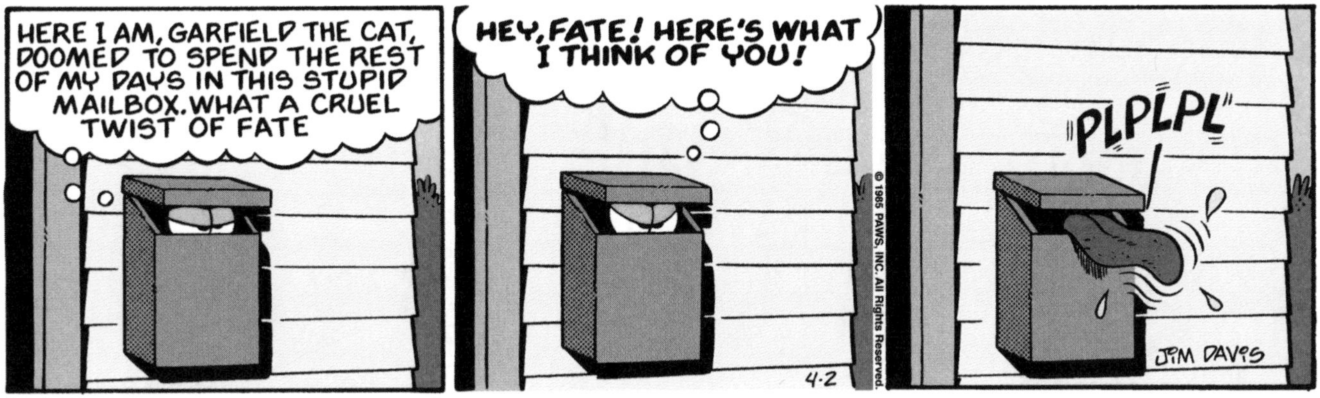
HERE I AM, GARFIELD THE CAT, DOOMED TO SPEND THE REST OF MY DAYS IN THIS STUPID MAILBOX. WHAT A CRUEL TWIST OF FATE
HEY, FATE! HERE'S WHAT I THINK OF YOU!
4-2
© 1985 PAWS, INC. All Rights Reserved.
PLPLPL
JIM DAVIS

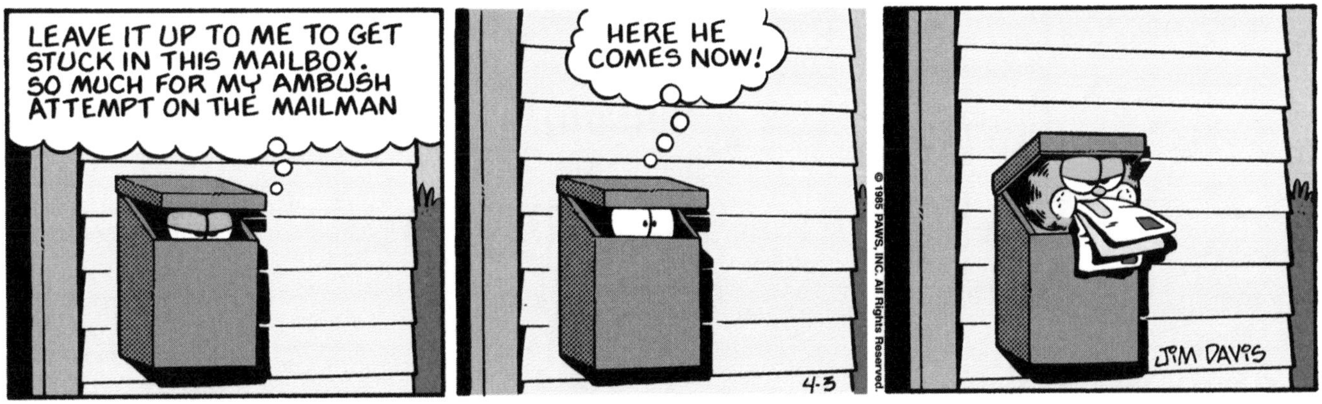
LEAVE IT UP TO ME TO GET STUCK IN THIS MAILBOX. SO MUCH FOR MY AMBUSH ATTEMPT ON THE MAILMAN
HERE HE COMES NOW!
4-3
© 1985 PAWS, INC. All Rights Reserved.
JIM DAVIS

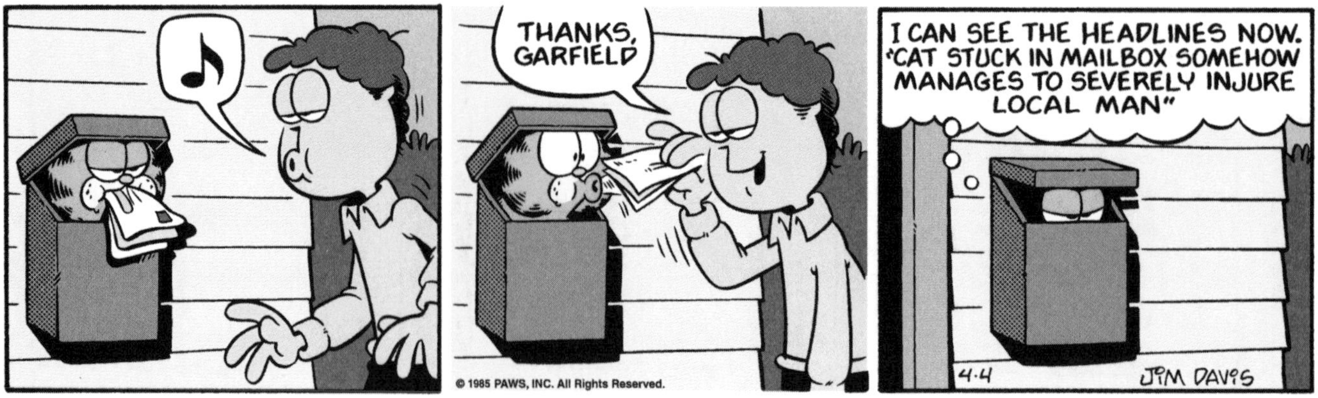
♪
THANKS, GARFIELD
© 1985 PAWS, INC. All Rights Reserved.
I CAN SEE THE HEADLINES NOW. "CAT STUCK IN MAILBOX SOMEHOW MANAGES TO SEVERELY INJURE LOCAL MAN"
4·4
JIM DAVIS

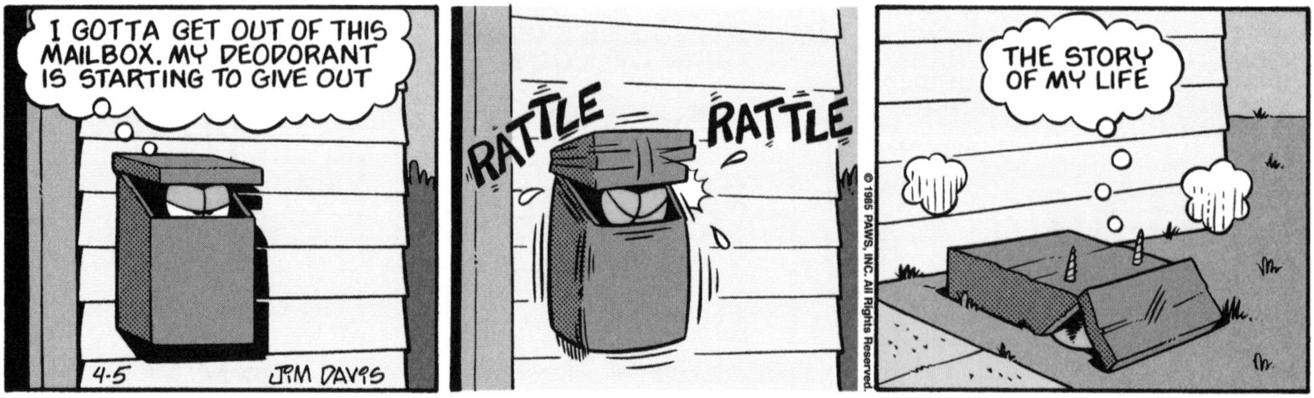
I GOTTA GET OUT OF THIS MAILBOX. MY DEODORANT IS STARTING TO GIVE OUT
4·5
JIM DAVIS
RATTLE
RATTLE
© 1985 PAWS, INC. All Rights Reserved.
THE STORY OF MY LIFE

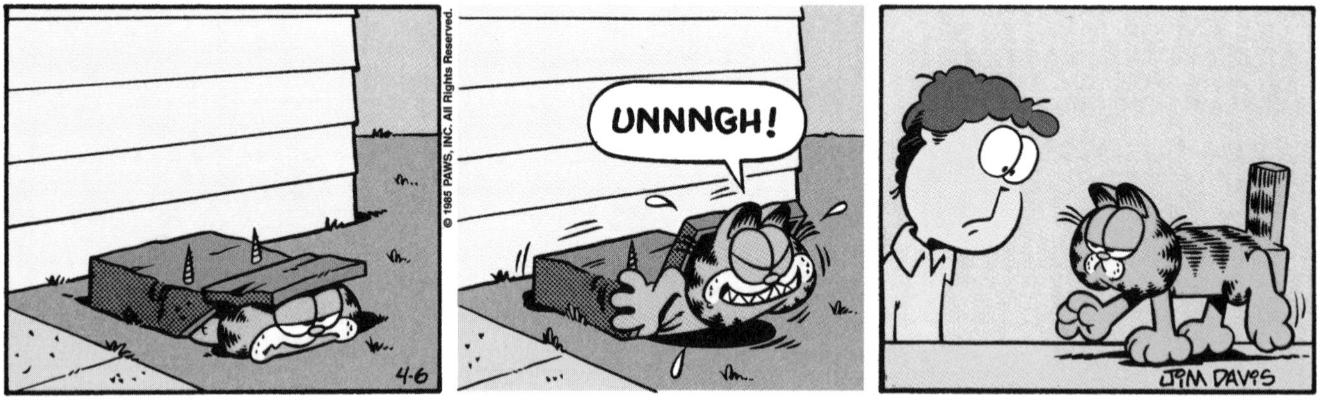
4·6
© 1985 PAWS, INC. All Rights Reserved.
UNNNGH!
JIM DAVIS

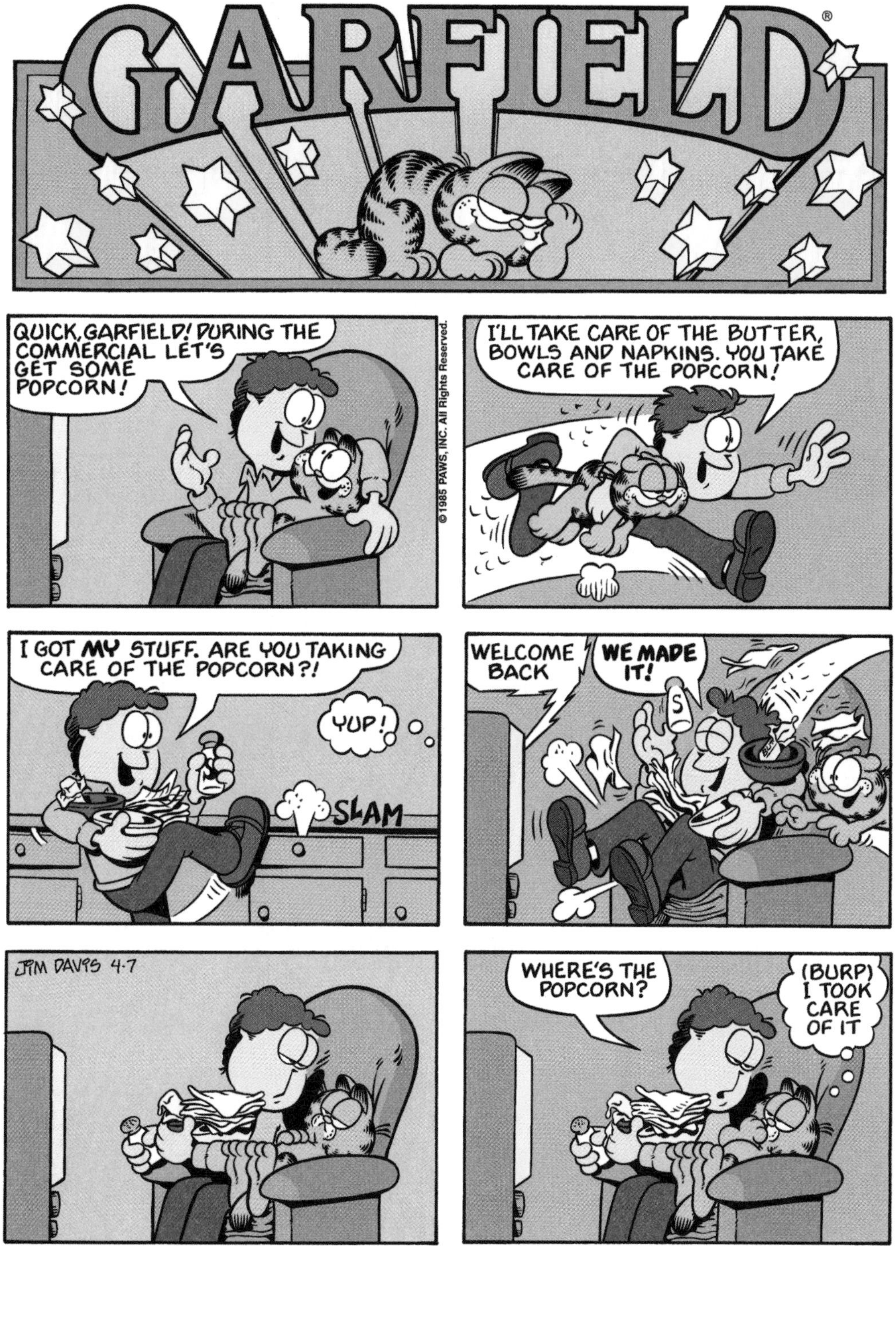
GARFIELD®
QUICK, GARFIELD! DURING THE COMMERCIAL LET'S GET SOME POPCORN!
©1985 PAWS, INC. All Rights Reserved.
I'LL TAKE CARE OF THE BUTTER, BOWLS AND NAPKINS. YOU TAKE CARE OF THE POPCORN!
I GOT **MY** STUFF. ARE YOU TAKING CARE OF THE POPCORN?!
YUP!
SLAM
WELCOME BACK
WE MADE IT!
S
JIM DAVIS 4-7
WHERE'S THE POPCORN?
(BURP) I TOOK CARE OF IT

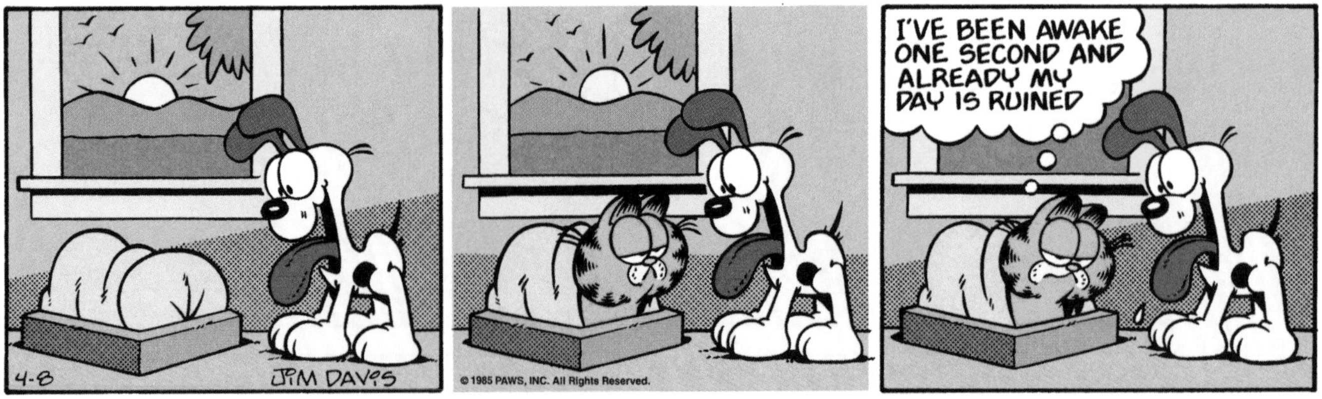
4-8
JIM DAVIS
© 1985 PAWS, INC. All Rights Reserved.
I'VE BEEN AWAKE ONE SECOND AND ALREADY MY DAY IS RUINED

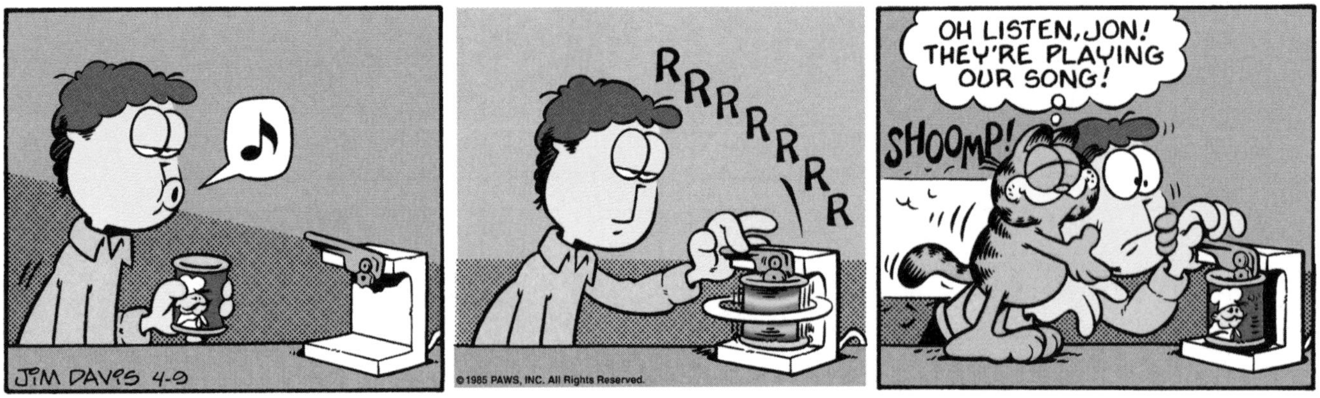
JIM DAVIS 4-9
RRRRRRRR
© 1985 PAWS, INC. All Rights Reserved.
OH LISTEN, JON! THEY'RE PLAYING OUR SONG!
SHOOMP!

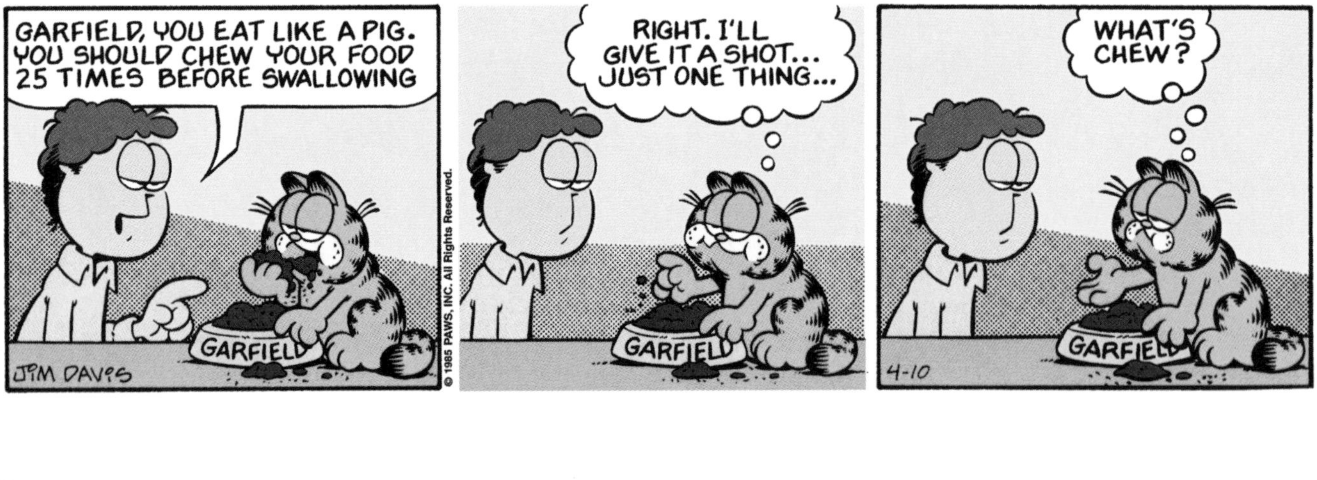
GARFIELD, YOU EAT LIKE A PIG. YOU SHOULD CHEW YOUR FOOD 25 TIMES BEFORE SWALLOWING
GARFIELD
JIM DAVIS
© 1985 PAWS, INC. All Rights Reserved.
RIGHT. I'LL GIVE IT A SHOT... JUST ONE THING...
GARFIELD
WHAT'S CHEW?
GARFIELD
4-10

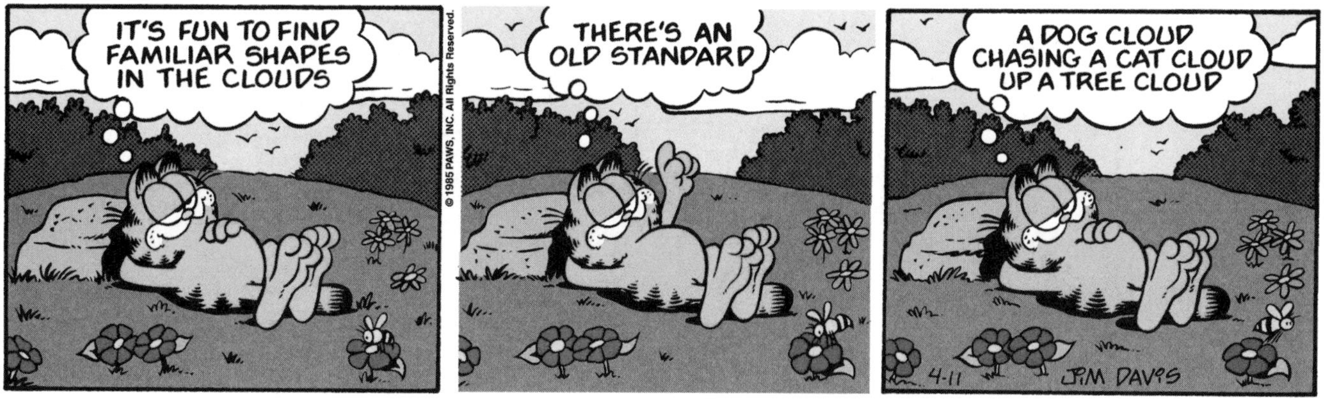
IT'S FUN TO FIND FAMILIAR SHAPES IN THE CLOUDS
© 1985 PAWS, INC. All Rights Reserved.
THERE'S AN OLD STANDARD
A DOG CLOUD CHASING A CAT CLOUD UP A TREE CLOUD
4-11
JIM DAVIS

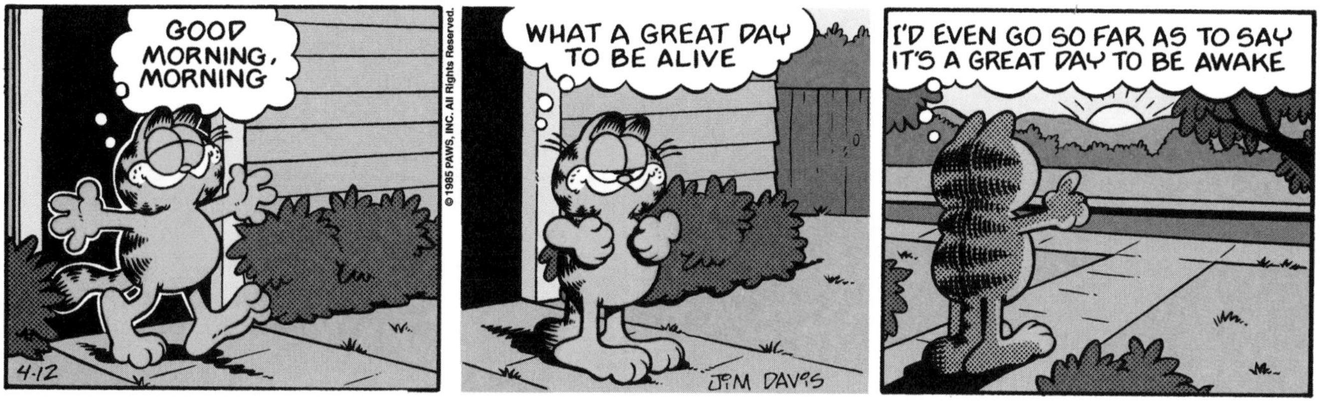
GOOD MORNING, MORNING
4-12
© 1985 PAWS, INC. All Rights Reserved.
WHAT A GREAT DAY TO BE ALIVE
JIM DAVIS
I'D EVEN GO SO FAR AS TO SAY IT'S A GREAT DAY TO BE AWAKE

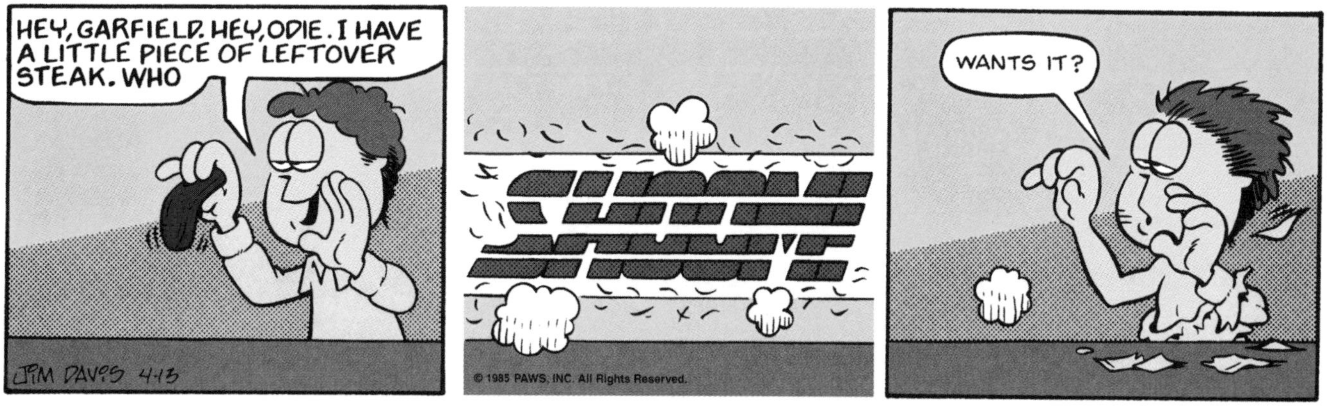
HEY, GARFIELD. HEY, ODIE. I HAVE A LITTLE PIECE OF LEFTOVER STEAK. WHO
JIM DAVIS 4-13
© 1985 PAWS, INC. All Rights Reserved.
WANTS IT?

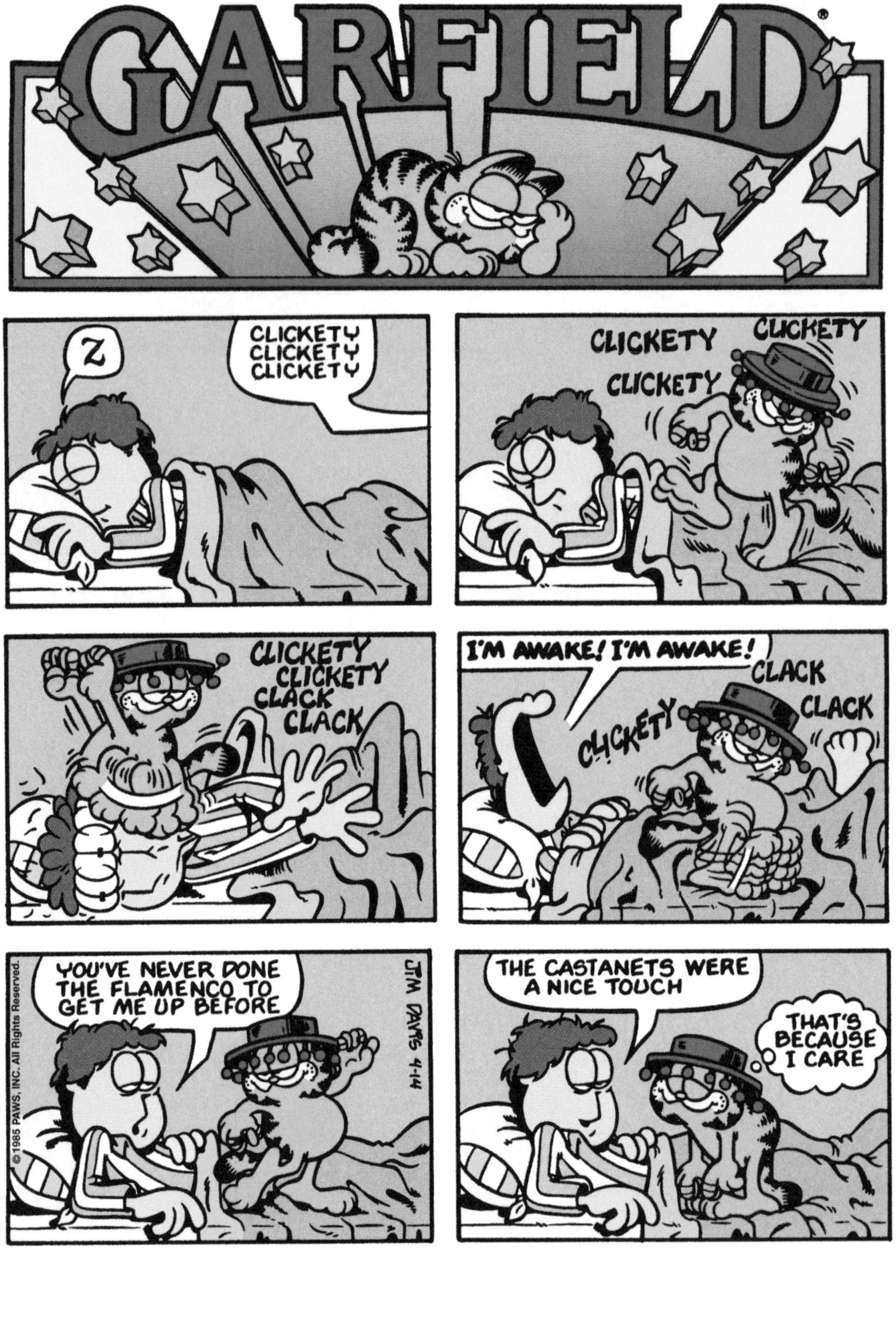
GARFIELD®
Z
CLICKETY CLICKETY CLICKETY
CLICKETY CLICKETY CLICKETY
CLICKETY CLICKETY CLACK CLACK
I'M AWAKE! I'M AWAKE!
CLICKETY CLACK CLACK
YOU'VE NEVER DONE THE FLAMENCO TO GET ME UP BEFORE
JIM DAVIS 4-14
THE CASTANETS WERE A NICE TOUCH
THAT'S BECAUSE I CARE

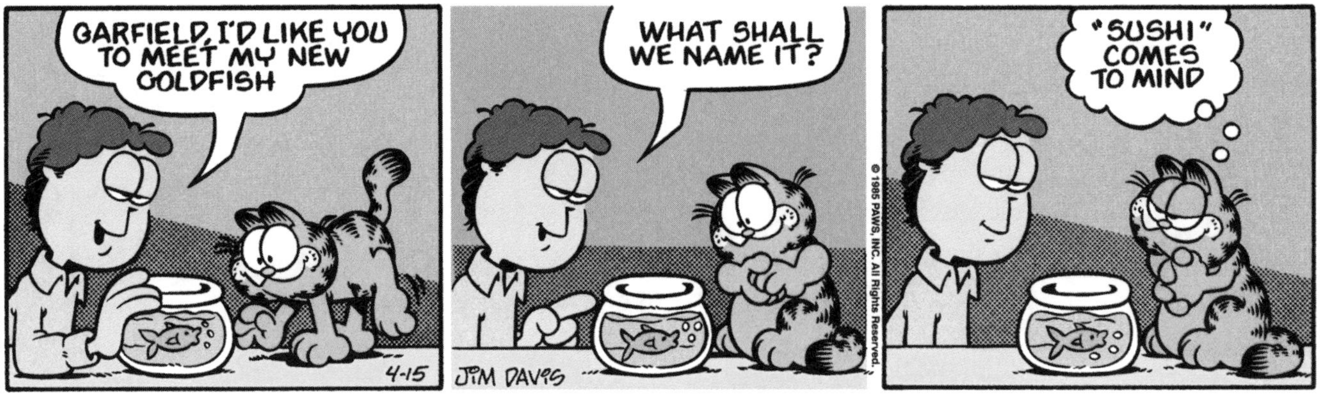
GARFIELD, I'D LIKE YOU TO MEET MY NEW GOLDFISH
4-15
WHAT SHALL WE NAME IT?
JIM DAVIS
© 1985 PAWS, INC. All Rights Reserved.
"SUSHI" COMES TO MIND

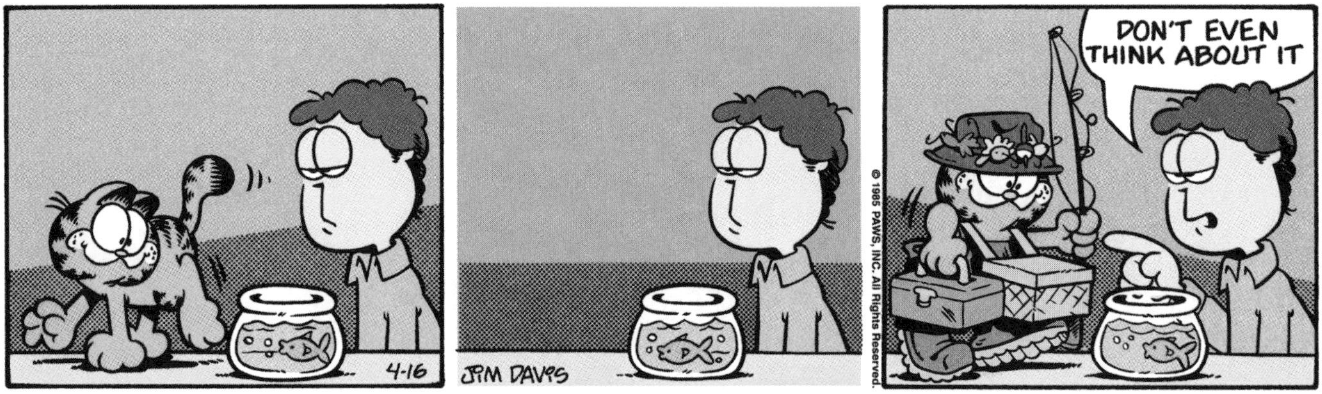
4-16
JIM DAVIS
© 1985 PAWS, INC. All Rights Reserved.
DON'T EVEN THINK ABOUT IT

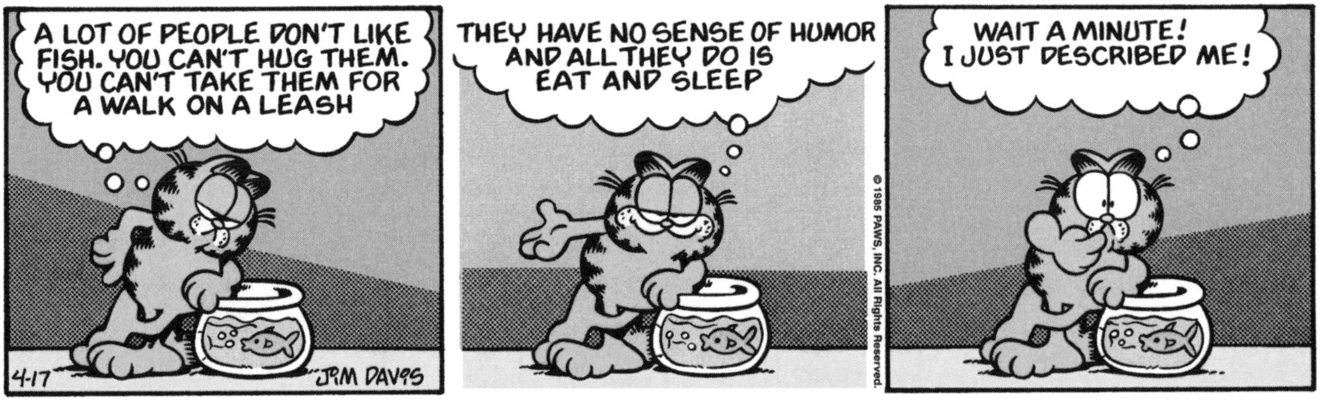
A LOT OF PEOPLE DON'T LIKE FISH. YOU CAN'T HUG THEM. YOU CAN'T TAKE THEM FOR A WALK ON A LEASH
4-17
JIM DAVIS
THEY HAVE NO SENSE OF HUMOR AND ALL THEY DO IS EAT AND SLEEP
© 1985 PAWS, INC. All Rights Reserved.
WAIT A MINUTE! I JUST DESCRIBED ME!

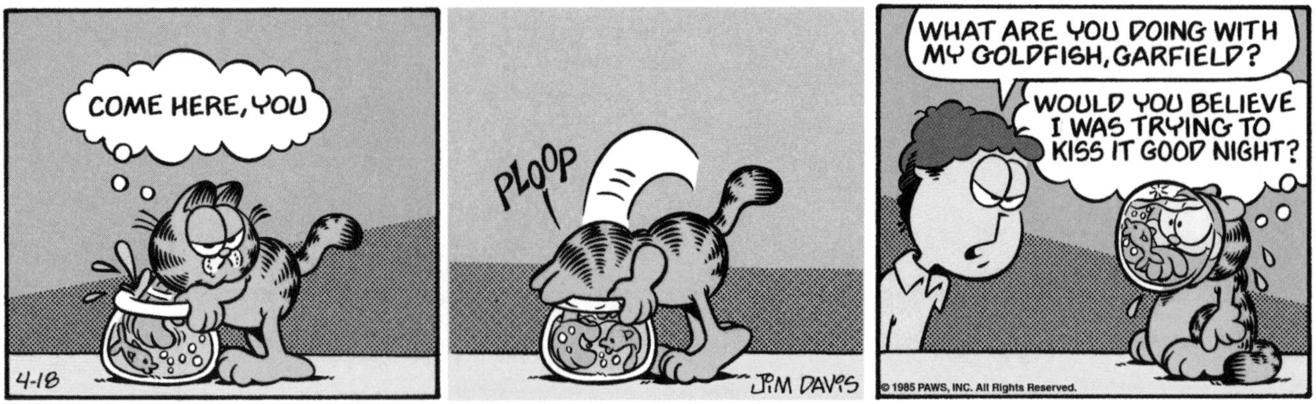
COME HERE, YOU
PLOOP
WHAT ARE YOU DOING WITH MY GOLDFISH, GARFIELD?
WOULD YOU BELIEVE I WAS TRYING TO KISS IT GOOD NIGHT?
4-18
JIM DAVIS
© 1985 PAWS, INC. All Rights Reserved.

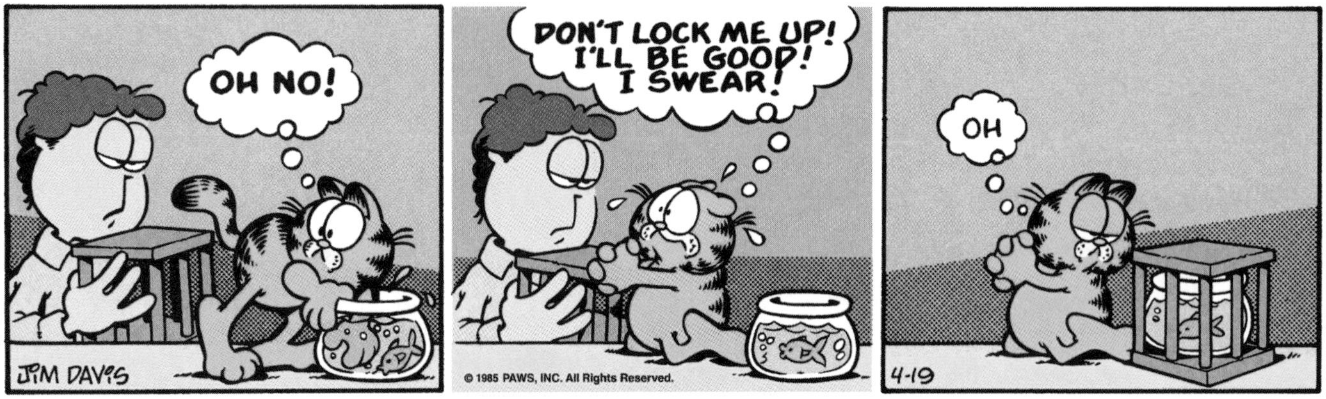
OH NO!
DON'T LOCK ME UP! I'LL BE GOOD! I SWEAR!
OH
JIM DAVIS
© 1985 PAWS, INC. All Rights Reserved.
4-19

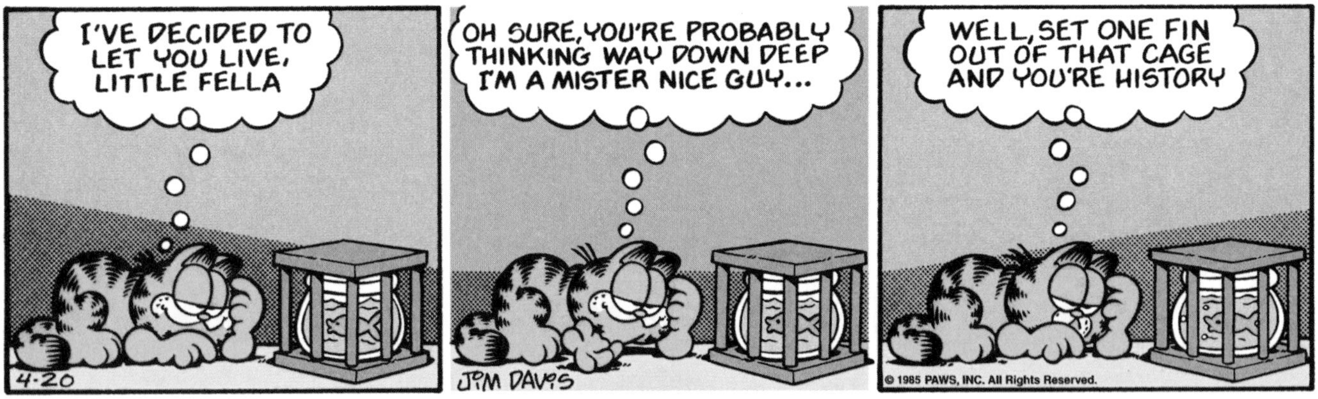
I'VE DECIDED TO LET YOU LIVE, LITTLE FELLA
OH SURE, YOU'RE PROBABLY THINKING WAY DOWN DEEP I'M A MISTER NICE GUY...
WELL, SET ONE FIN OUT OF THAT CAGE AND YOU'RE HISTORY
4-20
JIM DAVIS
© 1985 PAWS, INC. All Rights Reserved.

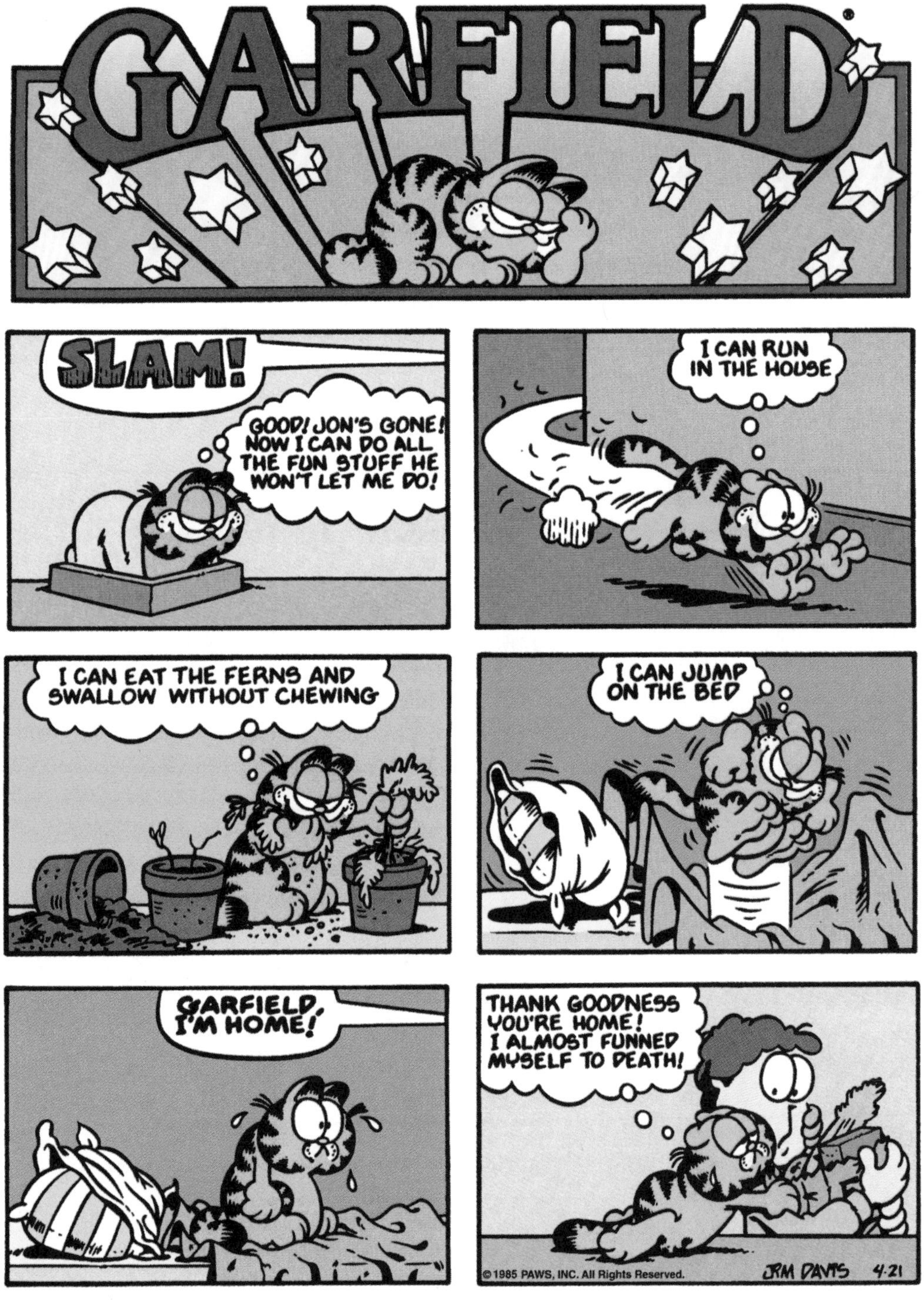
GARFIELD
SLAM!
GOOD! JON'S GONE! NOW I CAN DO ALL THE FUN STUFF HE WON'T LET ME DO!
I CAN RUN IN THE HOUSE
I CAN EAT THE FERNS AND SWALLOW WITHOUT CHEWING
I CAN JUMP ON THE BED
GARFIELD, I'M HOME!
THANK GOODNESS YOU'RE HOME! I ALMOST FUNNED MYSELF TO DEATH!
JIM DAVIS 4-21

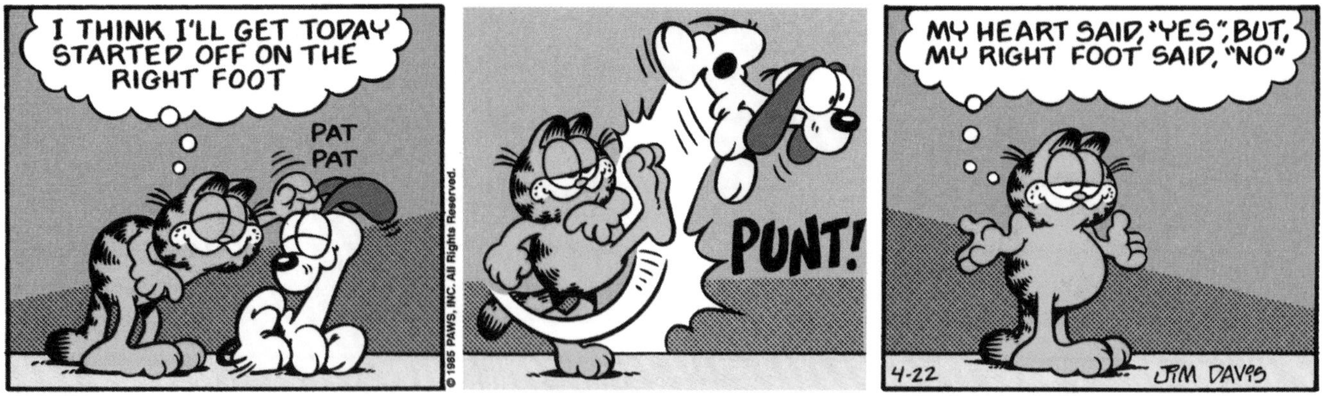
I THINK I'LL GET TODAY STARTED OFF ON THE RIGHT FOOT
PAT
PAT
© 1985 PAWS, INC. All Rights Reserved.
PUNT!
MY HEART SAID, "YES", BUT, MY RIGHT FOOT SAID, "NO"
4-22
JIM DAVIS

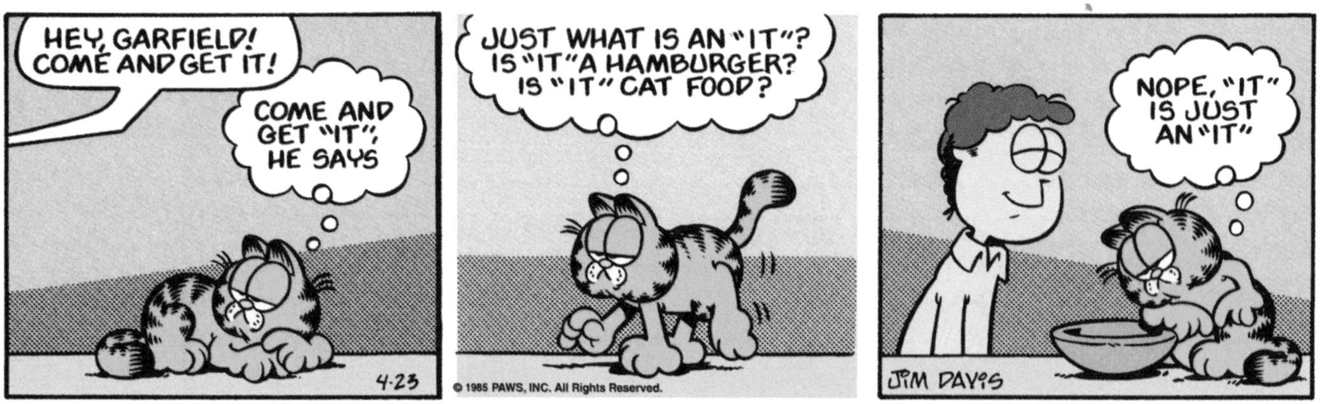
HEY, GARFIELD! COME AND GET IT!
COME AND GET "IT", HE SAYS
4-23
JUST WHAT IS AN "IT"? IS "IT" A HAMBURGER? IS "IT" CAT FOOD?
© 1985 PAWS, INC. All Rights Reserved.
NOPE, "IT" IS JUST AN "IT"
JIM DAVIS

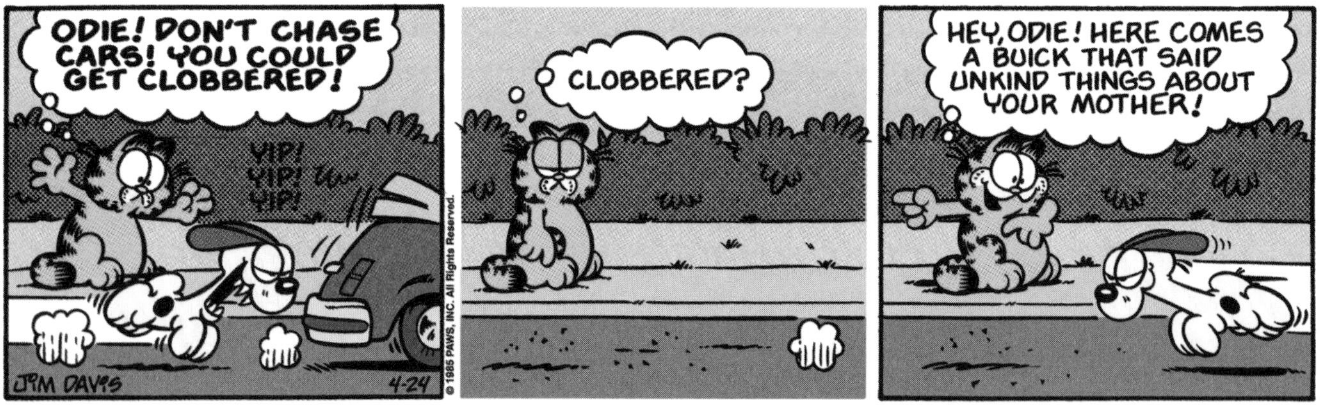
ODIE! DON'T CHASE CARS! YOU COULD GET CLOBBERED!
YIP! YIP! YIP!
JIM DAVIS
4-24
© 1985 PAWS, INC. All Rights Reserved.
CLOBBERED?
HEY, ODIE! HERE COMES A BUICK THAT SAID UNKIND THINGS ABOUT YOUR MOTHER!

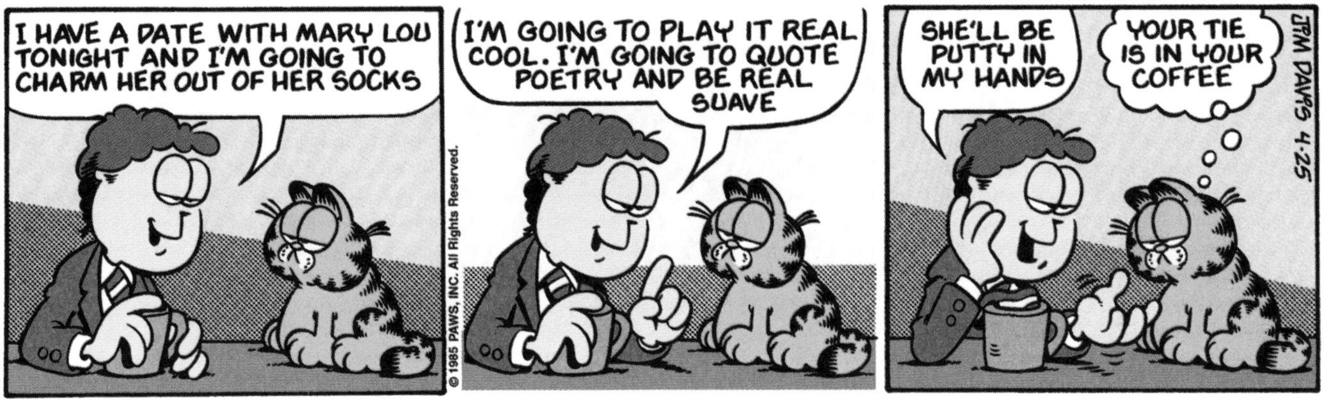
I HAVE A DATE WITH MARY LOU TONIGHT AND I'M GOING TO CHARM HER OUT OF HER SOCKS
© 1985 PAWS, INC. All Rights Reserved.
I'M GOING TO PLAY IT REAL COOL. I'M GOING TO QUOTE POETRY AND BE REAL SUAVE
SHE'LL BE PUTTY IN MY HANDS
YOUR TIE IS IN YOUR COFFEE
JIM DAVIS 4-25

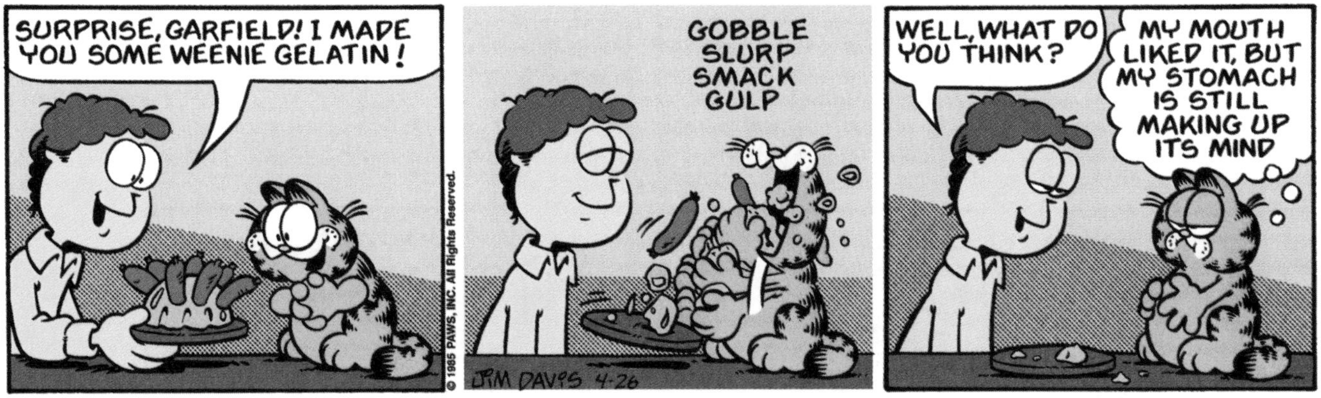
SURPRISE, GARFIELD! I MADE YOU SOME WEENIE GELATIN!
© 1985 PAWS, INC. All Rights Reserved.
GOBBLE
SLURP
SMACK
GULP
JIM DAVIS 4-26
WELL, WHAT DO YOU THINK?
MY MOUTH LIKED IT, BUT MY STOMACH IS STILL MAKING UP ITS MIND

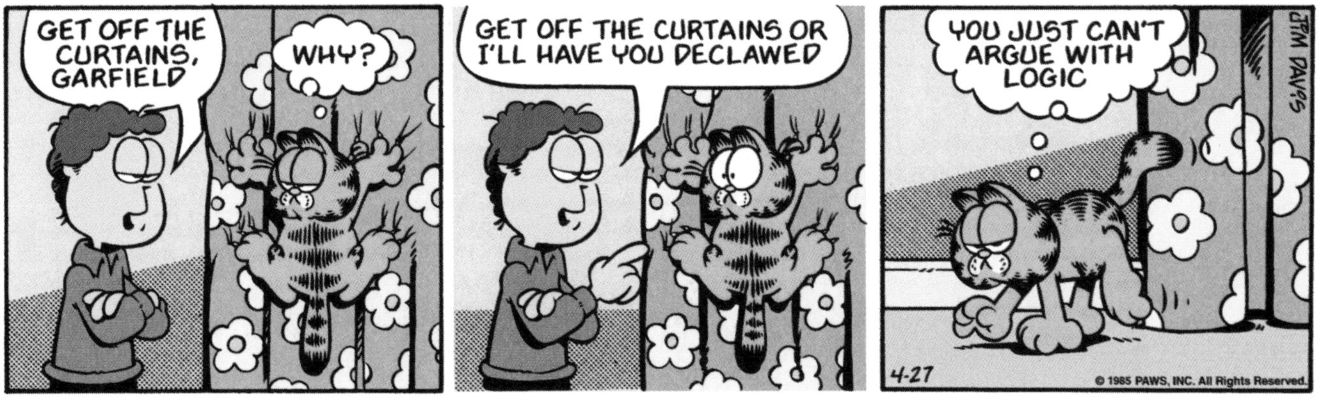
GET OFF THE CURTAINS, GARFIELD
WHY?
GET OFF THE CURTAINS OR I'LL HAVE YOU DECLAWED
YOU JUST CAN'T ARGUE WITH LOGIC
JIM DAVIS
4-27
© 1985 PAWS, INC. All Rights Reserved.

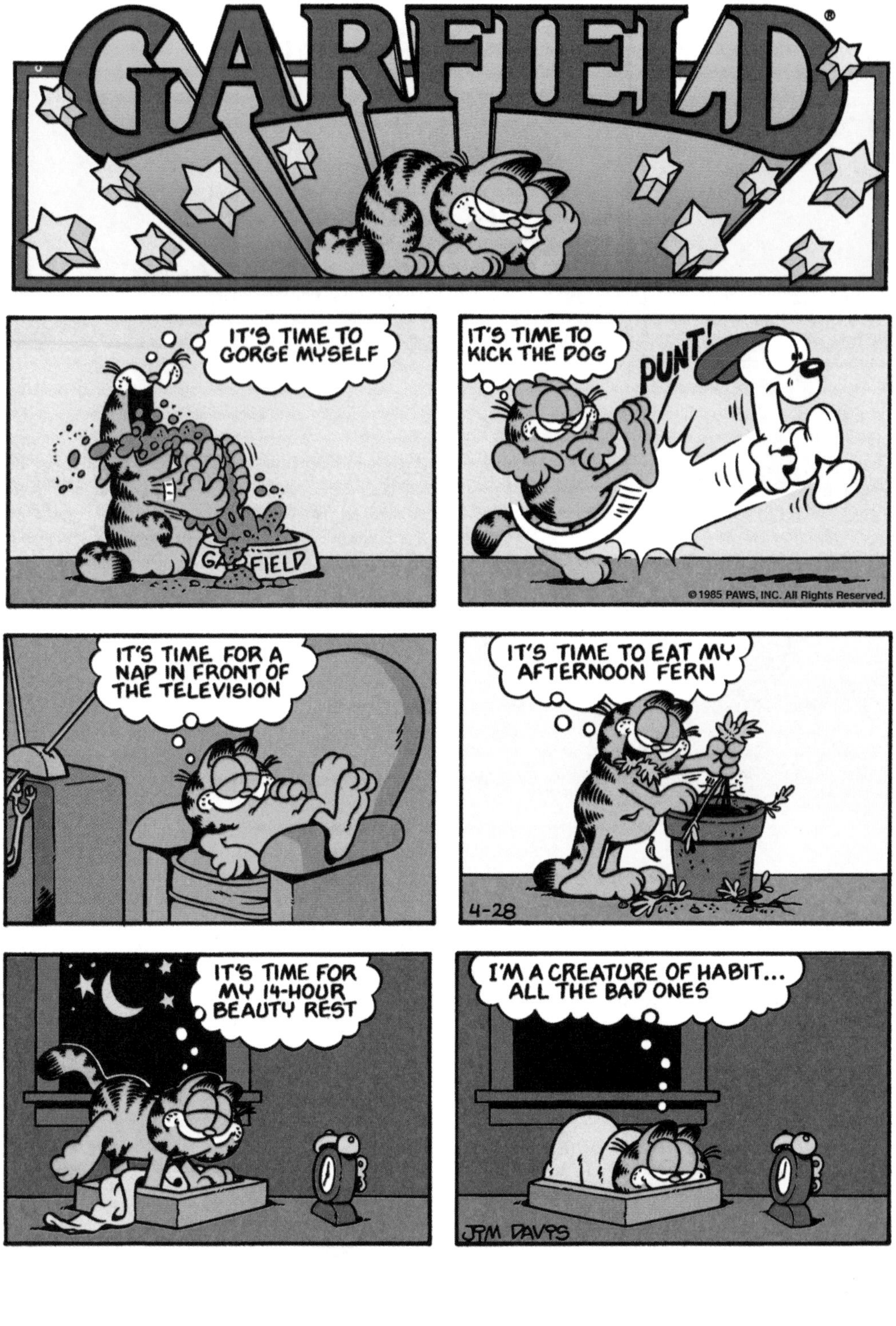
GARFIELD
IT'S TIME TO GORGE MYSELF
GARFIELD
IT'S TIME TO KICK THE DOG
PUNT!
© 1985 PAWS, INC. All Rights Reserved.
IT'S TIME FOR A NAP IN FRONT OF THE TELEVISION
IT'S TIME TO EAT MY AFTERNOON FERN
4-28
IT'S TIME FOR MY 14-HOUR BEAUTY REST
I'M A CREATURE OF HABIT... ALL THE BAD ONES
JIM DAVIS

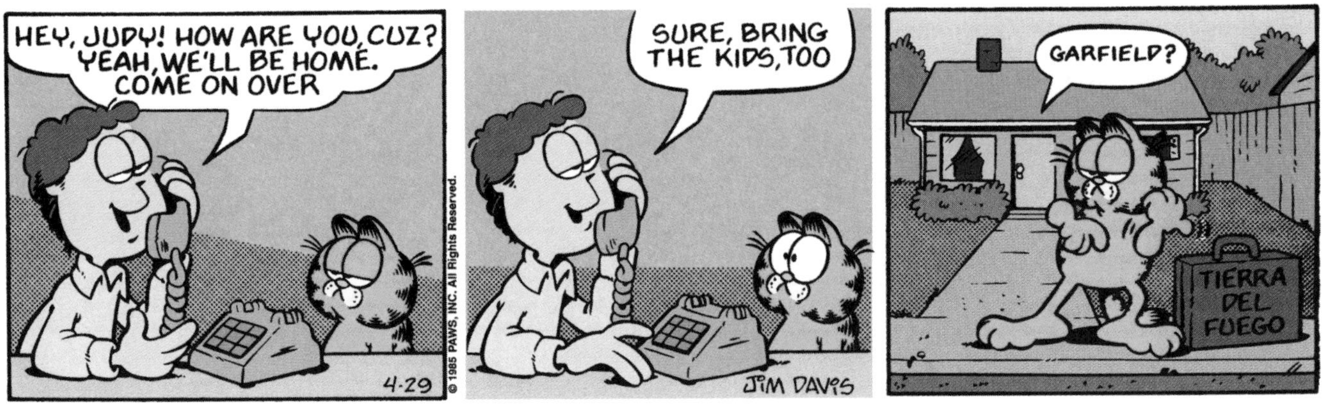
HEY, JUDY! HOW ARE YOU, CUZ? YEAH, WE'LL BE HOME. COME ON OVER
4-29
© 1985 PAWS, INC. All Rights Reserved.
SURE, BRING THE KIDS, TOO
JIM DAVIS
GARFIELD?
TIERRA DEL FUEGO

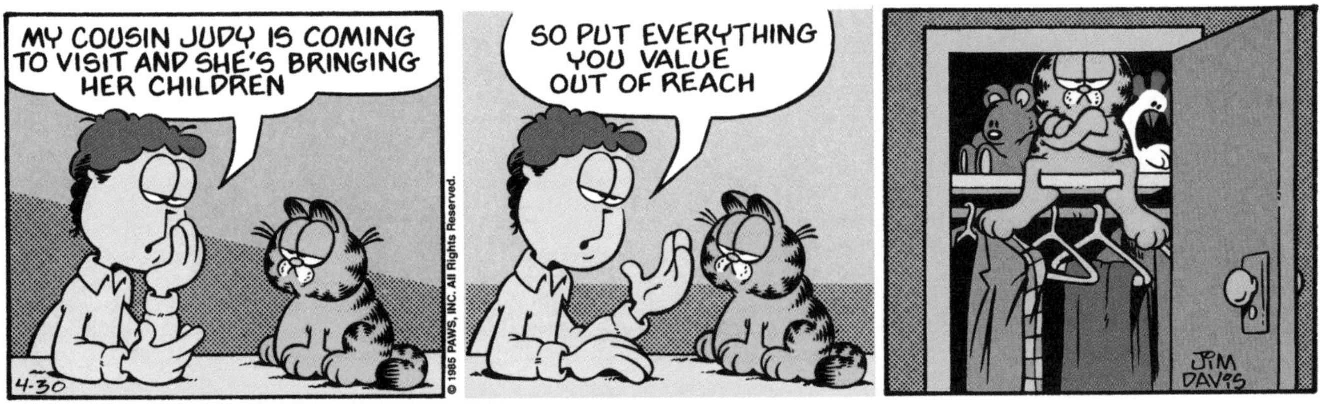
MY COUSIN JUDY IS COMING TO VISIT AND SHE'S BRINGING HER CHILDREN
4-30
© 1985 PAWS, INC. All Rights Reserved.
SO PUT EVERYTHING YOU VALUE OUT OF REACH
JIM DAVIS

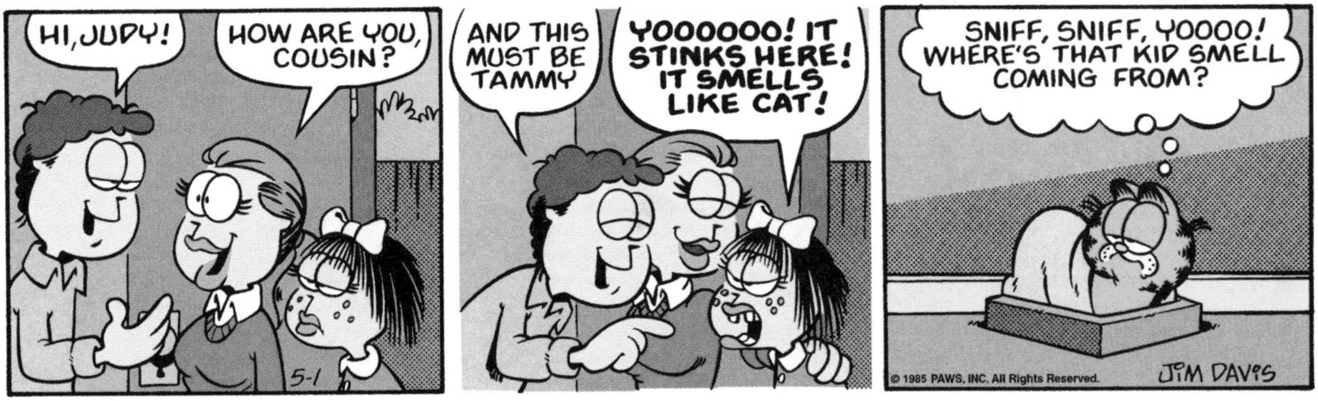
HI, JUDY!
HOW ARE YOU, COUSIN?
5-1
AND THIS MUST BE TAMMY
YOOOOOO! IT STINKS HERE! IT SMELLS LIKE CAT!
SNIFF, SNIFF, YOOOO! WHERE'S THAT KID SMELL COMING FROM?
© 1985 PAWS, INC. All Rights Reserved.
JIM DAVIS

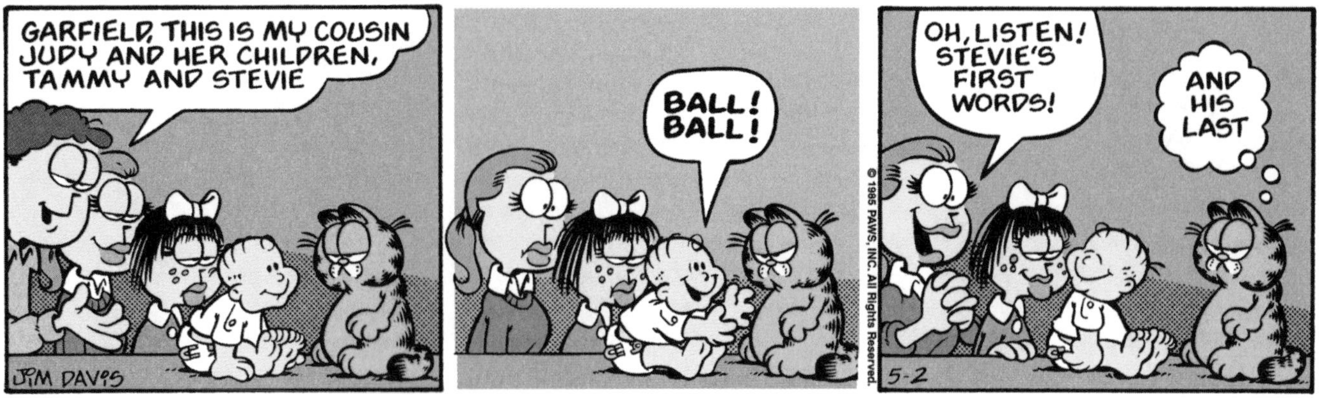
GARFIELD, THIS IS MY COUSIN JUDY AND HER CHILDREN, TAMMY AND STEVIE
JIM DAVIS
BALL! BALL!
© 1985 PAWS, INC. All Rights Reserved.
OH, LISTEN! STEVIE'S FIRST WORDS!
AND HIS LAST
5-2

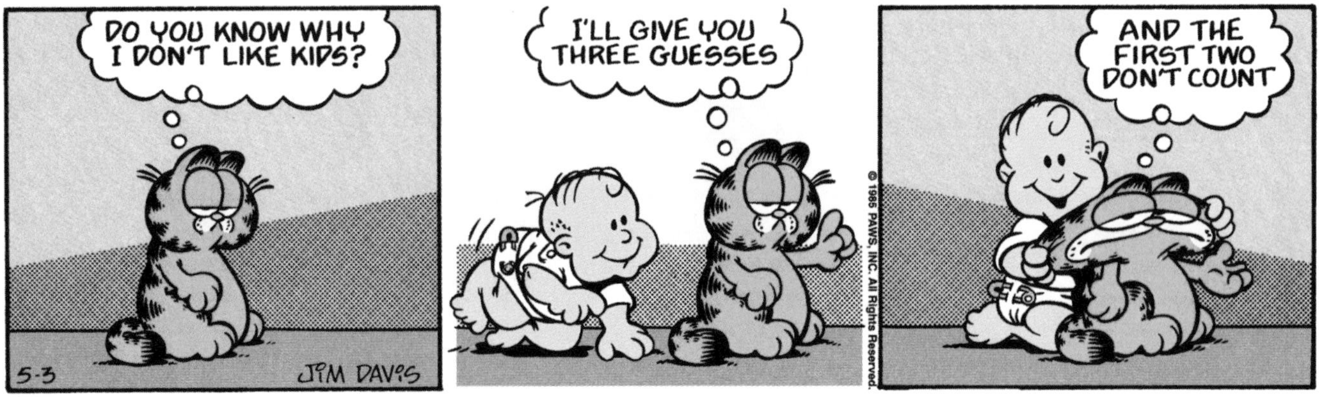
DO YOU KNOW WHY I DON'T LIKE KIDS?
5-3
JIM DAVIS
I'LL GIVE YOU THREE GUESSES
© 1985 PAWS, INC. All Rights Reserved.
AND THE FIRST TWO DON'T COUNT

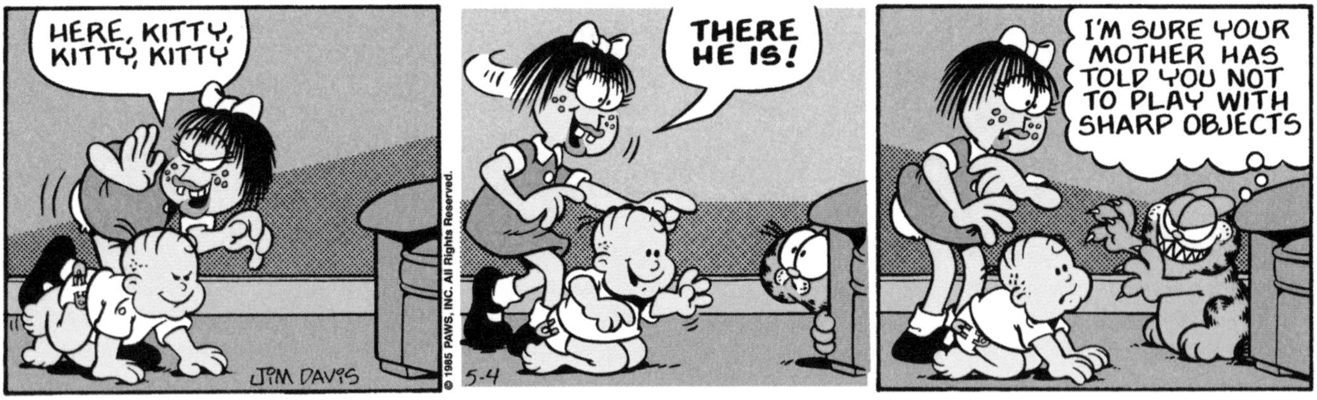
HERE, KITTY, KITTY, KITTY
JIM DAVIS
© 1985 PAWS, INC. All Rights Reserved.
THERE HE IS!
5-4
I'M SURE YOUR MOTHER HAS TOLD YOU NOT TO PLAY WITH SHARP OBJECTS

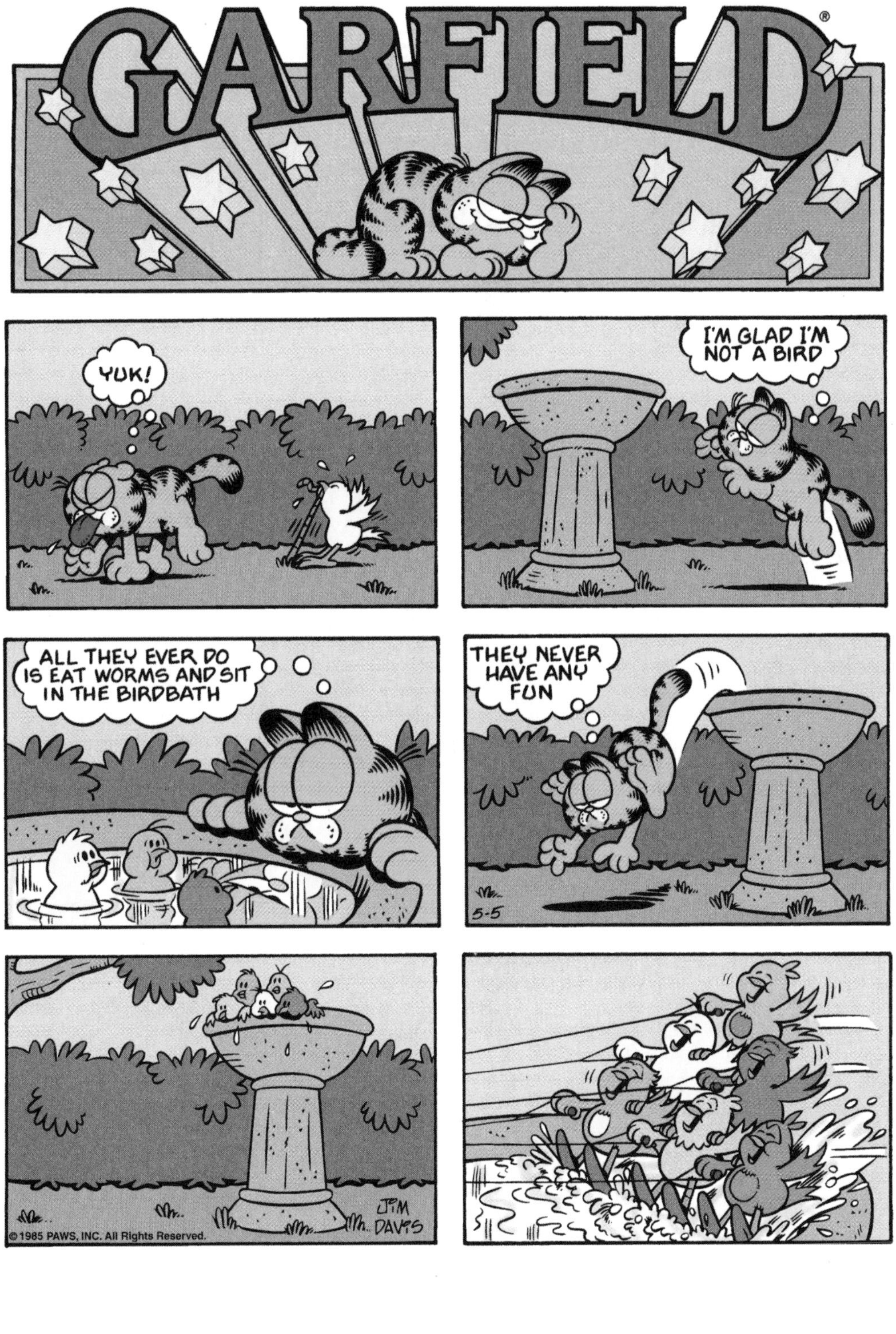
GARFIELD®
YUK!
I'M GLAD I'M NOT A BIRD
ALL THEY EVER DO IS EAT WORMS AND SIT IN THE BIRDBATH
THEY NEVER HAVE ANY FUN
5-5
JIM DAVIS
© 1985 PAWS, INC. All Rights Reserved.

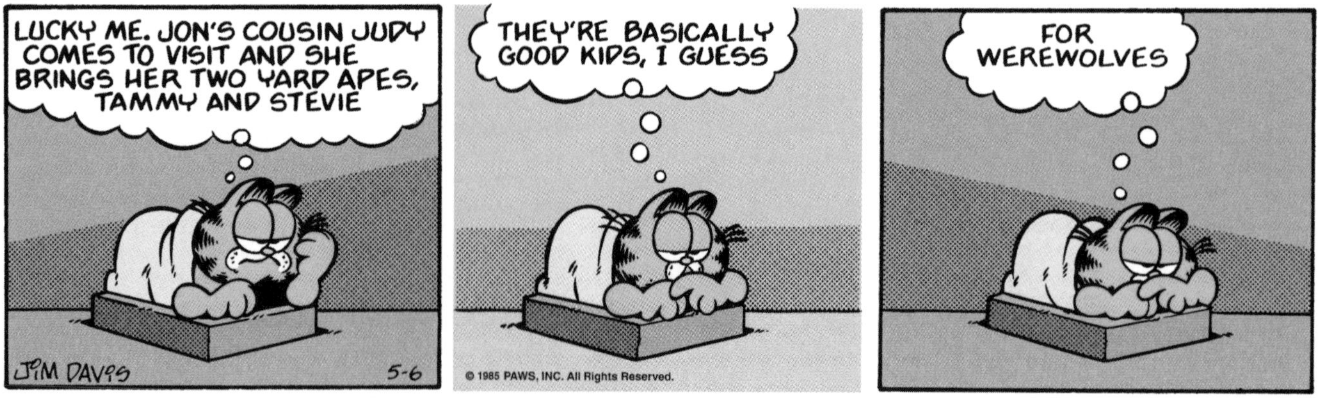
LUCKY ME. JON'S COUSIN JUDY COMES TO VISIT AND SHE BRINGS HER TWO YARD APES, TAMMY AND STEVIE
JIM DAVIS
5-6
THEY'RE BASICALLY GOOD KIDS, I GUESS
© 1985 PAWS, INC. All Rights Reserved.
FOR WEREWOLVES

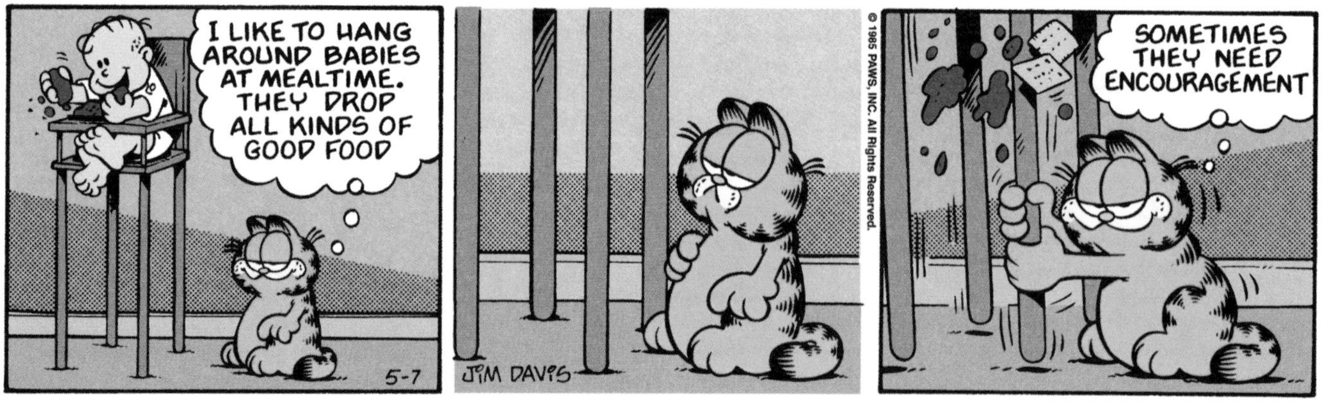
I LIKE TO HANG AROUND BABIES AT MEALTIME. THEY DROP ALL KINDS OF GOOD FOOD
5-7
JIM DAVIS
© 1985 PAWS, INC. All Rights Reserved.
SOMETIMES THEY NEED ENCOURAGEMENT

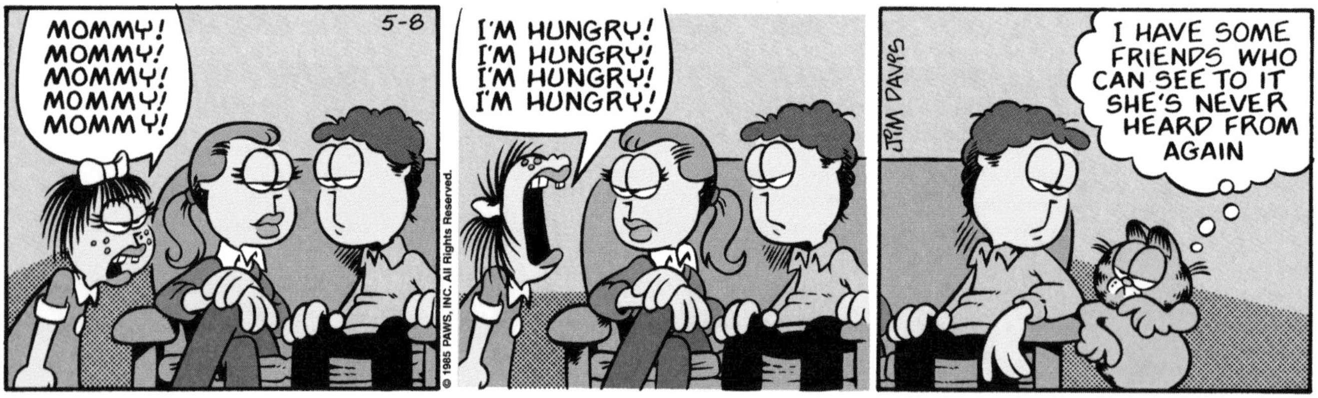
MOMMY! MOMMY! MOMMY! MOMMY! MOMMY!
5-8
© 1985 PAWS, INC. All Rights Reserved.
I'M HUNGRY! I'M HUNGRY! I'M HUNGRY! I'M HUNGRY!
JIM DAVIS
I HAVE SOME FRIENDS WHO CAN SEE TO IT SHE'S NEVER HEARD FROM AGAIN

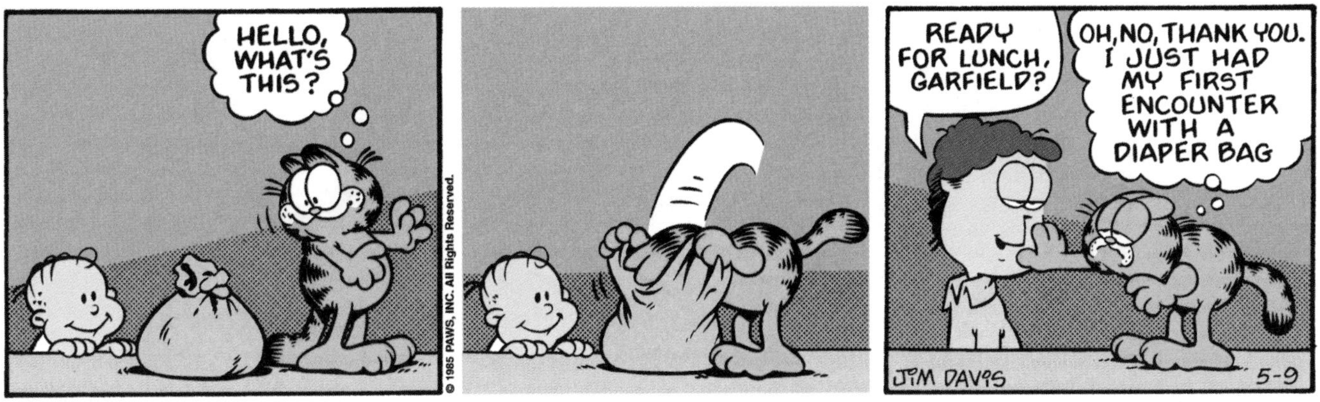
HELLO, WHAT'S THIS?
© 1985 PAWS, INC. All Rights Reserved.
READY FOR LUNCH, GARFIELD?
OH, NO, THANK YOU. I JUST HAD MY FIRST ENCOUNTER WITH A DIAPER BAG
JIM DAVIS 5-9

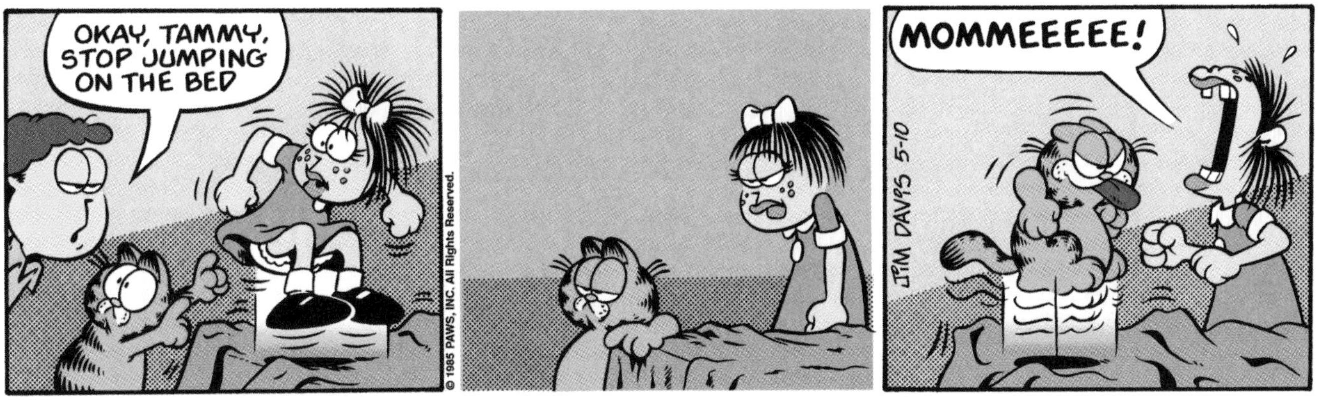
OKAY, TAMMY, STOP JUMPING ON THE BED
© 1985 PAWS, INC. All Rights Reserved.
MOMMEEEEE!
JIM DAVIS 5-10

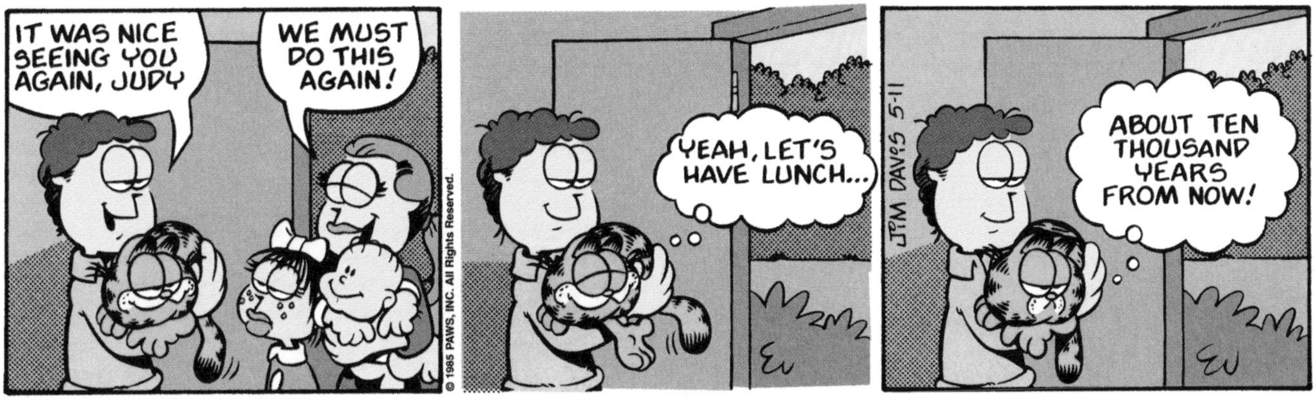
IT WAS NICE SEEING YOU AGAIN, JUDY
WE MUST DO THIS AGAIN!
© 1985 PAWS, INC. All Rights Reserved.
YEAH, LET'S HAVE LUNCH...
JIM DAVIS 5-11
ABOUT TEN THOUSAND YEARS FROM NOW!

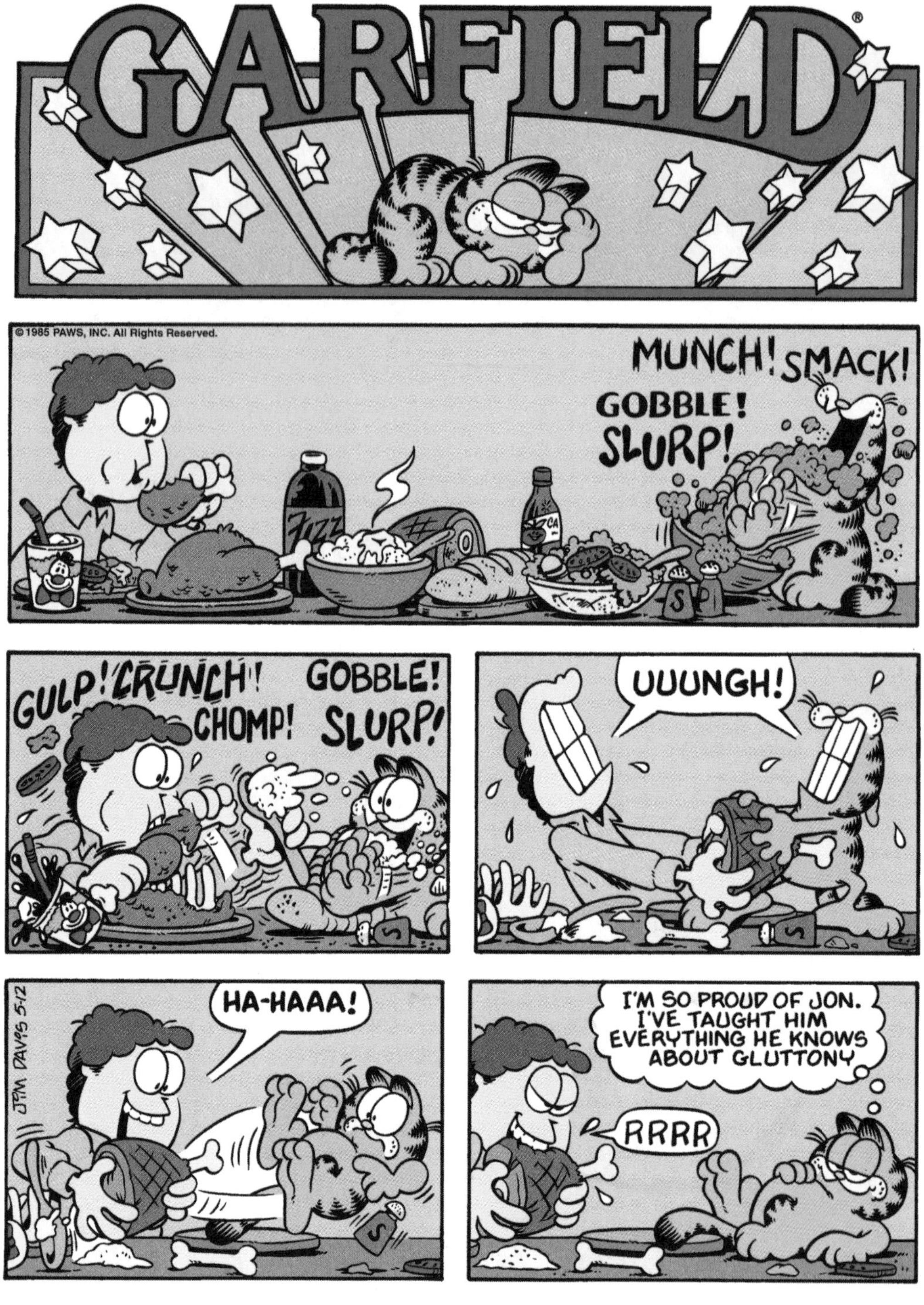
GARFIELD
© 1985 PAWS, INC. All Rights Reserved.
MUNCH! SMACK!
GOBBLE!
SLURP!
GULP! CRUNCH!
CHOMP!
GOBBLE!
SLURP!
UUUNGH!
JIM DAVIS 5-12
HA-HAAA!
I'M SO PROUD OF JON. I'VE TAUGHT HIM EVERYTHING HE KNOWS ABOUT GLUTTONY
RRRR

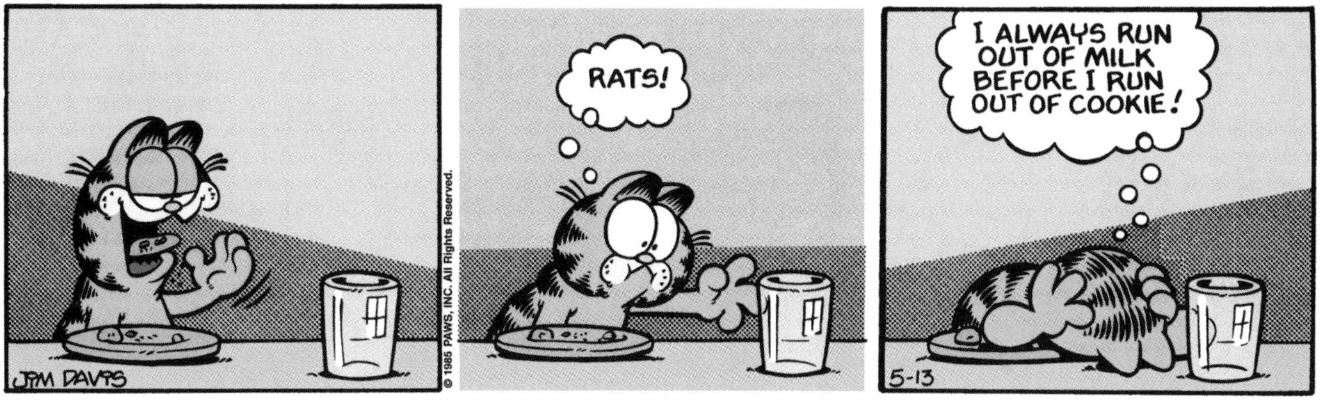
JIM DAVIS
© 1985 PAWS, INC. All Rights Reserved.
RATS!
I ALWAYS RUN OUT OF MILK BEFORE I RUN OUT OF COOKIE!
5-13

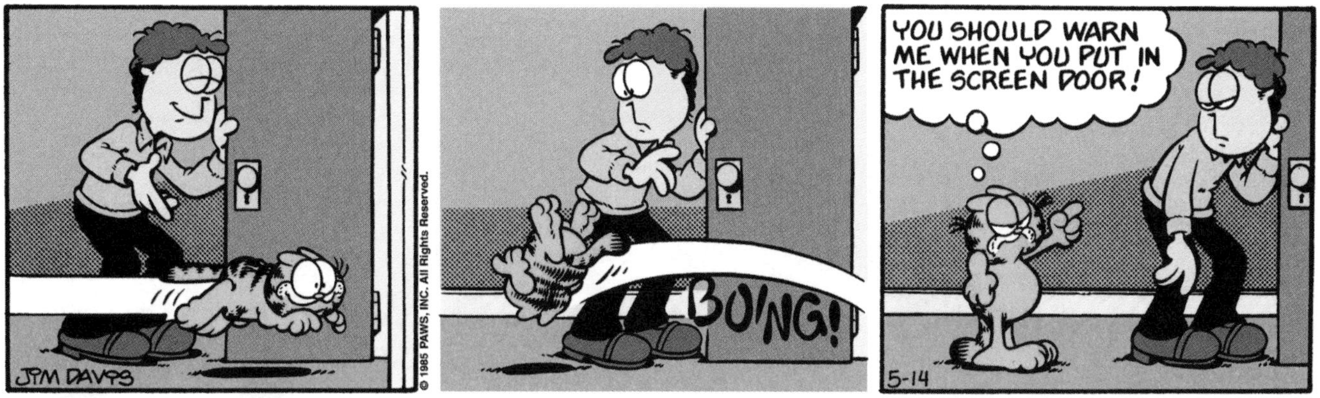
JIM DAVIS
© 1985 PAWS, INC. All Rights Reserved.
BOING!
YOU SHOULD WARN ME WHEN YOU PUT IN THE SCREEN DOOR!
5-14

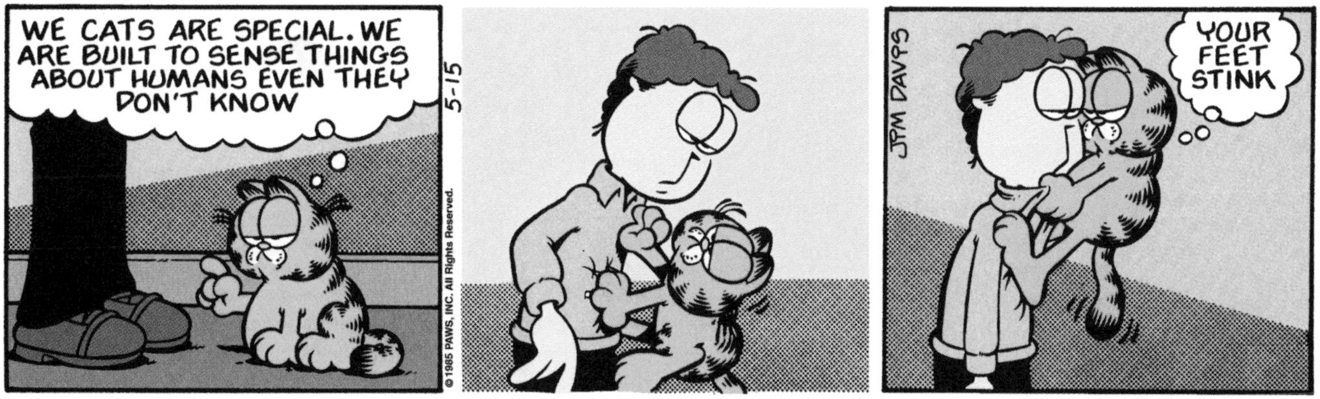
WE CATS ARE SPECIAL. WE ARE BUILT TO SENSE THINGS ABOUT HUMANS EVEN THEY DON'T KNOW
5-15
© 1985 PAWS, INC. All Rights Reserved.
JIM DAVIS
YOUR FEET STINK

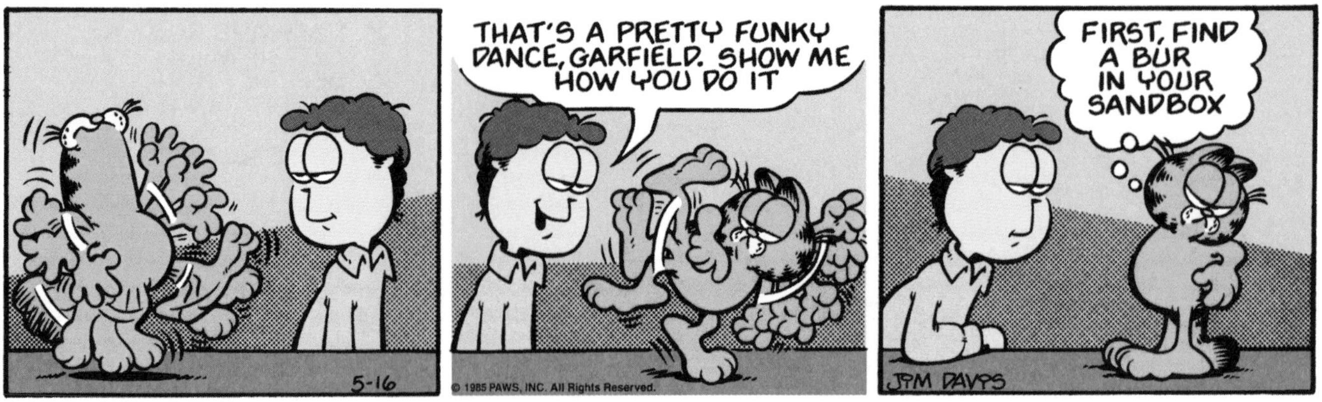
THAT'S A PRETTY FUNKY DANCE, GARFIELD. SHOW ME HOW YOU DO IT
FIRST, FIND A BUR IN YOUR SANDBOX
5-16
© 1985 PAWS, INC. All Rights Reserved.
JIM DAVIS

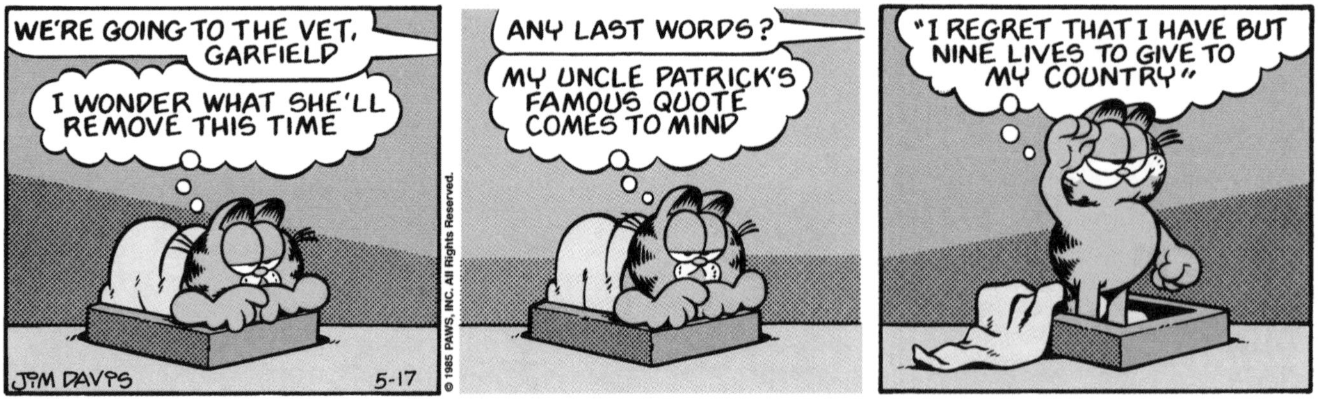
WE'RE GOING TO THE VET, GARFIELD
I WONDER WHAT SHE'LL REMOVE THIS TIME
JIM DAVIS
5-17
© 1985 PAWS, INC. All Rights Reserved.
ANY LAST WORDS?
MY UNCLE PATRICK'S FAMOUS QUOTE COMES TO MIND
"I REGRET THAT I HAVE BUT NINE LIVES TO GIVE TO MY COUNTRY"

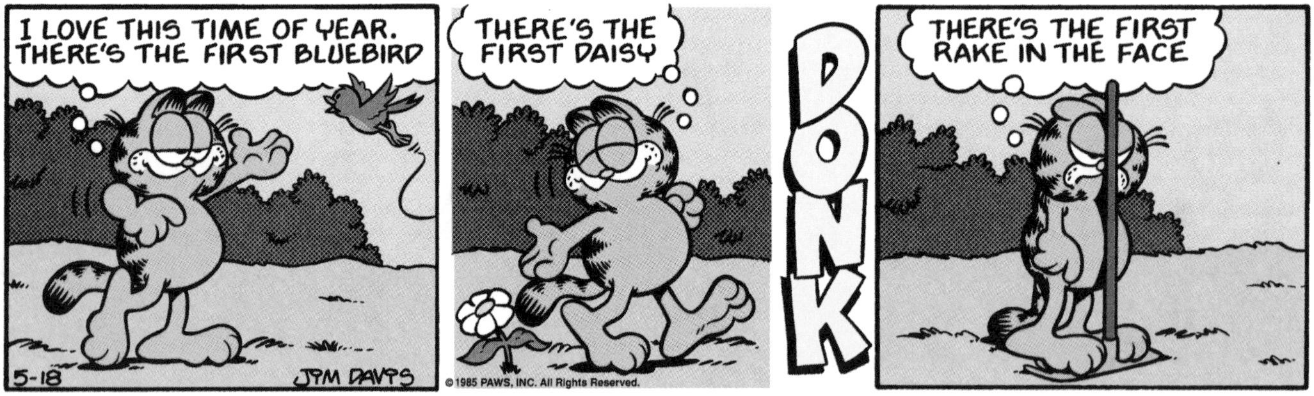
I LOVE THIS TIME OF YEAR. THERE'S THE FIRST BLUEBIRD
5-18
JIM DAVIS
THERE'S THE FIRST DAISY
© 1985 PAWS, INC. All Rights Reserved.
DONK
THERE'S THE FIRST RAKE IN THE FACE

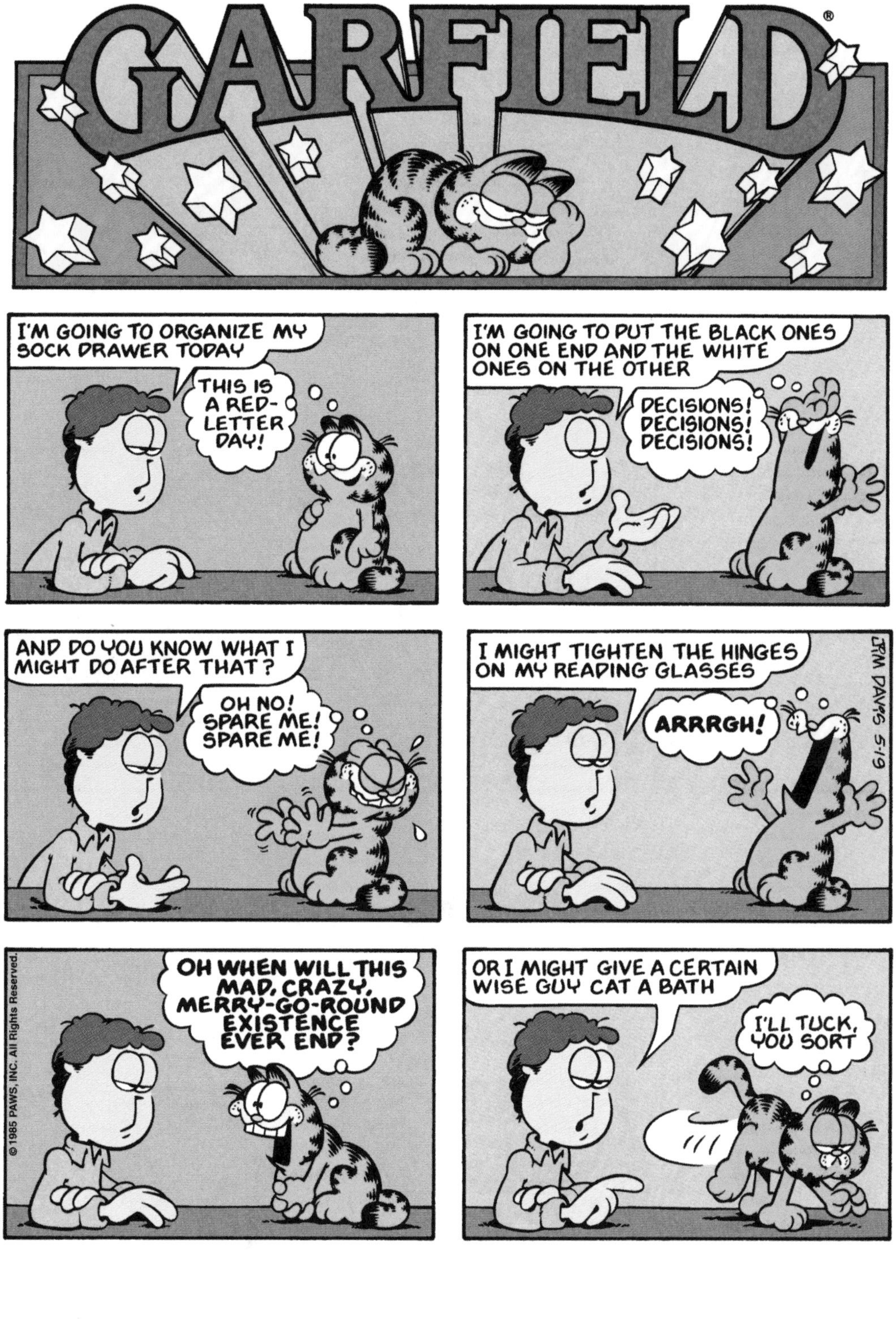
GARFIELD®
I'M GOING TO ORGANIZE MY SOCK DRAWER TODAY
THIS IS A RED-LETTER DAY!
I'M GOING TO PUT THE BLACK ONES ON ONE END AND THE WHITE ONES ON THE OTHER
DECISIONS! DECISIONS! DECISIONS!
AND DO YOU KNOW WHAT I MIGHT DO AFTER THAT?
OH NO! SPARE ME! SPARE ME!
I MIGHT TIGHTEN THE HINGES ON MY READING GLASSES
ARRRGH!
JIM DAVIS 5-19
© 1985 PAWS, INC. All Rights Reserved.
OH WHEN WILL THIS MAD, CRAZY, MERRY-GO-ROUND EXISTENCE EVER END?
OR I MIGHT GIVE A CERTAIN WISE GUY CAT A BATH
I'LL TUCK, YOU SORT

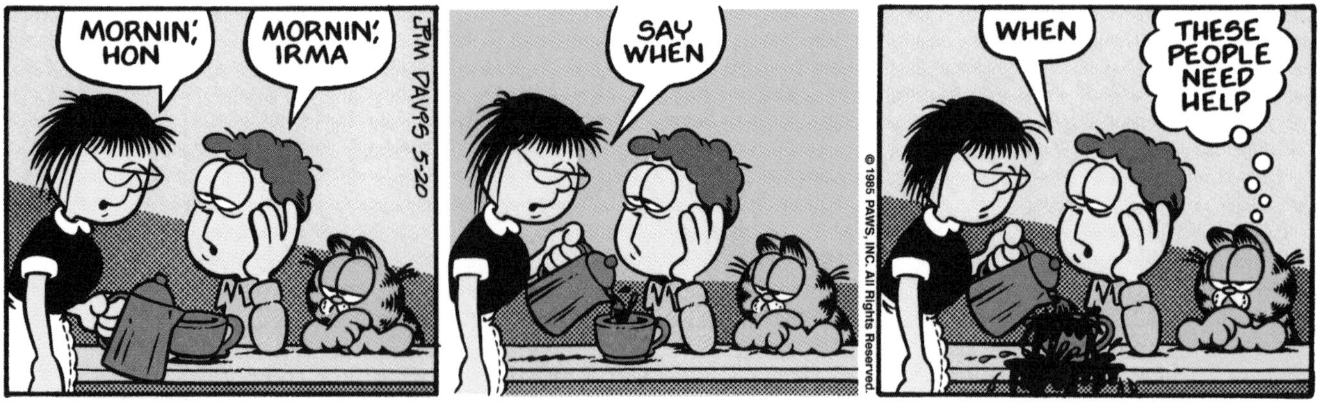
MORNIN', HON
MORNIN', IRMA
JIM DAVIS 5-20
SAY WHEN
© 1985 PAWS, INC. All Rights Reserved.
WHEN
THESE PEOPLE NEED HELP

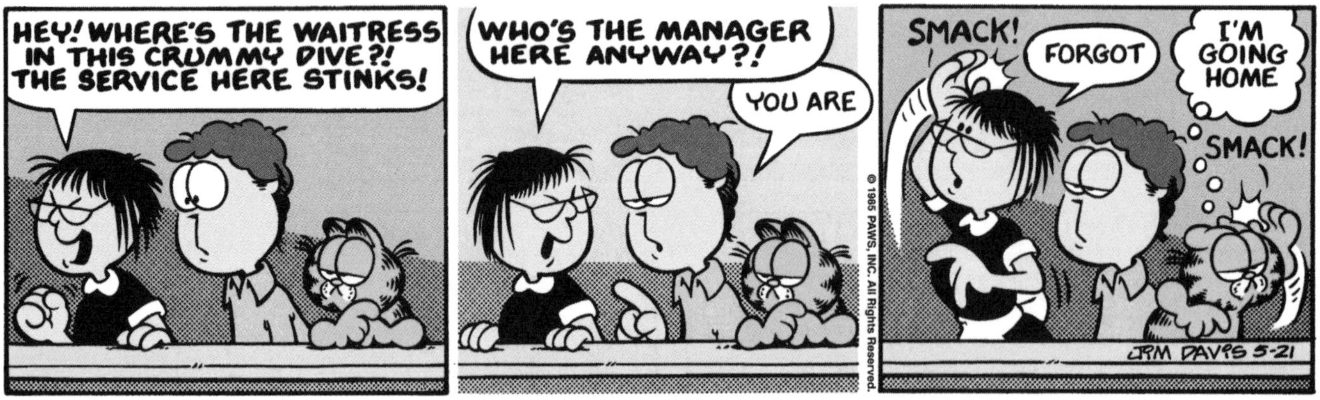
HEY! WHERE'S THE WAITRESS IN THIS CRUMMY DIVE?! THE SERVICE HERE STINKS!
WHO'S THE MANAGER HERE ANYWAY?!
YOU ARE
© 1985 PAWS, INC. All Rights Reserved.
SMACK!
FORGOT
I'M GOING HOME
SMACK!
JIM DAVIS 5-21

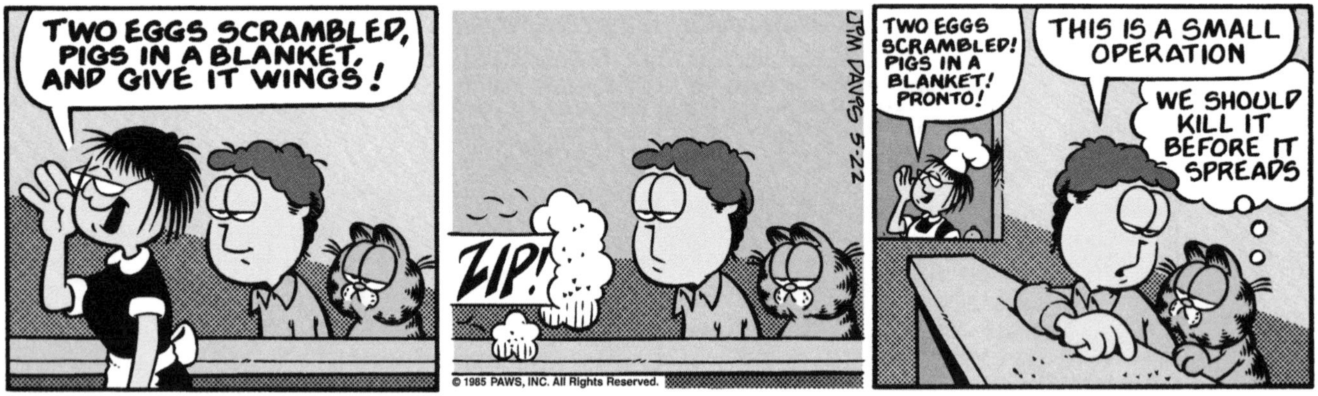
TWO EGGS SCRAMBLED, PIGS IN A BLANKET, AND GIVE IT WINGS!
ZIP!
JIM DAVIS 5-22
© 1985 PAWS, INC. All Rights Reserved.
TWO EGGS SCRAMBLED! PIGS IN A BLANKET! PRONTO!
THIS IS A SMALL OPERATION
WE SHOULD KILL IT BEFORE IT SPREADS

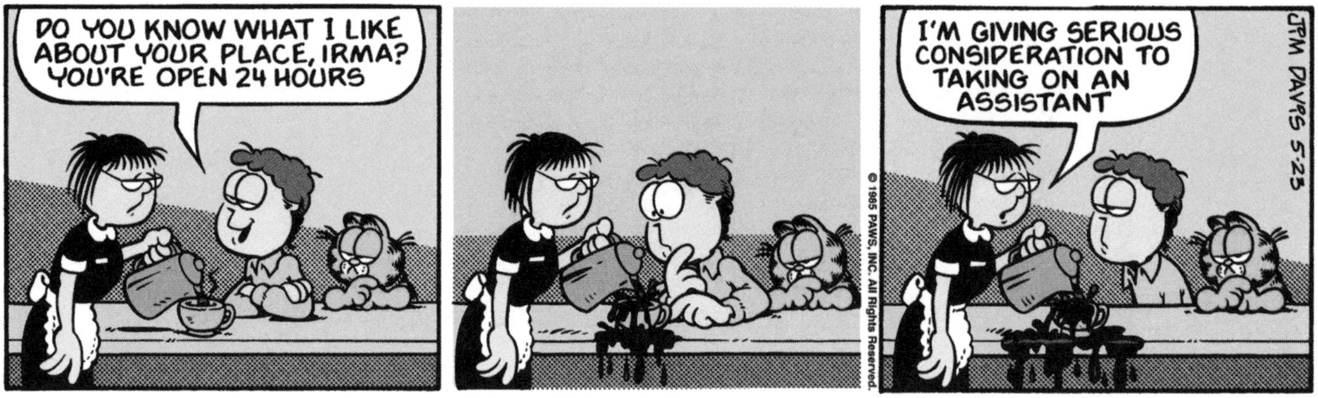
DO YOU KNOW WHAT I LIKE ABOUT YOUR PLACE, IRMA? YOU'RE OPEN 24 HOURS
© 1985 PAWS, INC. All Rights Reserved.
I'M GIVING SERIOUS CONSIDERATION TO TAKING ON AN ASSISTANT
JIM DAVIS 5-23

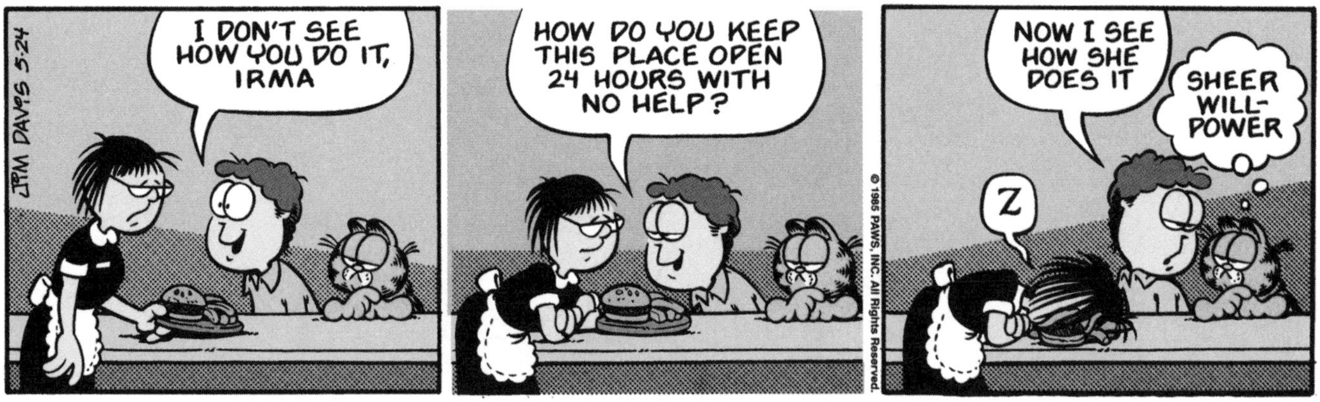
JIM DAVIS 5-24
I DON'T SEE HOW YOU DO IT, IRMA
HOW DO YOU KEEP THIS PLACE OPEN 24 HOURS WITH NO HELP?
© 1985 PAWS, INC. All Rights Reserved.
NOW I SEE HOW SHE DOES IT
SHEER WILL-POWER
Z

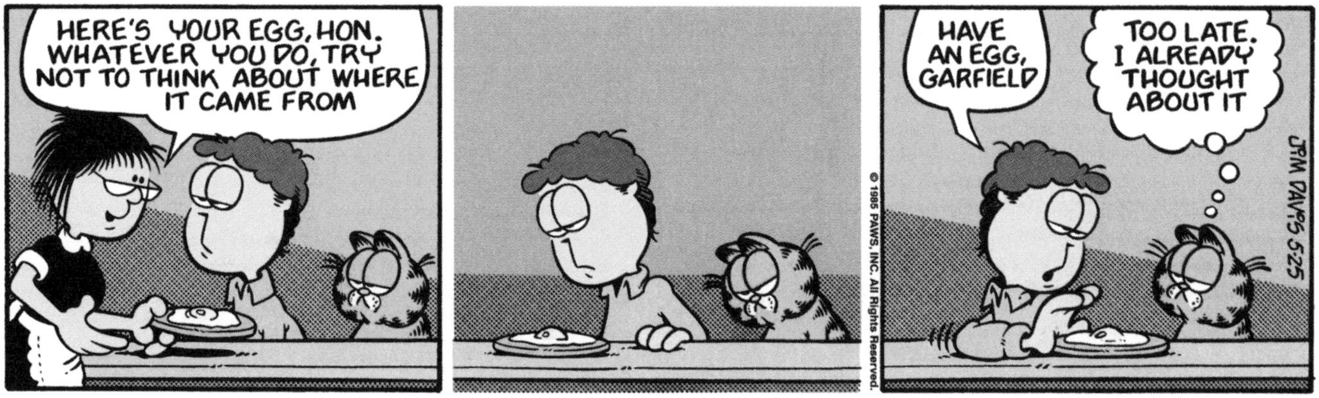
HERE'S YOUR EGG, HON. WHATEVER YOU DO, TRY NOT TO THINK ABOUT WHERE IT CAME FROM
© 1985 PAWS, INC. All Rights Reserved.
HAVE AN EGG, GARFIELD
TOO LATE. I ALREADY THOUGHT ABOUT IT
JIM DAVIS 5-25

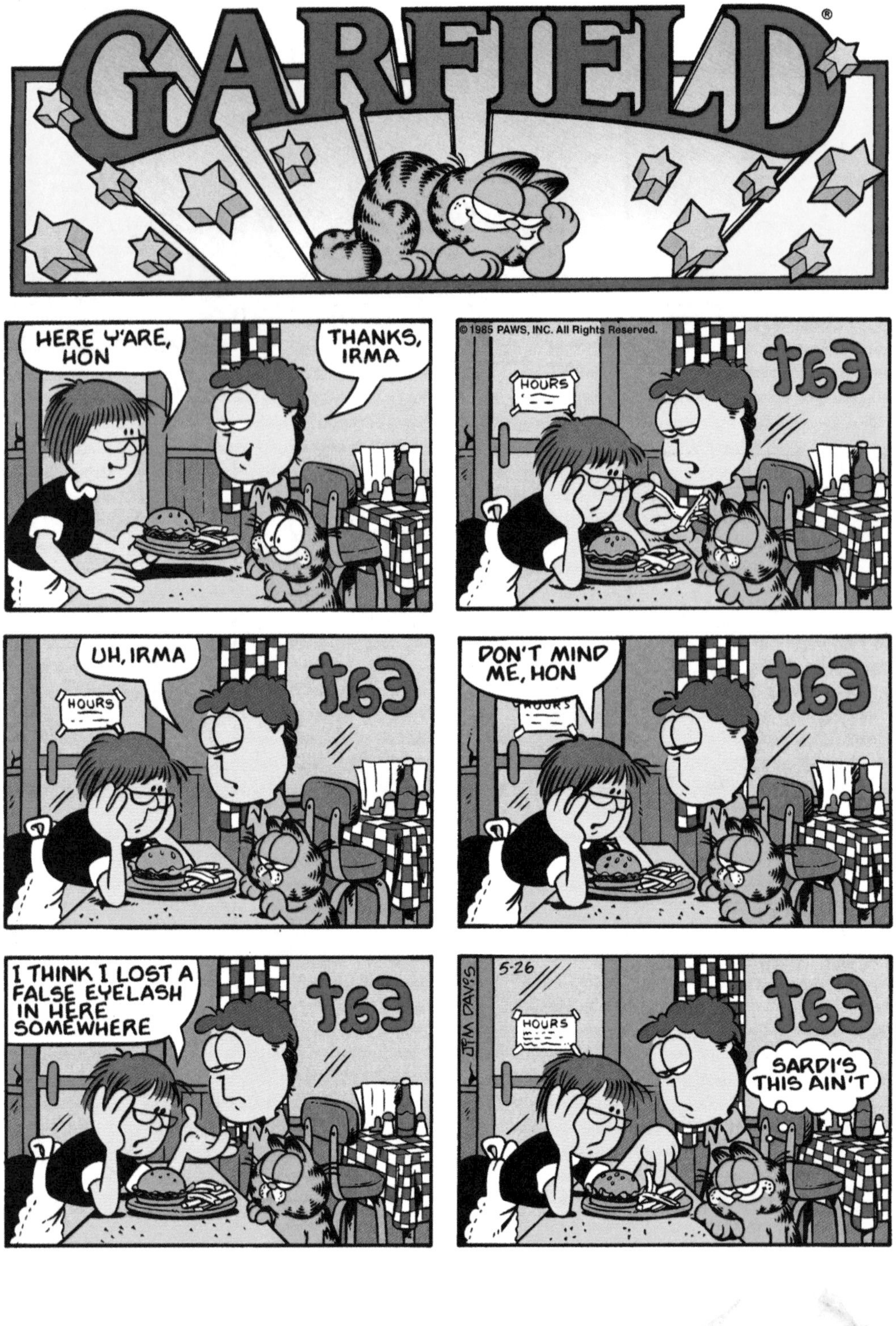
GARFIELD®
HERE Y'ARE, HON
THANKS, IRMA
© 1985 PAWS, INC. All Rights Reserved.
HOURS
UH, IRMA
DON'T MIND ME, HON
I THINK I LOST A FALSE EYELASH IN HERE SOMEWHERE
JPM DAVIS 5-26
SARDI'S THIS AIN'T

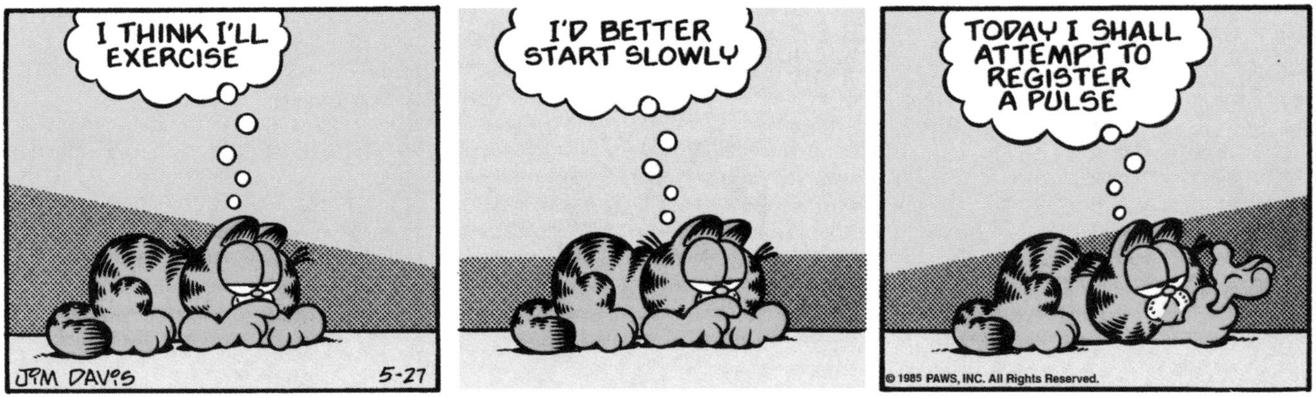
I THINK I'LL EXERCISE
JIM DAVIS
5-27
I'D BETTER START SLOWLY
TODAY I SHALL ATTEMPT TO REGISTER A PULSE
© 1985 PAWS, INC. All Rights Reserved.

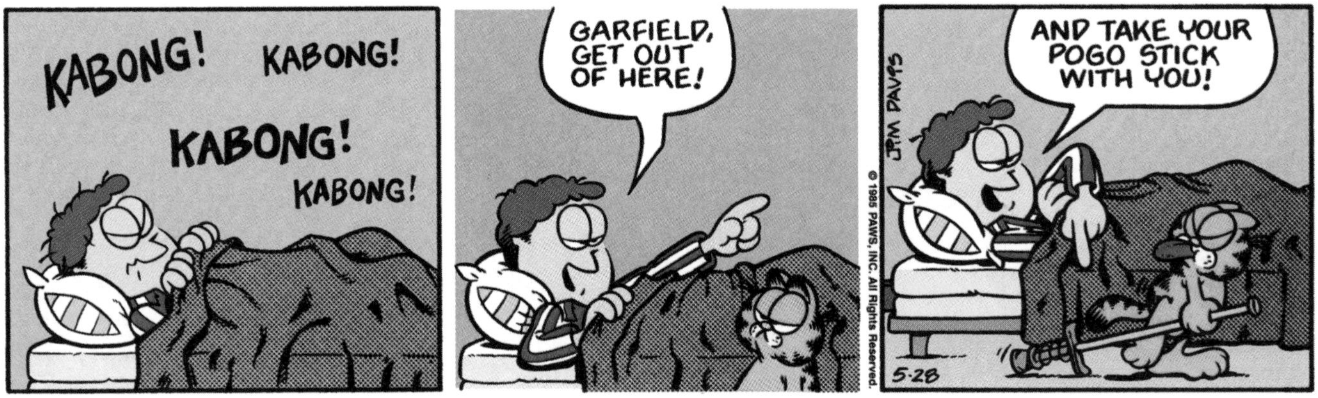
KABONG!
KABONG!
KABONG!
KABONG!
GARFIELD, GET OUT OF HERE!
© 1985 PAWS, INC. All Rights Reserved.
JIM DAVIS
AND TAKE YOUR POGO STICK WITH YOU!
5-28

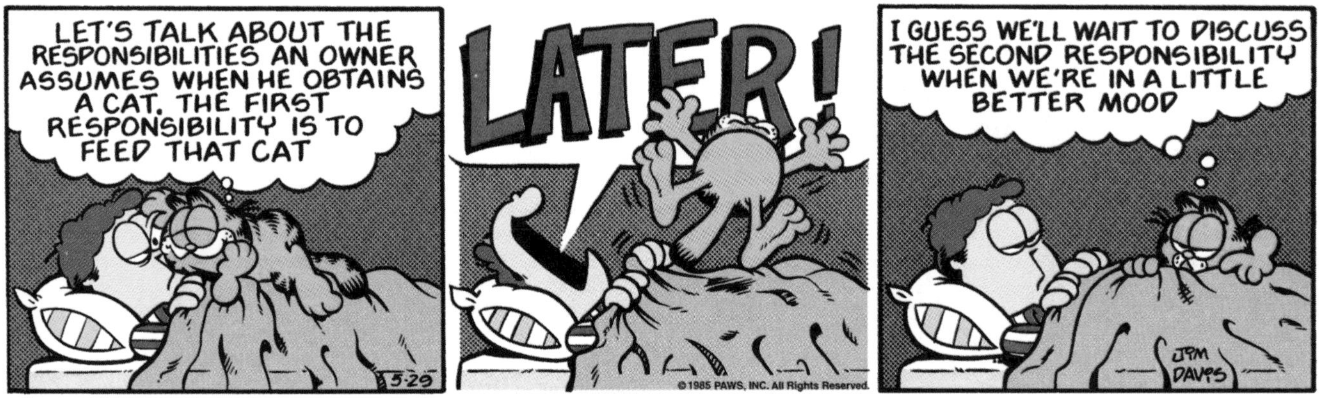
LET'S TALK ABOUT THE RESPONSIBILITIES AN OWNER ASSUMES WHEN HE OBTAINS A CAT. THE FIRST RESPONSIBILITY IS TO FEED THAT CAT
5-29
LATER!
© 1985 PAWS, INC. All Rights Reserved.
I GUESS WE'LL WAIT TO DISCUSS THE SECOND RESPONSIBILITY WHEN WE'RE IN A LITTLE BETTER MOOD
JIM DAVIS

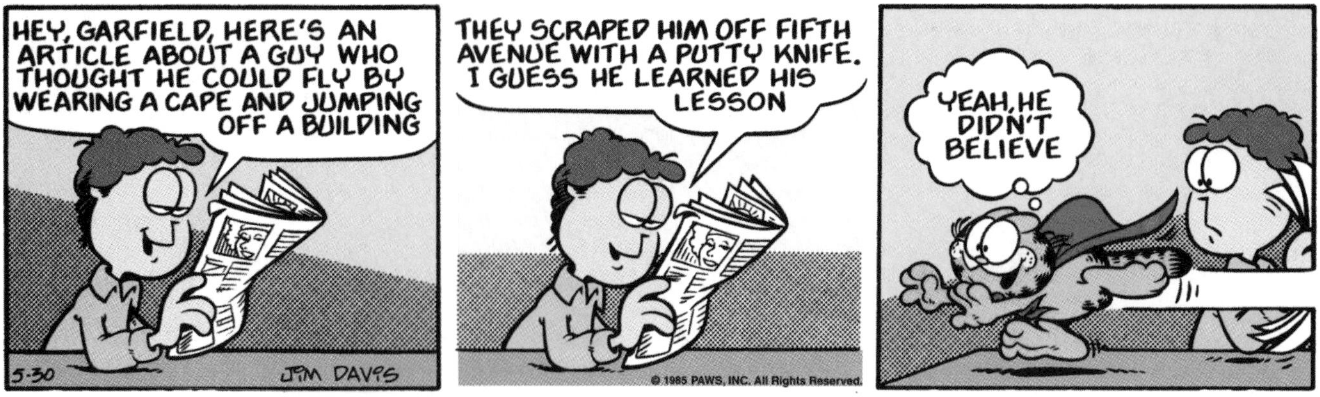
HEY, GARFIELD, HERE'S AN ARTICLE ABOUT A GUY WHO THOUGHT HE COULD FLY BY WEARING A CAPE AND JUMPING OFF A BUILDING
5-30
JIM DAVIS
THEY SCRAPED HIM OFF FIFTH AVENUE WITH A PUTTY KNIFE. I GUESS HE LEARNED HIS LESSON
© 1985 PAWS, INC. All Rights Reserved.
YEAH, HE DIDN'T BELIEVE

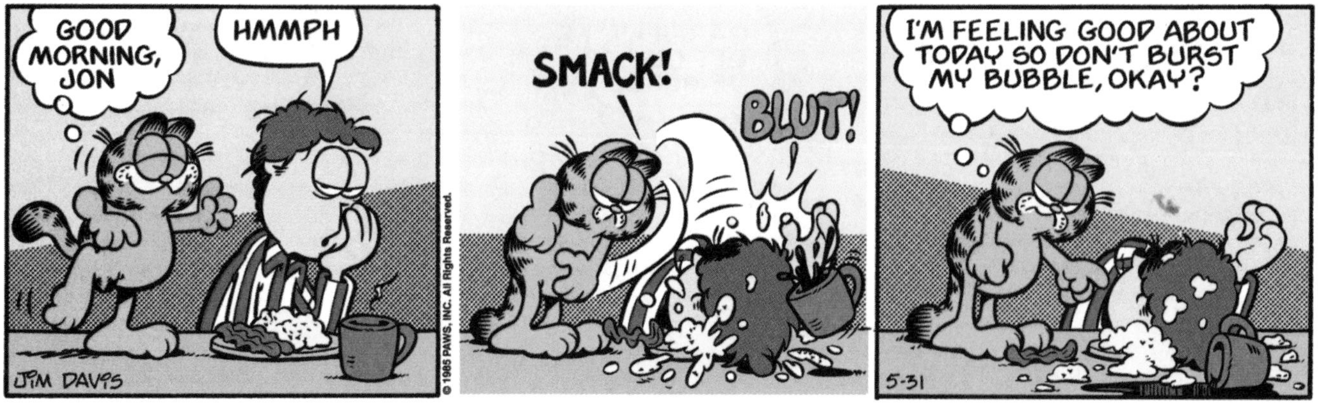
GOOD MORNING, JON
HMMPH
JIM DAVIS
© 1985 PAWS, INC. All Rights Reserved.
SMACK!
BLUT!
I'M FEELING GOOD ABOUT TODAY SO DON'T BURST MY BUBBLE, OKAY?
5-31

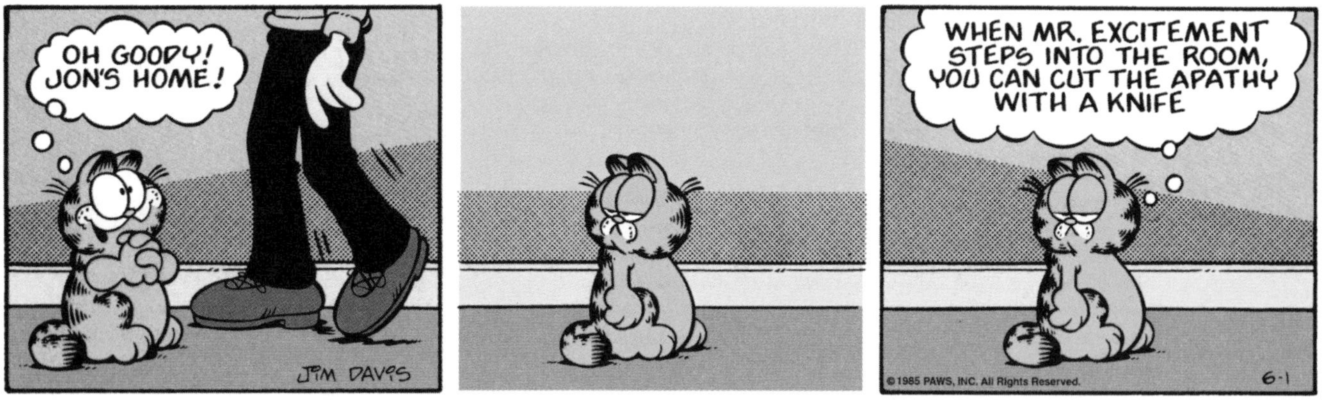
OH GOODY! JON'S HOME!
JIM DAVIS
WHEN MR. EXCITEMENT STEPS INTO THE ROOM, YOU CAN CUT THE APATHY WITH A KNIFE
© 1985 PAWS, INC. All Rights Reserved.
6-1

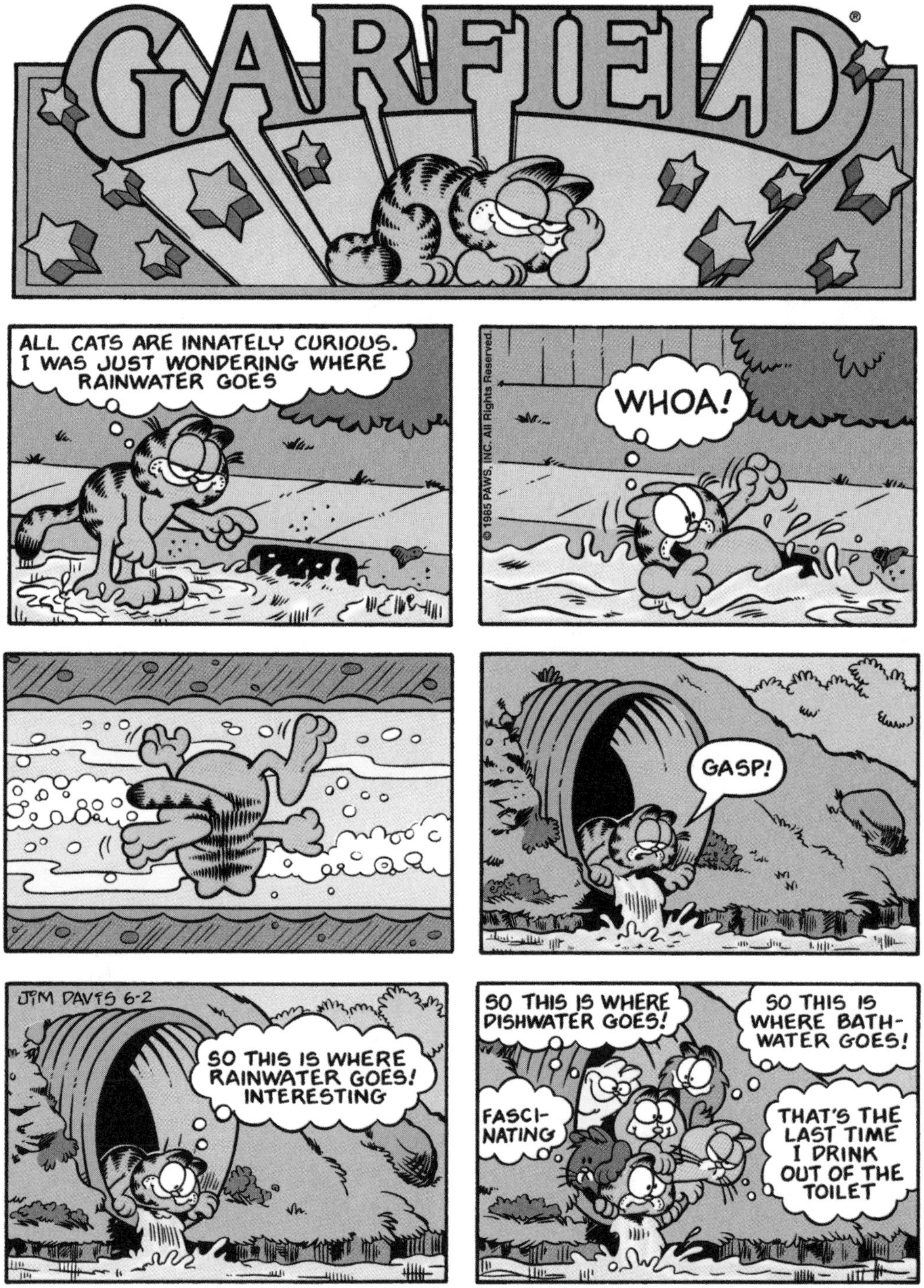
GARFIELD®
ALL CATS ARE INNATELY CURIOUS. I WAS JUST WONDERING WHERE RAINWATER GOES
© 1985 PAWS, INC. All Rights Reserved.
WHOA!
GASP!
JIM DAVIS 6-2
SO THIS IS WHERE RAINWATER GOES! INTERESTING
SO THIS IS WHERE DISHWATER GOES!
SO THIS IS WHERE BATH-WATER GOES!
FASCI-NATING
THAT'S THE LAST TIME I DRINK OUT OF THE TOILET

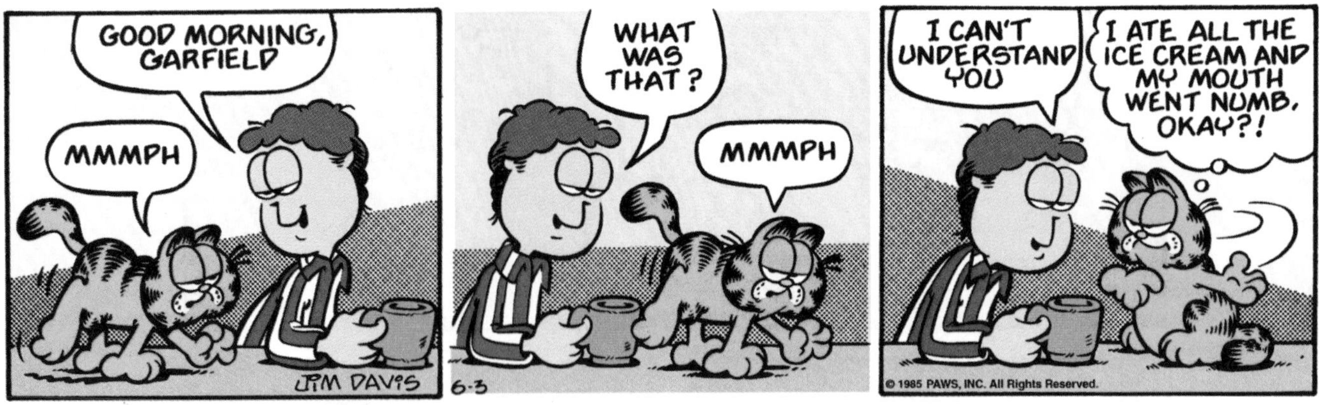
GOOD MORNING, GARFIELD
MMMPH
JIM DAVIS
WHAT WAS THAT?
MMMPH
6-3
I CAN'T UNDERSTAND YOU
I ATE ALL THE ICE CREAM AND MY MOUTH WENT NUMB, OKAY?!
© 1985 PAWS, INC. All Rights Reserved.

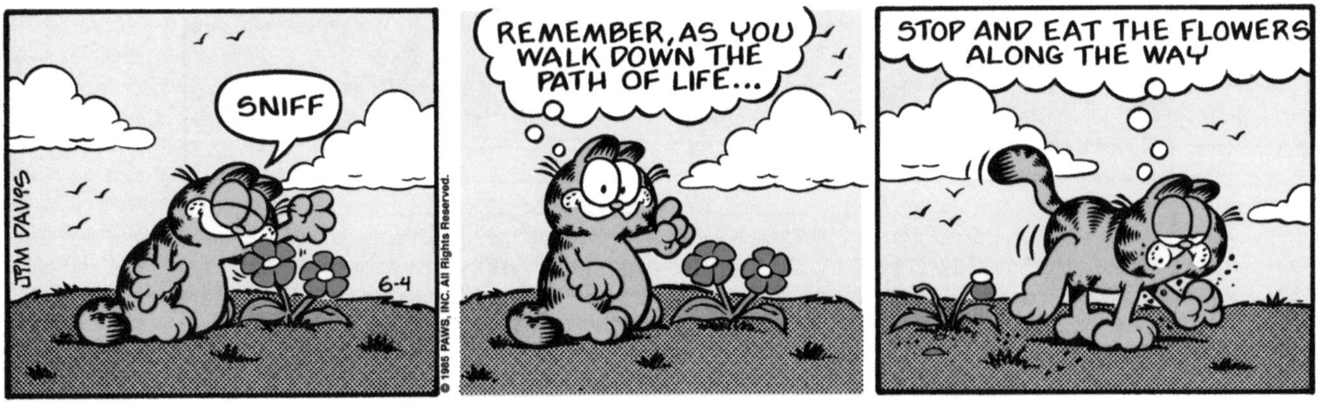
SNIFF
JIM DAVIS
6-4
© 1985 PAWS, INC. All Rights Reserved.
REMEMBER, AS YOU WALK DOWN THE PATH OF LIFE...
STOP AND EAT THE FLOWERS ALONG THE WAY

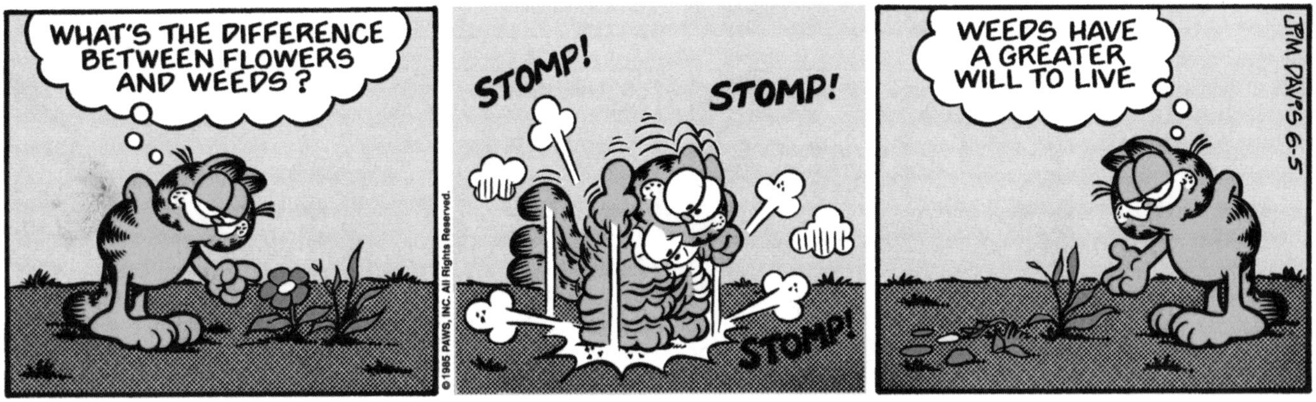
WHAT'S THE DIFFERENCE BETWEEN FLOWERS AND WEEDS?
© 1985 PAWS, INC. All Rights Reserved.
STOMP!
STOMP!
STOMP!
WEEDS HAVE A GREATER WILL TO LIVE
JIM DAVIS 6-5

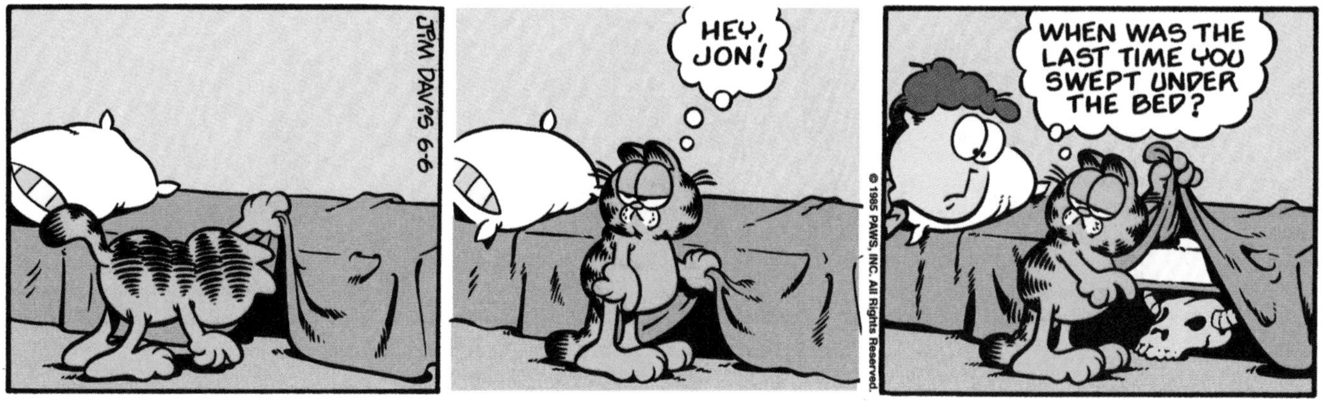
JIM DAVIS 6-6
HEY, JON!
© 1985 PAWS, INC. All Rights Reserved.
WHEN WAS THE LAST TIME YOU SWEPT UNDER THE BED?

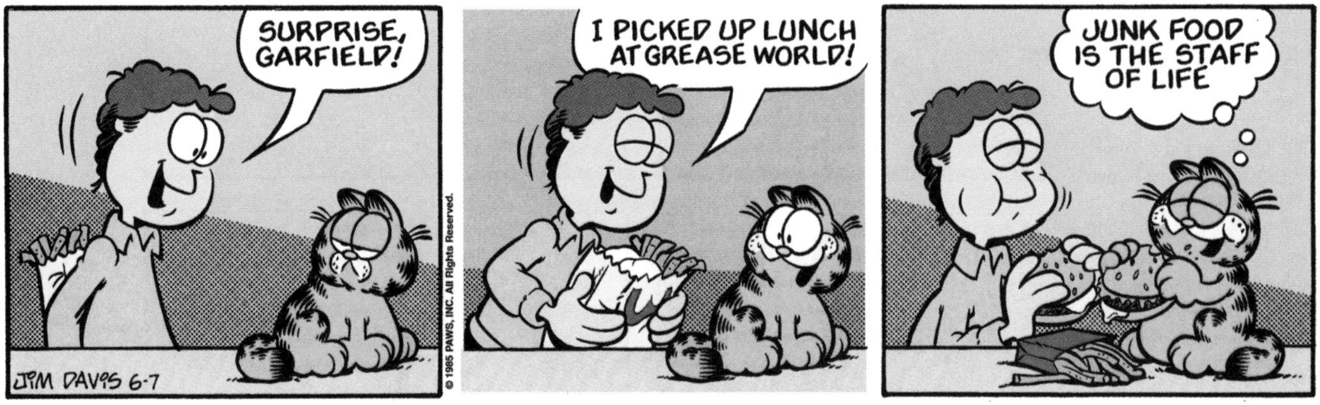
SURPRISE, GARFIELD!
JIM DAVIS 6-7
© 1985 PAWS, INC. All Rights Reserved.
I PICKED UP LUNCH AT GREASE WORLD!
JUNK FOOD IS THE STAFF OF LIFE

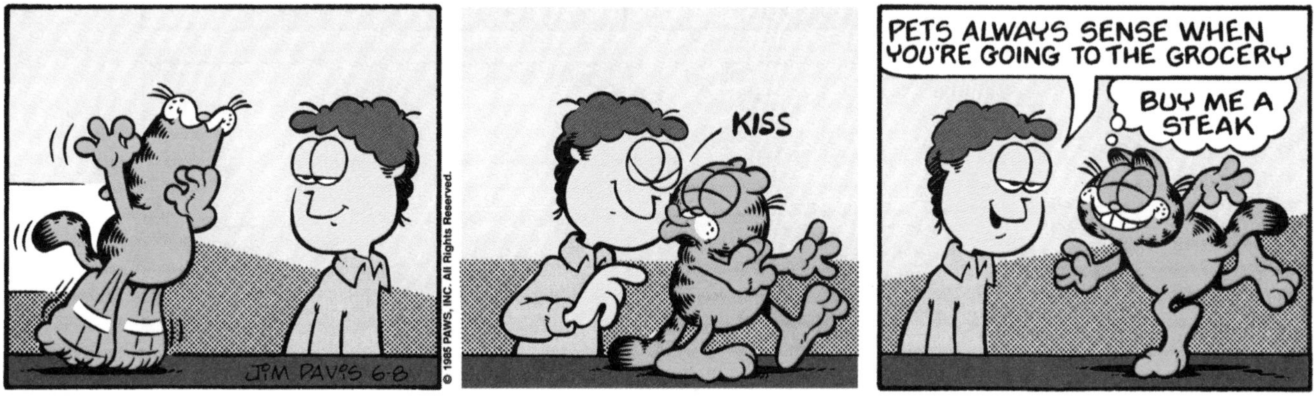
JIM DAVIS 6-8
© 1985 PAWS, INC. All Rights Reserved.
KISS
PETS ALWAYS SENSE WHEN YOU'RE GOING TO THE GROCERY
BUY ME A STEAK

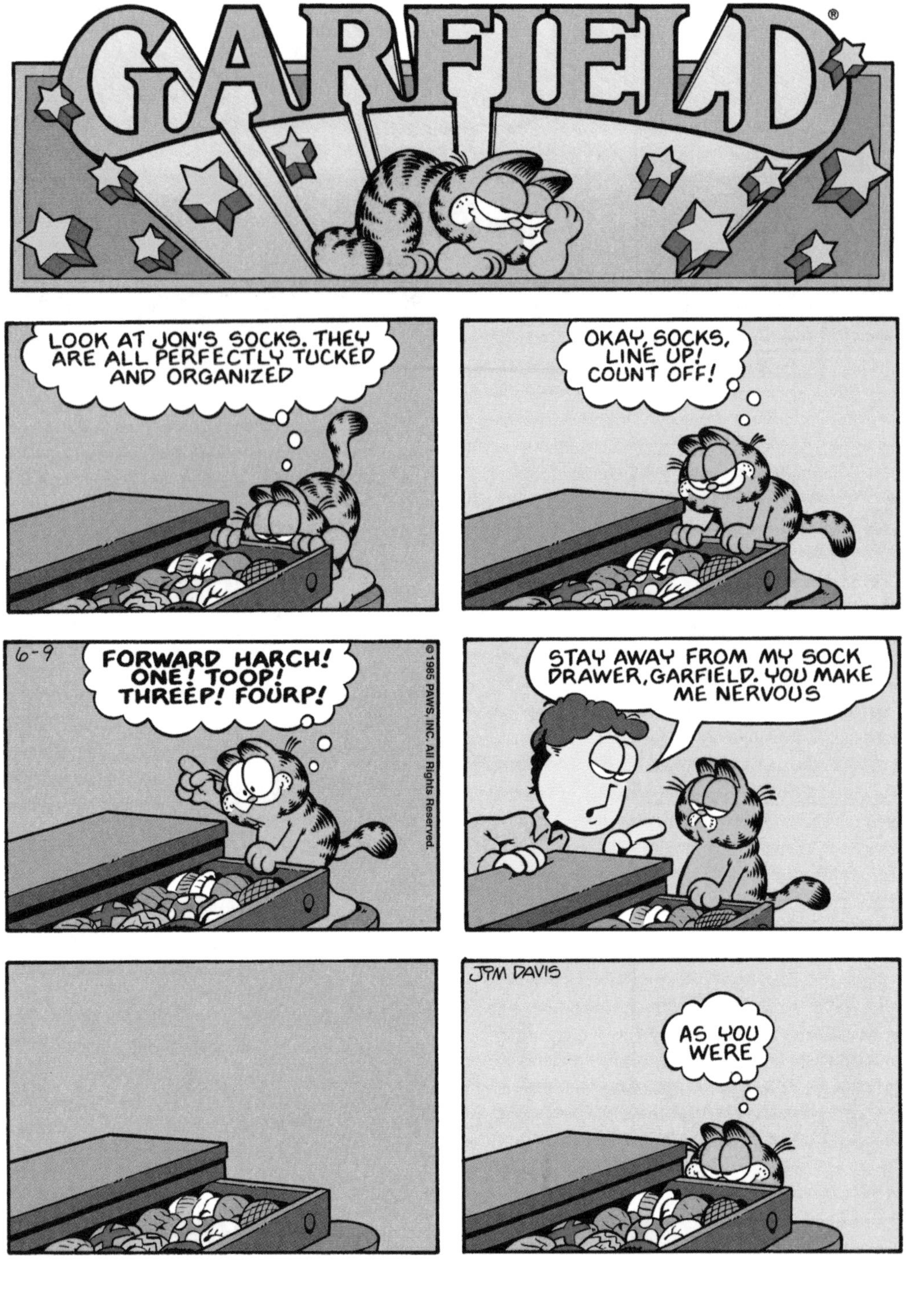
GARFIELD®
LOOK AT JON'S SOCKS. THEY ARE ALL PERFECTLY TUCKED AND ORGANIZED
OKAY, SOCKS, LINE UP! COUNT OFF!
6-9
FORWARD HARCH! ONE! TOOP! THREEP! FOURP!
© 1985 PAWS, INC. All Rights Reserved.
STAY AWAY FROM MY SOCK DRAWER, GARFIELD. YOU MAKE ME NERVOUS
JIM DAVIS
AS YOU WERE

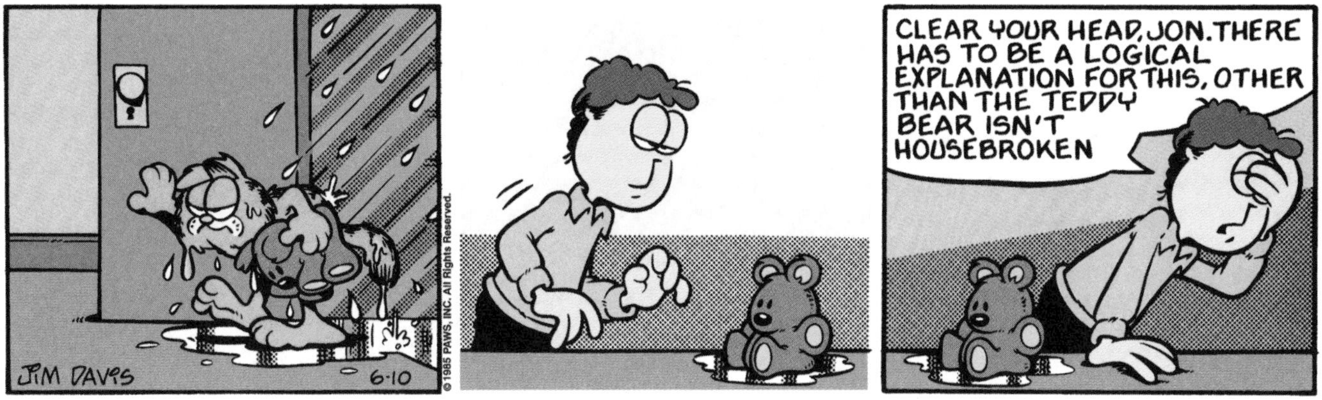
JIM DAVIS
6-10
© 1985 PAWS, INC. All Rights Reserved.
CLEAR YOUR HEAD, JON. THERE HAS TO BE A LOGICAL EXPLANATION FOR THIS, OTHER THAN THE TEDDY BEAR ISN'T HOUSEBROKEN

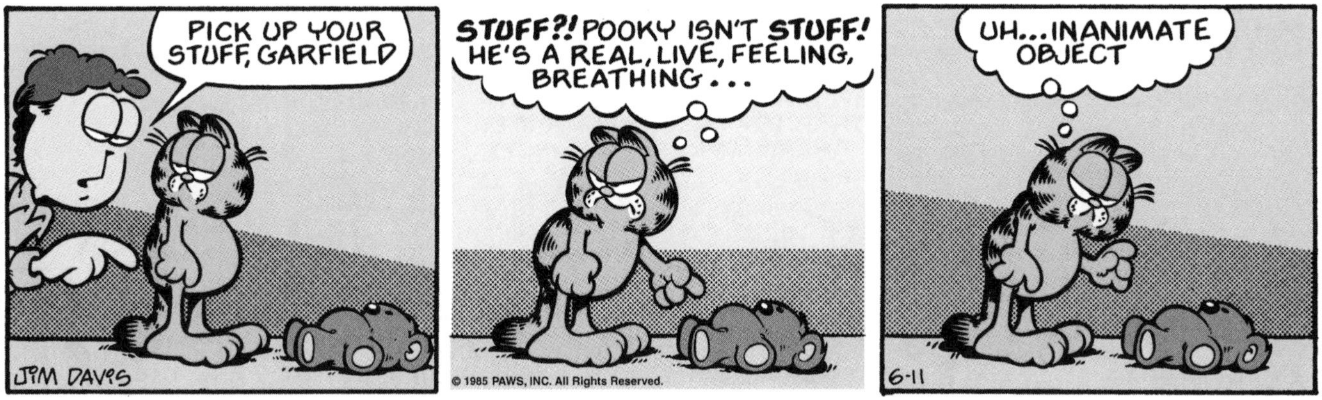
PICK UP YOUR STUFF, GARFIELD
JIM DAVIS
STUFF?! POOKY ISN'T STUFF! HE'S A REAL, LIVE, FEELING, BREATHING...
© 1985 PAWS, INC. All Rights Reserved.
UH...INANIMATE OBJECT
6-11

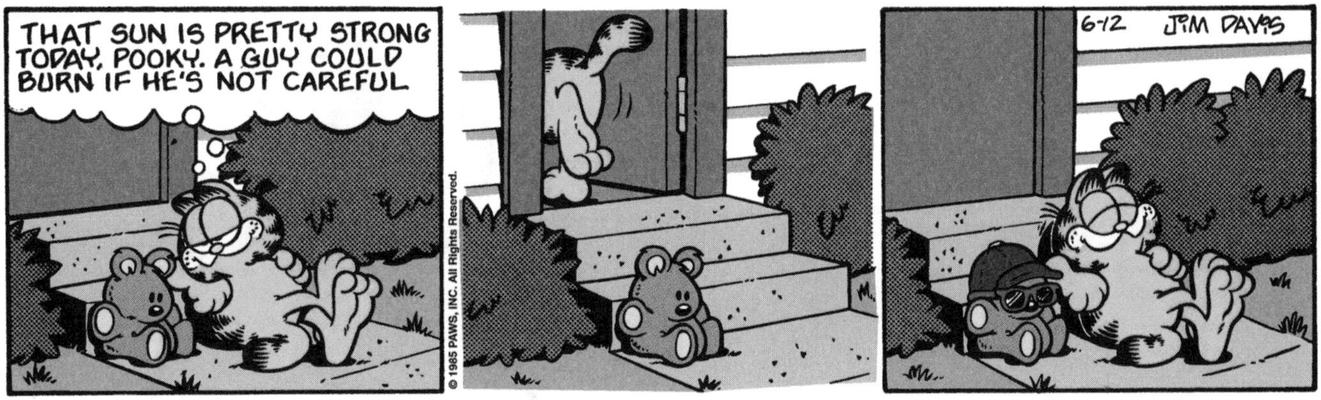
THAT SUN IS PRETTY STRONG TODAY, POOKY. A GUY COULD BURN IF HE'S NOT CAREFUL
© 1985 PAWS, INC. All Rights Reserved.
6-12
JIM DAVIS

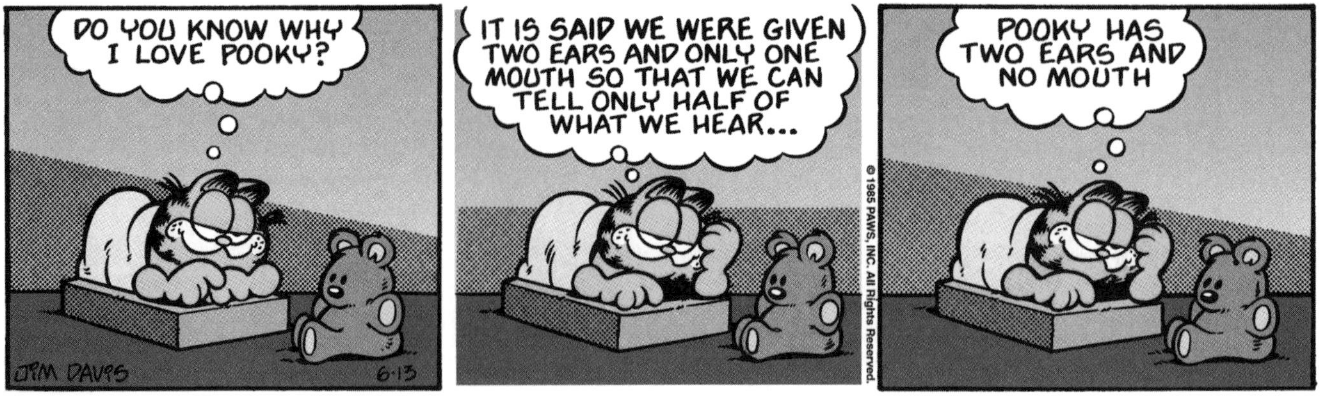
DO YOU KNOW WHY I LOVE POOKY?
JIM DAVIS
6-13
IT IS SAID WE WERE GIVEN TWO EARS AND ONLY ONE MOUTH SO THAT WE CAN TELL ONLY HALF OF WHAT WE HEAR...
© 1985 PAWS, INC. All Rights Reserved.
POOKY HAS TWO EARS AND NO MOUTH

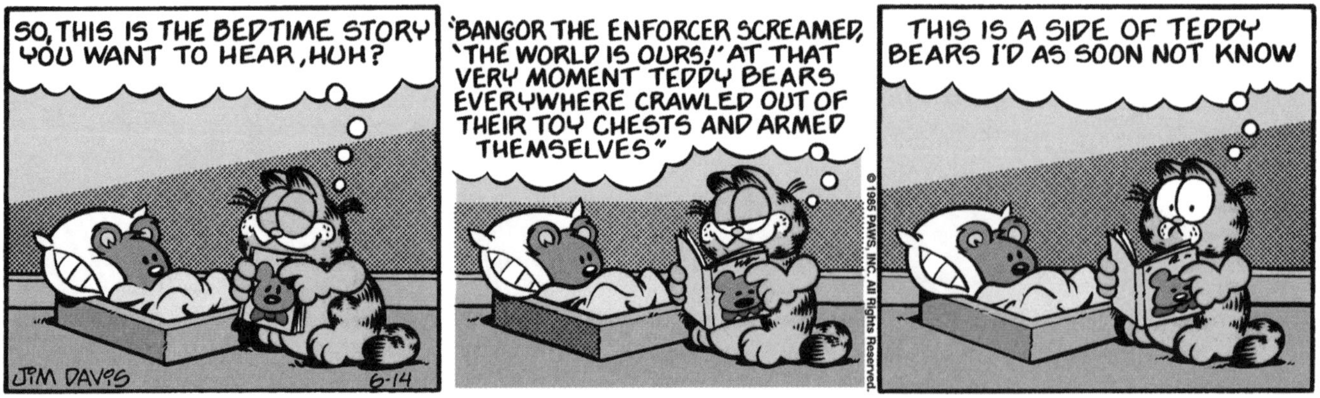
SO, THIS IS THE BEDTIME STORY YOU WANT TO HEAR, HUH?
JIM DAVIS
6-14
"BANGOR THE ENFORCER SCREAMED, 'THE WORLD IS OURS!' AT THAT VERY MOMENT TEDDY BEARS EVERYWHERE CRAWLED OUT OF THEIR TOY CHESTS AND ARMED THEMSELVES"
© 1985 PAWS, INC. All Rights Reserved.
THIS IS A SIDE OF TEDDY BEARS I'D AS SOON NOT KNOW

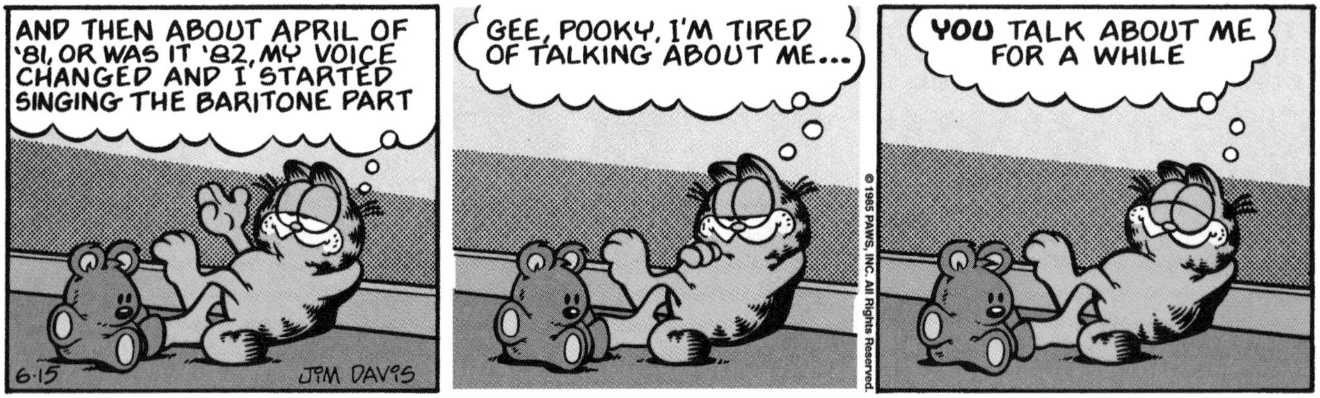
AND THEN ABOUT APRIL OF '81, OR WAS IT '82, MY VOICE CHANGED AND I STARTED SINGING THE BARITONE PART
6-15
JIM DAVIS
GEE, POOKY, I'M TIRED OF TALKING ABOUT ME...
© 1985 PAWS, INC. All Rights Reserved.
YOU TALK ABOUT ME FOR A WHILE

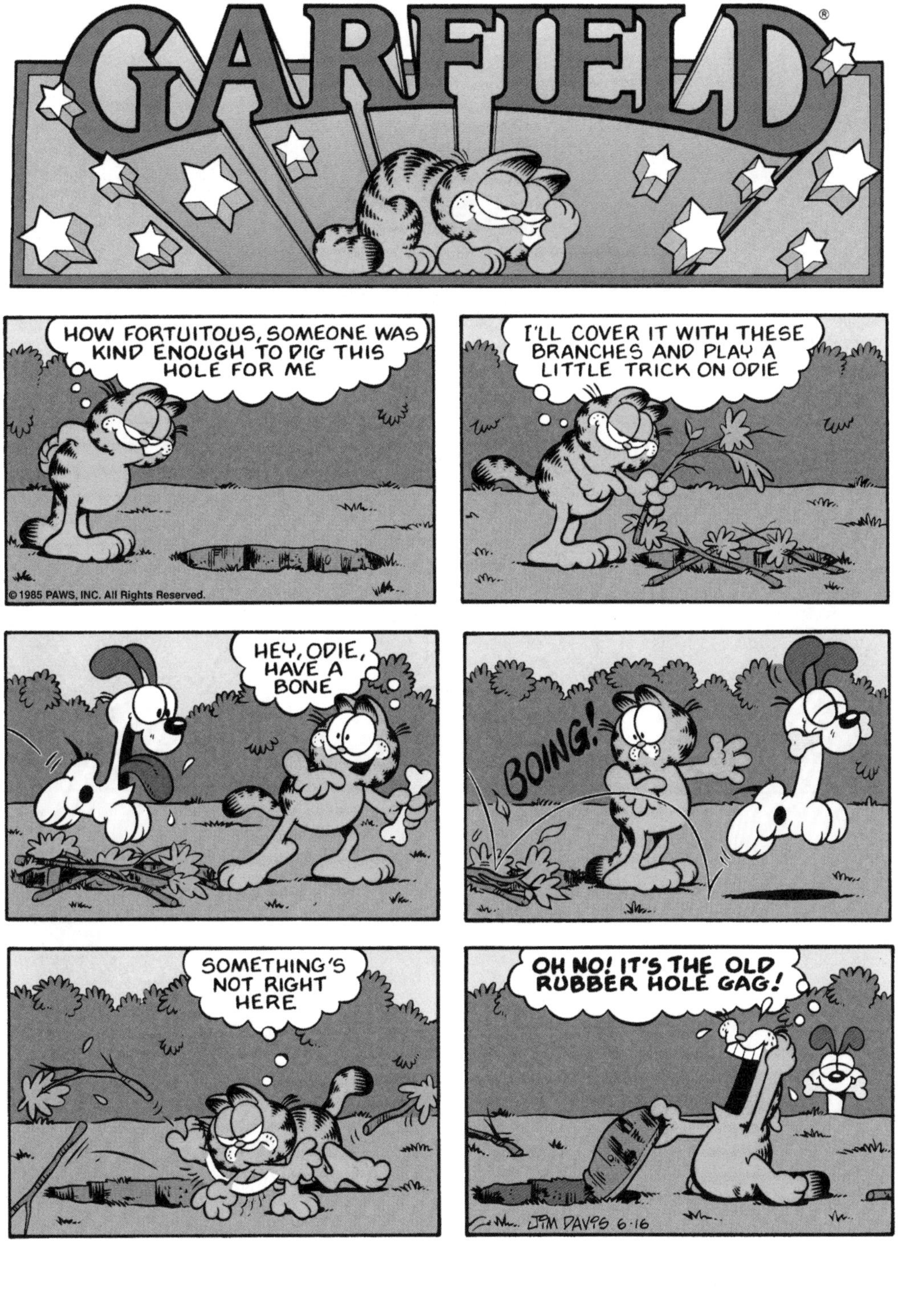
GARFIELD®
HOW FORTUITOUS, SOMEONE WAS KIND ENOUGH TO DIG THIS HOLE FOR ME
© 1985 PAWS, INC. All Rights Reserved.
I'LL COVER IT WITH THESE BRANCHES AND PLAY A LITTLE TRICK ON ODIE
HEY, ODIE, HAVE A BONE
BOING!
SOMETHING'S NOT RIGHT HERE
OH NO! IT'S THE OLD RUBBER HOLE GAG!
JIM DAVIS 6-16

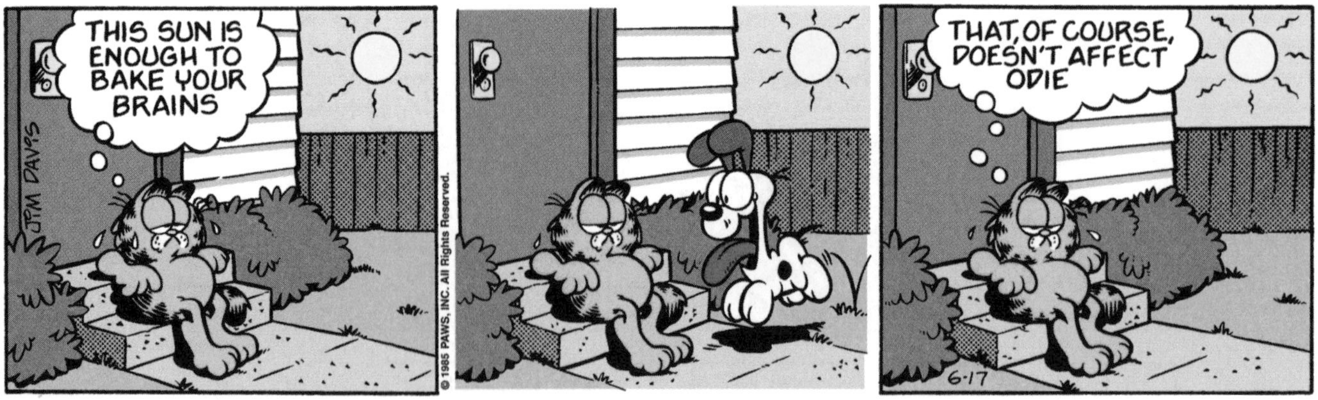
JIM DAVIS
THIS SUN IS ENOUGH TO BAKE YOUR BRAINS
© 1985 PAWS, INC. All Rights Reserved.
THAT, OF COURSE, DOESN'T AFFECT ODIE
6-17

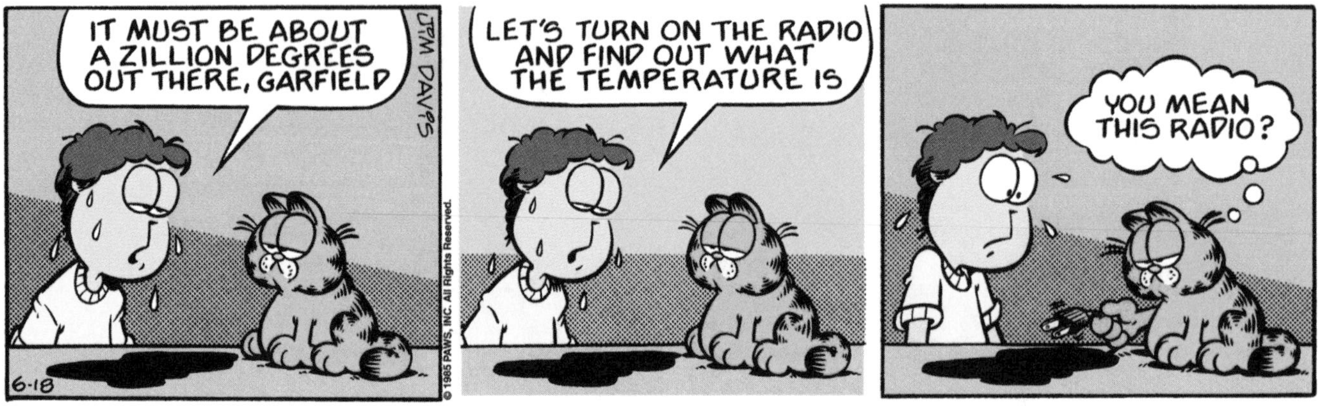
IT MUST BE ABOUT A ZILLION DEGREES OUT THERE, GARFIELD
JIM DAVIS
6-18
© 1985 PAWS, INC. All Rights Reserved.
LET'S TURN ON THE RADIO AND FIND OUT WHAT THE TEMPERATURE IS
YOU MEAN THIS RADIO?

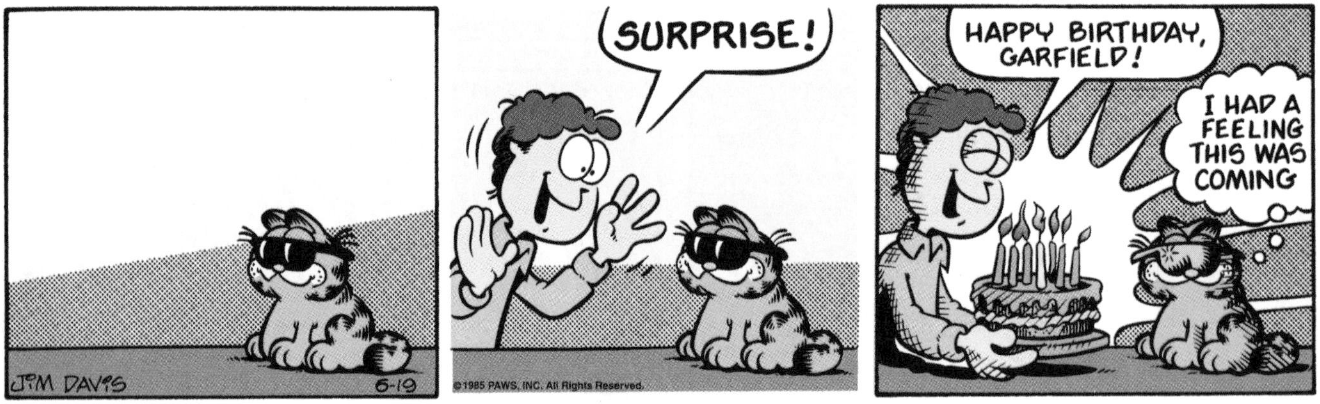
JIM DAVIS
6-19
SURPRISE!
©1985 PAWS, INC. All Rights Reserved.
HAPPY BIRTHDAY, GARFIELD!
I HAD A FEELING THIS WAS COMING

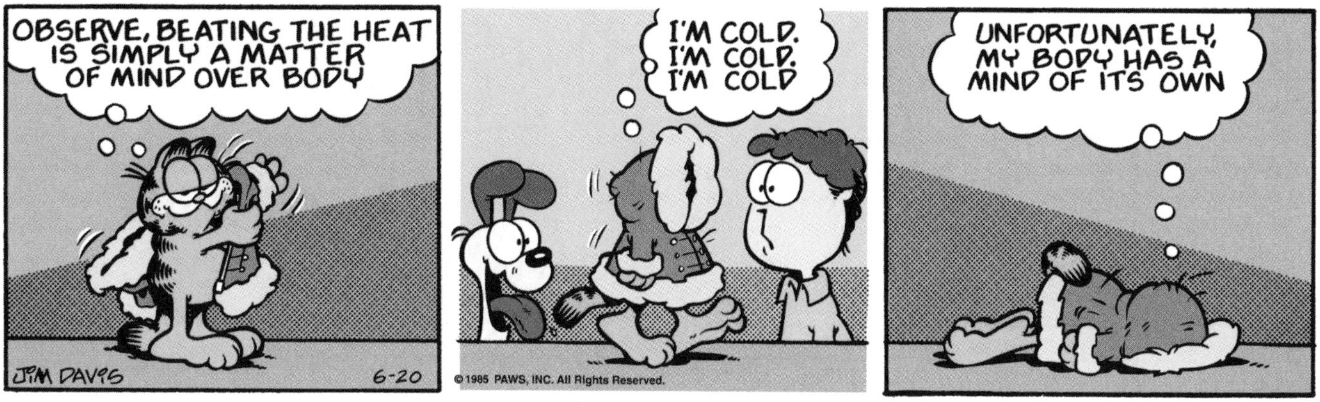
OBSERVE, BEATING THE HEAT IS SIMPLY A MATTER OF MIND OVER BODY
JIM DAVIS 6-20
I'M COLD. I'M COLD. I'M COLD
© 1985 PAWS, INC. All Rights Reserved.
UNFORTUNATELY, MY BODY HAS A MIND OF ITS OWN

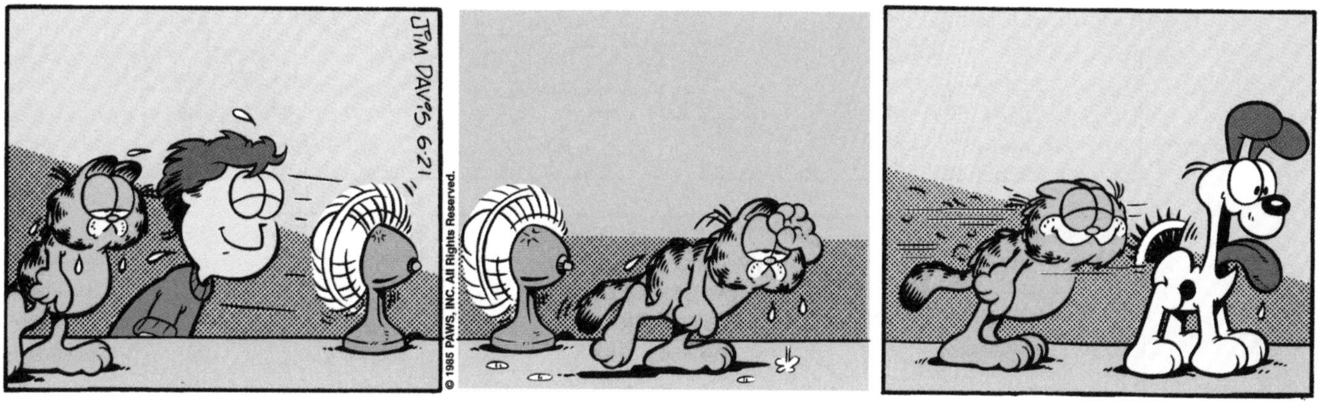
JIM DAVIS 6-21
© 1985 PAWS, INC. All Rights Reserved.

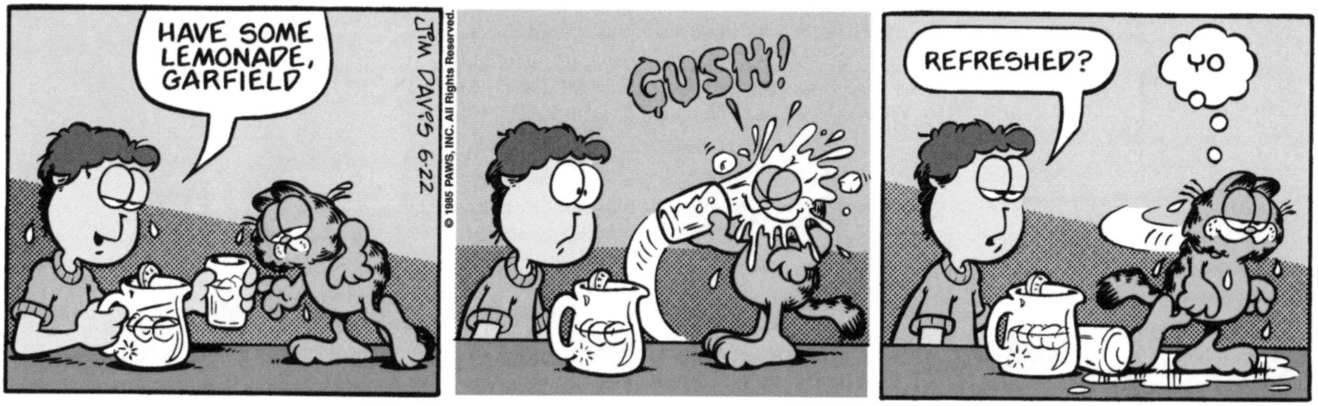
HAVE SOME LEMONADE, GARFIELD
JIM DAVIS 6-22
© 1985 PAWS, INC. All Rights Reserved.
GUSH!
REFRESHED?
YO

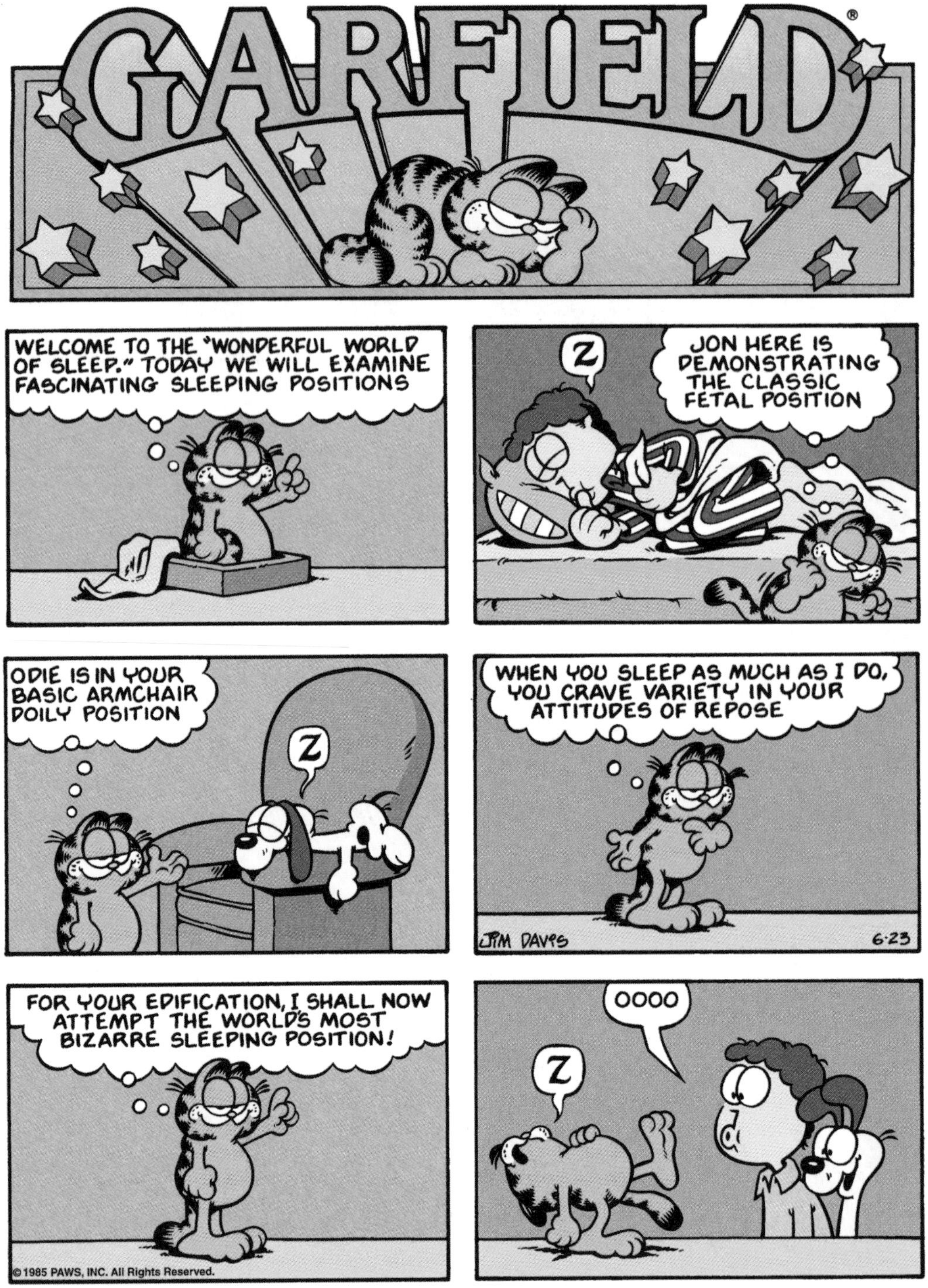
GARFIELD®
WELCOME TO THE "WONDERFUL WORLD OF SLEEP." TODAY WE WILL EXAMINE FASCINATING SLEEPING POSITIONS
Z
JON HERE IS DEMONSTRATING THE CLASSIC FETAL POSITION
ODIE IS IN YOUR BASIC ARMCHAIR DOILY POSITION
Z
WHEN YOU SLEEP AS MUCH AS I DO, YOU CRAVE VARIETY IN YOUR ATTITUDES OF REPOSE
JIM DAVIS 6·23
FOR YOUR EDIFICATION, I SHALL NOW ATTEMPT THE WORLD'S MOST BIZARRE SLEEPING POSITION!
Z
OOOO

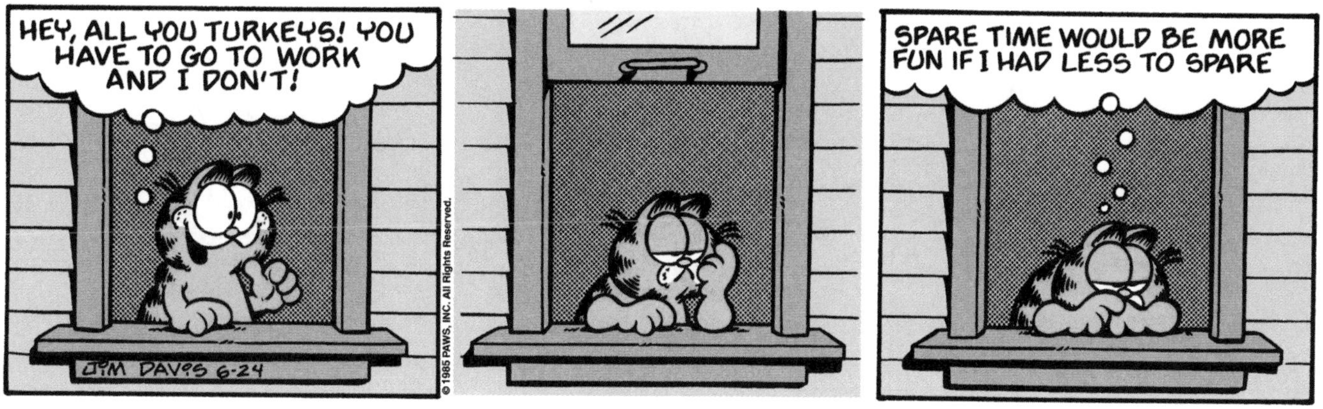
HEY, ALL YOU TURKEYS! YOU HAVE TO GO TO WORK AND I DON'T!
JIM DAVIS 6-24
© 1985 PAWS, INC. All Rights Reserved.
SPARE TIME WOULD BE MORE FUN IF I HAD LESS TO SPARE

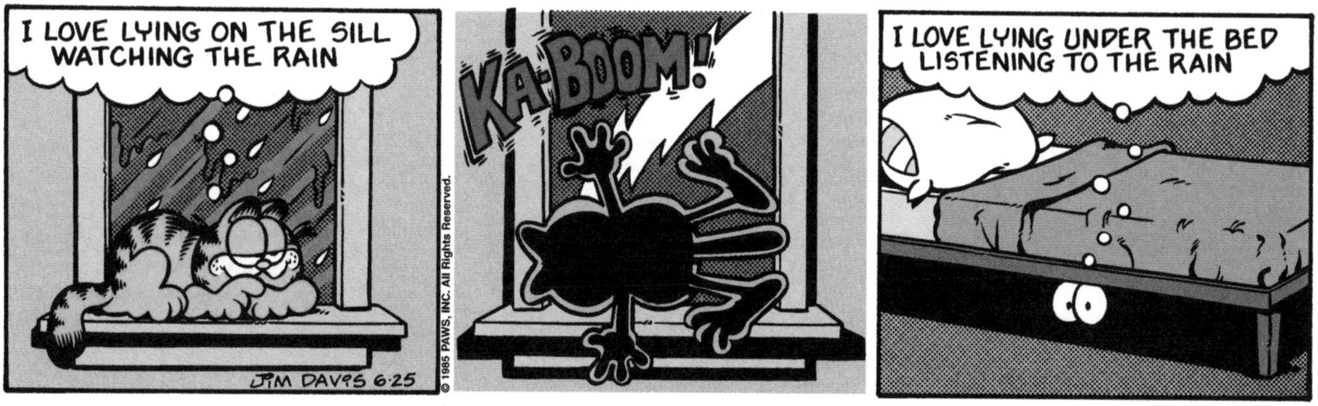
I LOVE LYING ON THE SILL WATCHING THE RAIN
JIM DAVIS 6-25
© 1985 PAWS, INC. All Rights Reserved.
KA-BOOM!
I LOVE LYING UNDER THE BED LISTENING TO THE RAIN

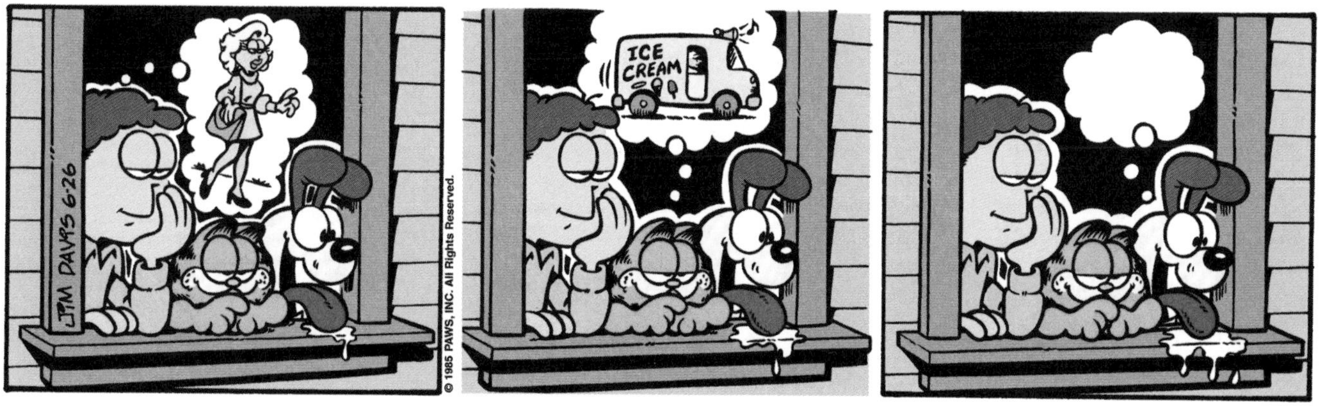
JIM DAVIS 6-26
© 1985 PAWS, INC. All Rights Reserved.
ICE CREAM

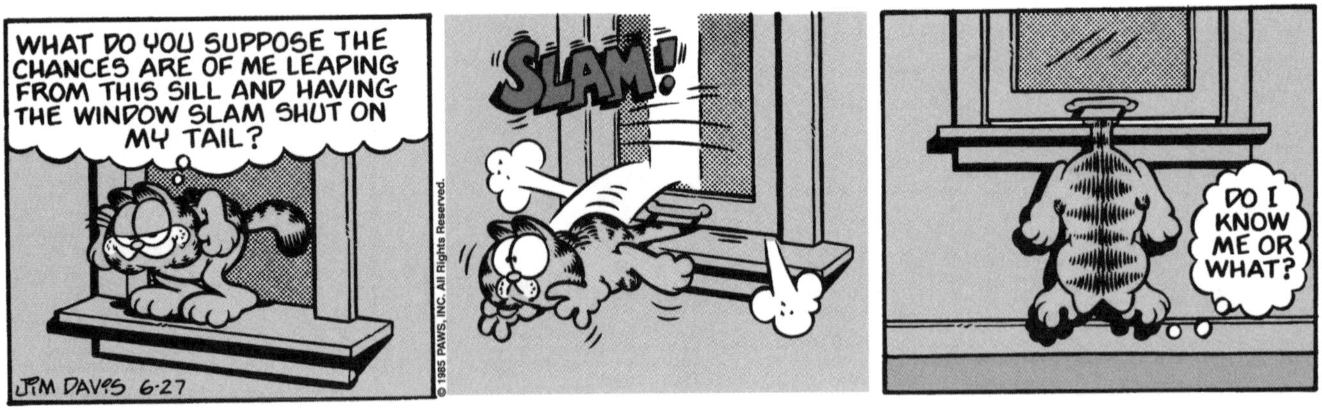
WHAT DO YOU SUPPOSE THE CHANCES ARE OF ME LEAPING FROM THIS SILL AND HAVING THE WINDOW SLAM SHUT ON MY TAIL?
JIM DAVIS 6-27
SLAM!
© 1985 PAWS, INC. All Rights Reserved.
DO I KNOW ME OR WHAT?

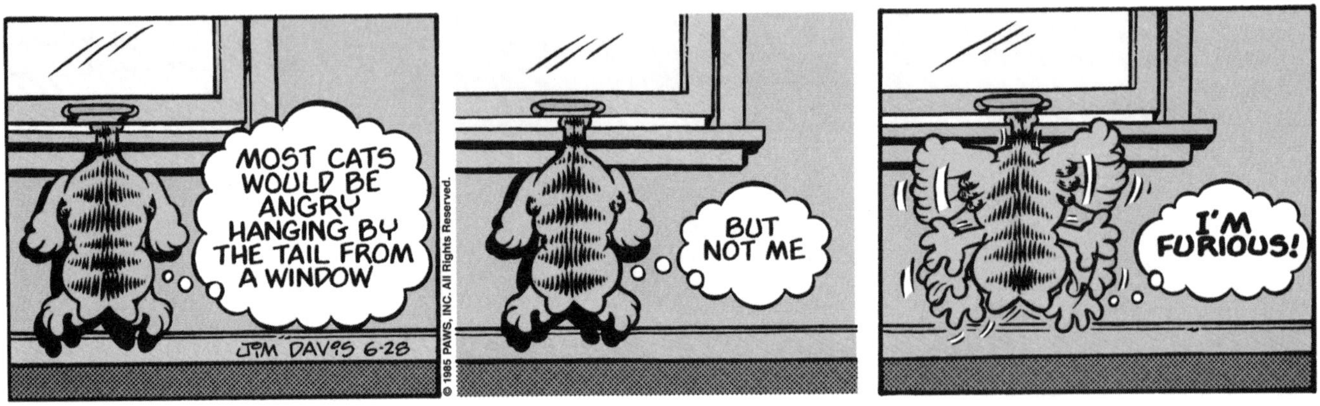
MOST CATS WOULD BE ANGRY HANGING BY THE TAIL FROM A WINDOW
JIM DAVIS 6-28
© 1985 PAWS, INC. All Rights Reserved.
BUT NOT ME
I'M FURIOUS!

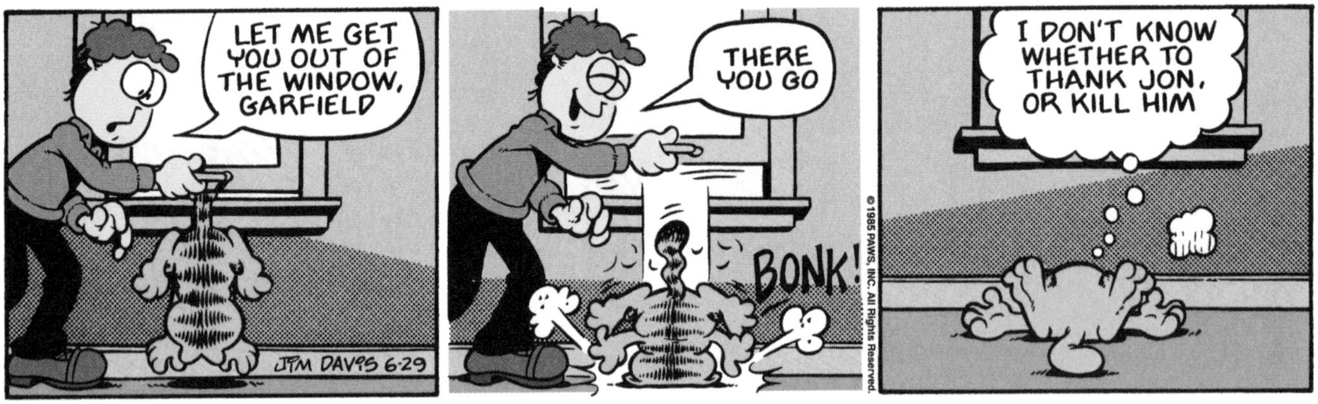
LET ME GET YOU OUT OF THE WINDOW, GARFIELD
JIM DAVIS 6-29
THERE YOU GO
BONK!
© 1985 PAWS, INC. All Rights Reserved.
I DON'T KNOW WHETHER TO THANK JON, OR KILL HIM

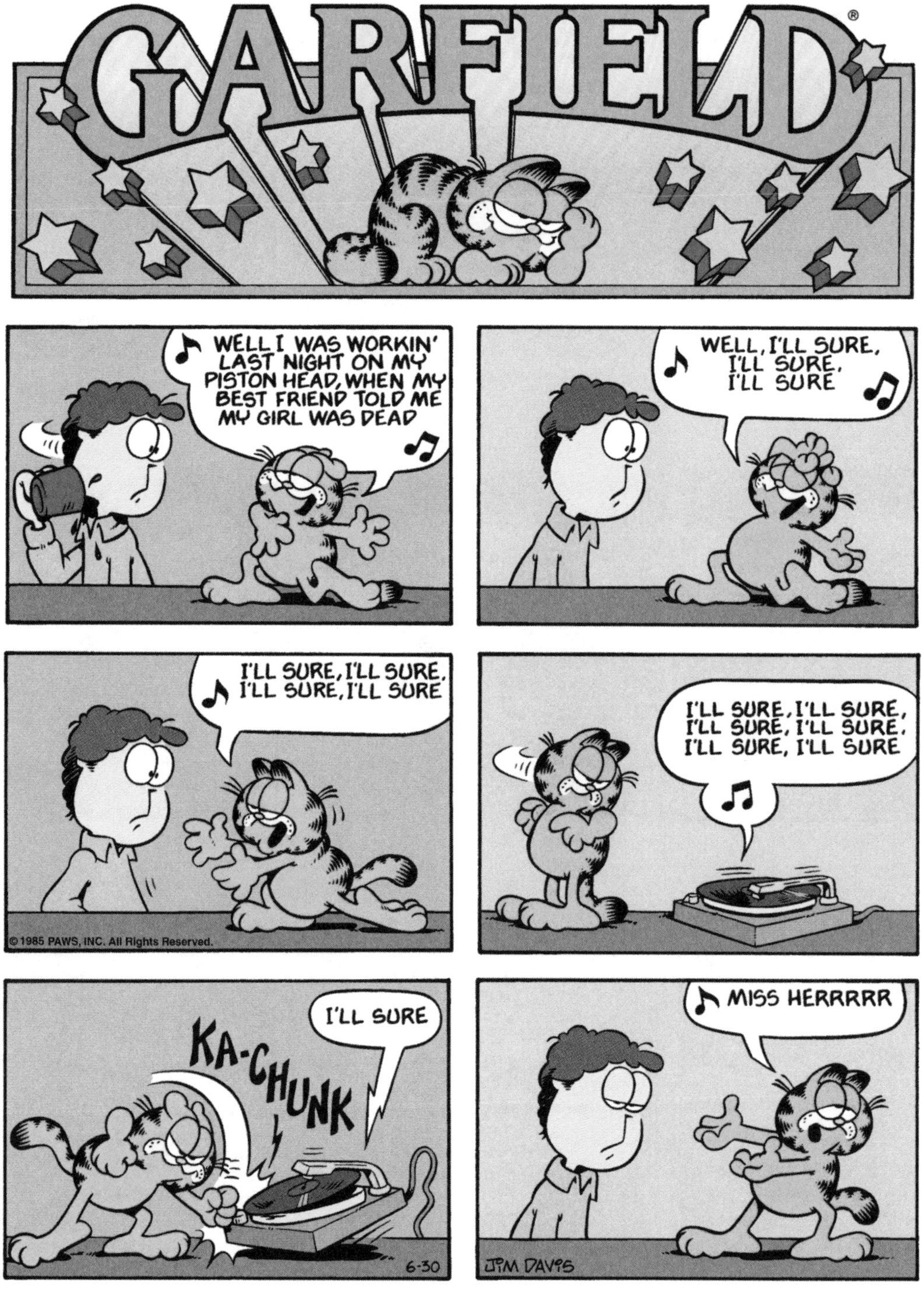
GARFIELD®
WELL I WAS WORKIN' LAST NIGHT ON MY PISTON HEAD, WHEN MY BEST FRIEND TOLD ME MY GIRL WAS DEAD
WELL, I'LL SURE, I'LL SURE, I'LL SURE
I'LL SURE, I'LL SURE, I'LL SURE, I'LL SURE
© 1985 PAWS, INC. All Rights Reserved.
I'LL SURE, I'LL SURE, I'LL SURE, I'LL SURE, I'LL SURE, I'LL SURE
I'LL SURE
KA-CHUNK
6-30
MISS HERRRRR
JIM DAVIS

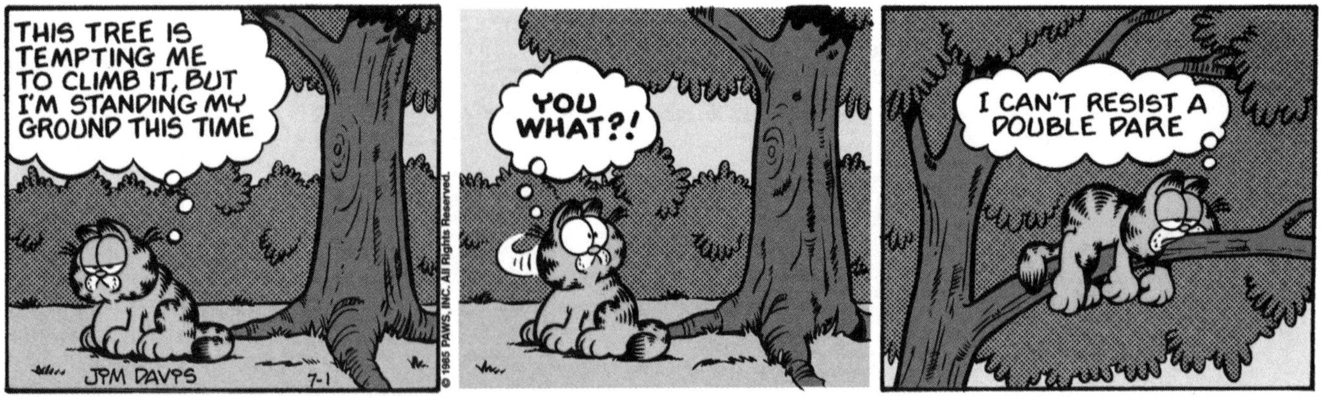
THIS TREE IS TEMPTING ME TO CLIMB IT, BUT I'M STANDING MY GROUND THIS TIME
JIM DAVIS
7-1
© 1985 PAWS, INC. All Rights Reserved.
YOU WHAT?!
I CAN'T RESIST A DOUBLE DARE

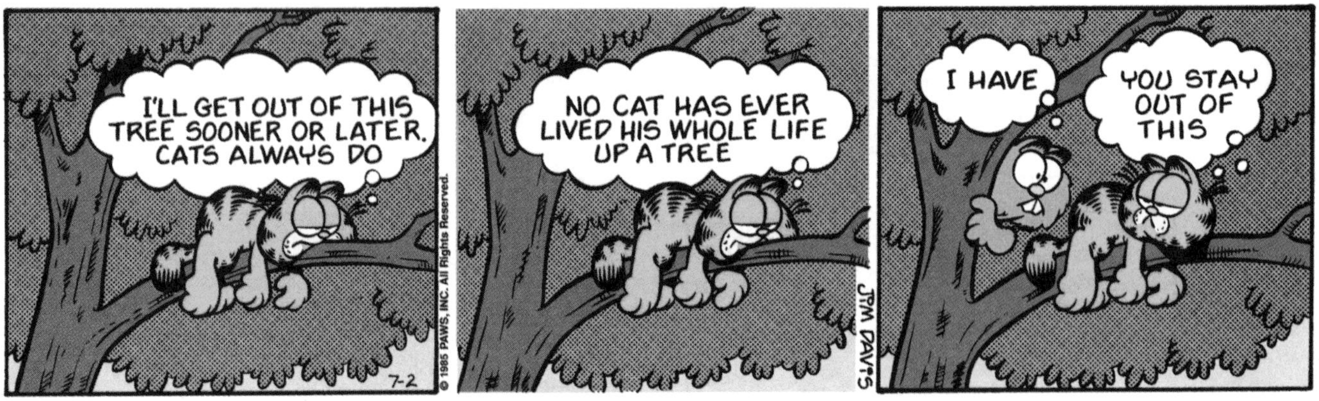
I'LL GET OUT OF THIS TREE SOONER OR LATER. CATS ALWAYS DO
7-2
© 1985 PAWS, INC. All Rights Reserved.
NO CAT HAS EVER LIVED HIS WHOLE LIFE UP A TREE
JIM DAVIS
I HAVE
YOU STAY OUT OF THIS

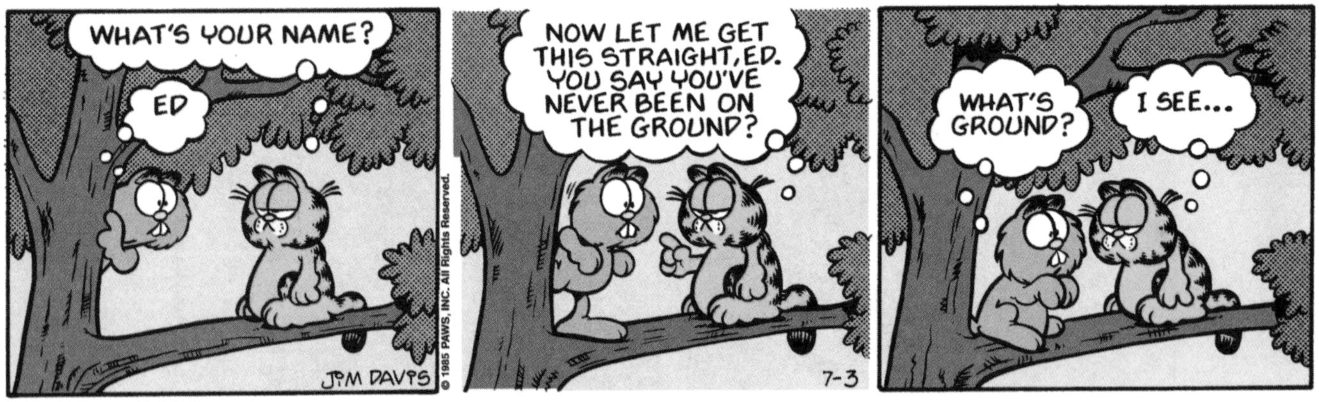
WHAT'S YOUR NAME?
ED
JIM DAVIS
© 1985 PAWS, INC. All Rights Reserved.
NOW LET ME GET THIS STRAIGHT, ED. YOU SAY YOU'VE NEVER BEEN ON THE GROUND?
7-3
WHAT'S GROUND?
I SEE...

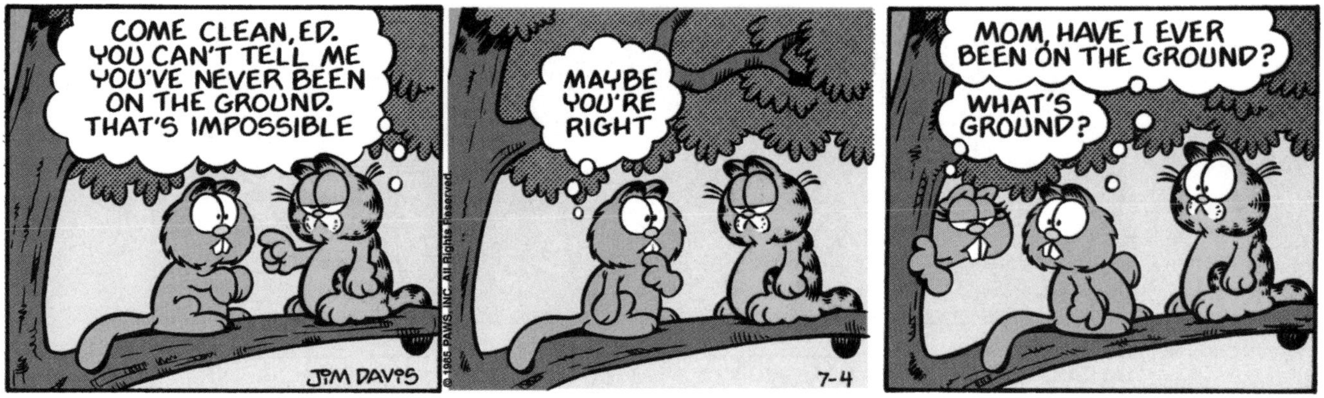
COME CLEAN, ED. YOU CAN'T TELL ME YOU'VE NEVER BEEN ON THE GROUND. THAT'S IMPOSSIBLE
JIM DAVIS
© 1985 PAWS, INC. All Rights Reserved.
MAYBE YOU'RE RIGHT
7-4
MOM, HAVE I EVER BEEN ON THE GROUND?
WHAT'S GROUND?

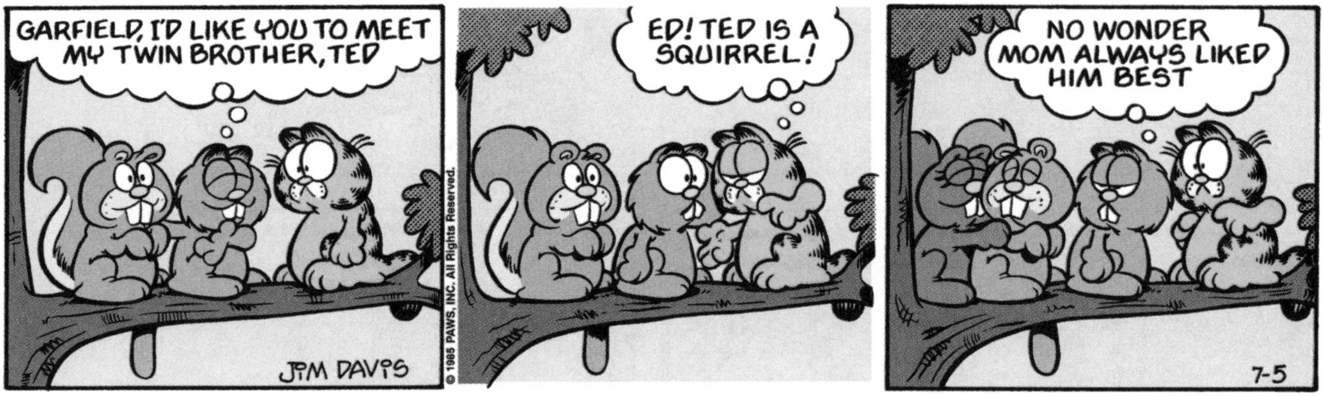
GARFIELD, I'D LIKE YOU TO MEET MY TWIN BROTHER, TED
JIM DAVIS
© 1985 PAWS, INC. All Rights Reserved.
ED! TED IS A SQUIRREL!
NO WONDER MOM ALWAYS LIKED HIM BEST
7-5

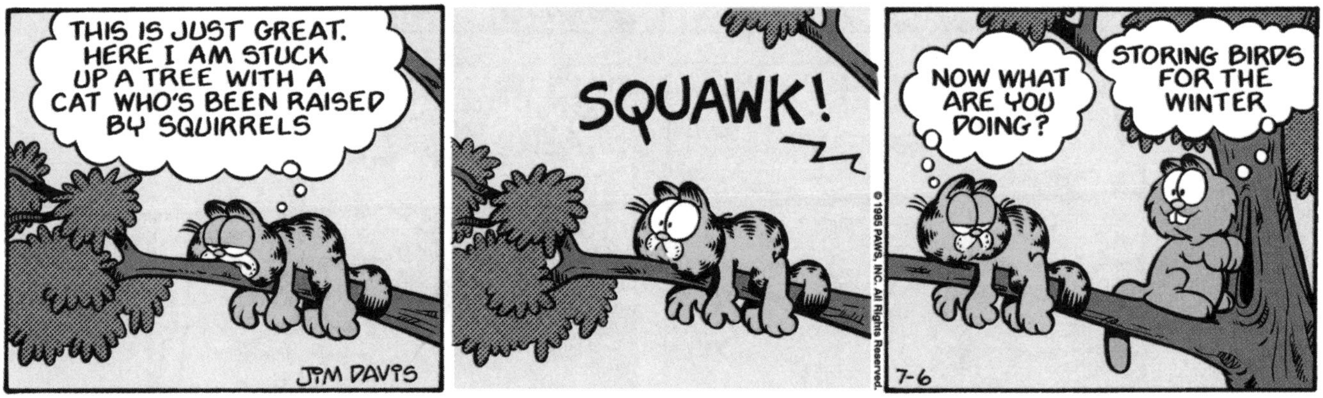
THIS IS JUST GREAT. HERE I AM STUCK UP A TREE WITH A CAT WHO'S BEEN RAISED BY SQUIRRELS
JIM DAVIS
SQUAWK!
© 1985 PAWS, INC. All Rights Reserved.
NOW WHAT ARE YOU DOING?
STORING BIRDS FOR THE WINTER
7-6

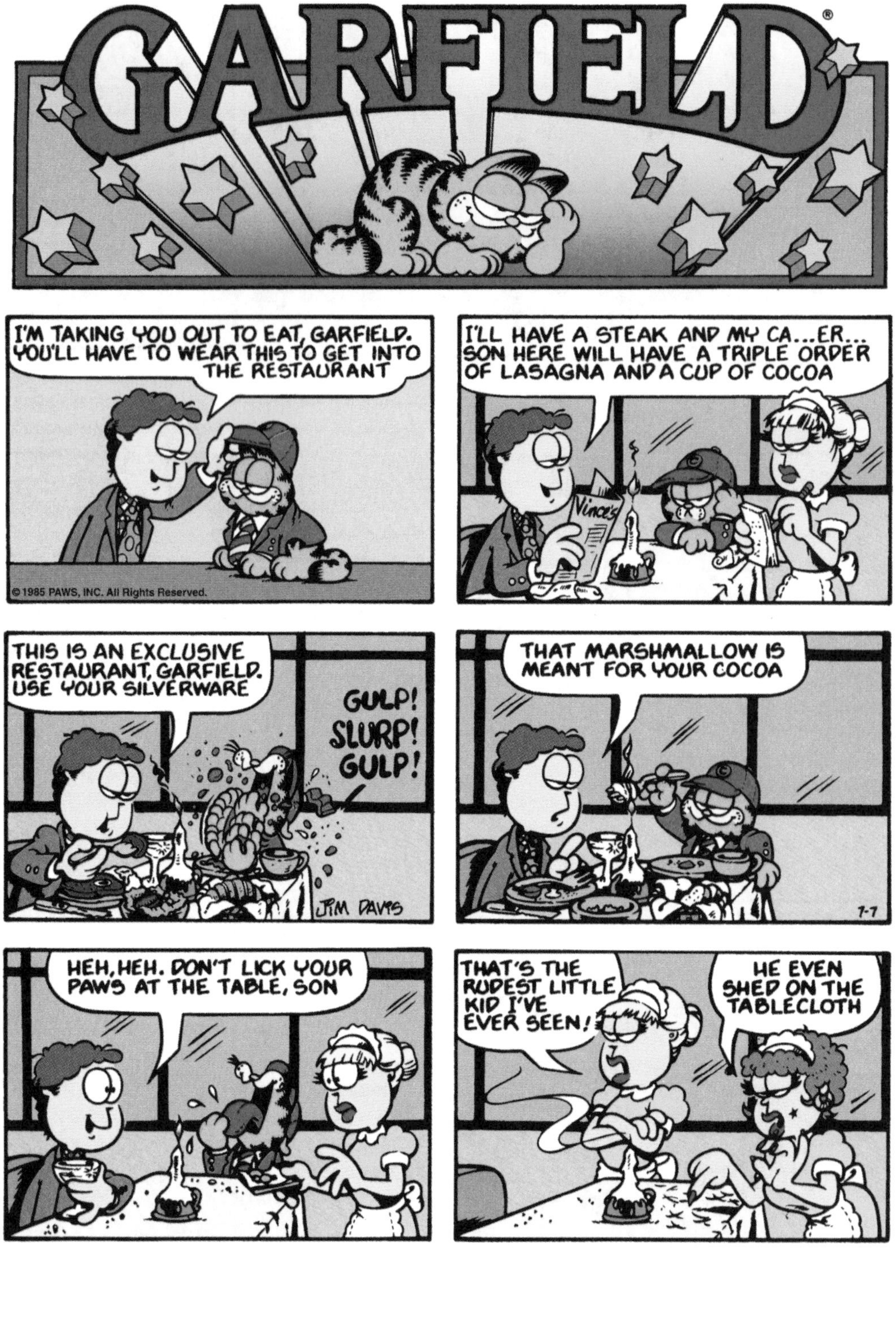
GARFIELD®
I'M TAKING YOU OUT TO EAT, GARFIELD. YOU'LL HAVE TO WEAR THIS TO GET INTO THE RESTAURANT
© 1985 PAWS, INC. All Rights Reserved.
I'LL HAVE A STEAK AND MY CA...ER... SON HERE WILL HAVE A TRIPLE ORDER OF LASAGNA AND A CUP OF COCOA
Vince's
THIS IS AN EXCLUSIVE RESTAURANT, GARFIELD. USE YOUR SILVERWARE
GULP! SLURP! GULP!
JIM DAVIS
THAT MARSHMALLOW IS MEANT FOR YOUR COCOA
7-7
HEH, HEH. DON'T LICK YOUR PAWS AT THE TABLE, SON
THAT'S THE RUDEST LITTLE KID I'VE EVER SEEN!
HE EVEN SHED ON THE TABLECLOTH

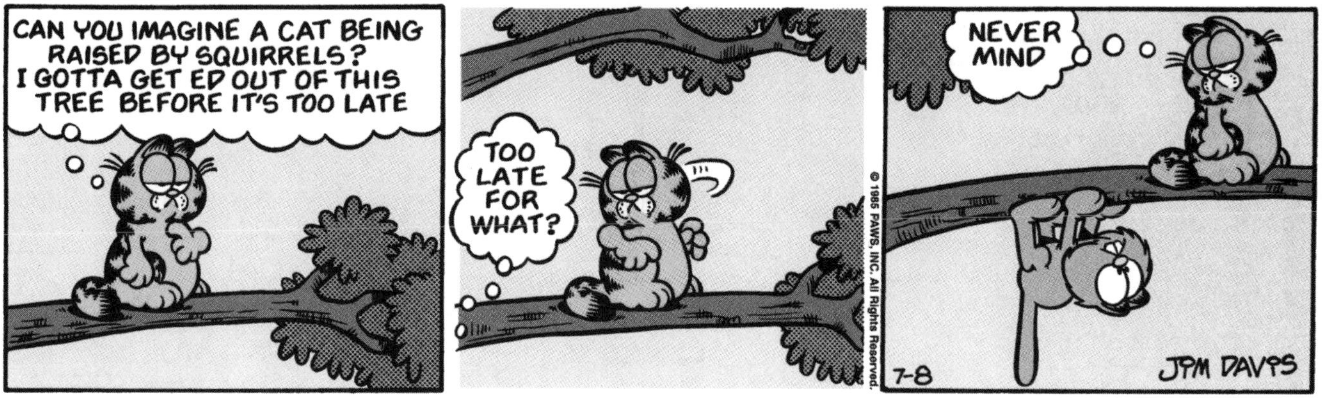
CAN YOU IMAGINE A CAT BEING RAISED BY SQUIRRELS? I GOTTA GET ED OUT OF THIS TREE BEFORE IT'S TOO LATE
TOO LATE FOR WHAT?
NEVER MIND
© 1985 PAWS, INC. All Rights Reserved.
7-8
JPM DAVPS

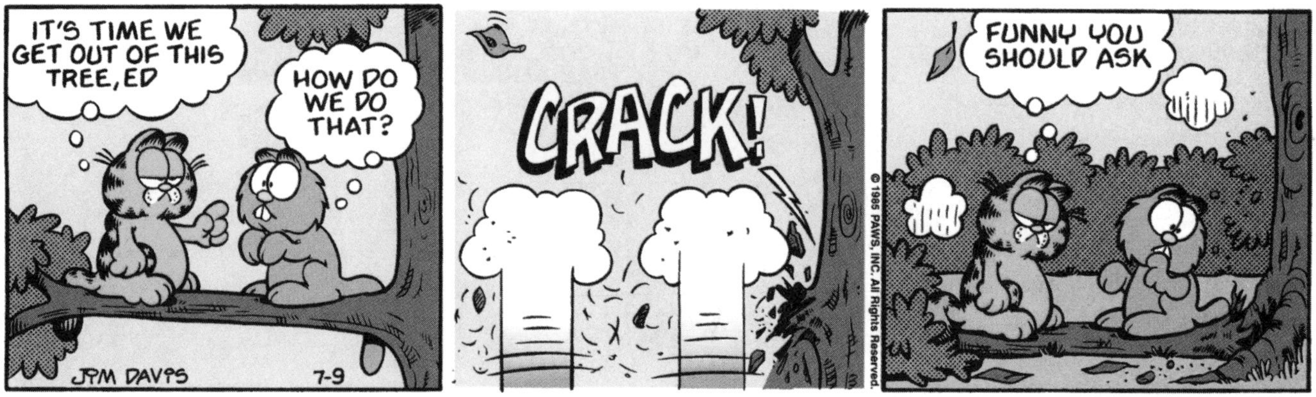
IT'S TIME WE GET OUT OF THIS TREE, ED
HOW DO WE DO THAT?
JPM DAVPS
7-9
CRACK!
FUNNY YOU SHOULD ASK
© 1985 PAWS, INC. All Rights Reserved.

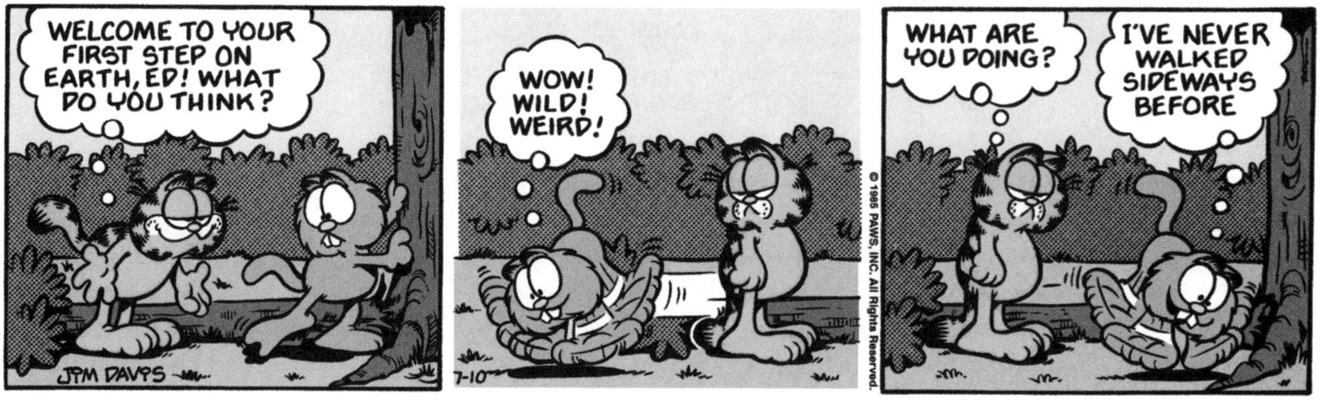
WELCOME TO YOUR FIRST STEP ON EARTH, ED! WHAT DO YOU THINK?
JPM DAVPS
WOW! WILD! WEIRD!
7-10
WHAT ARE YOU DOING?
I'VE NEVER WALKED SIDEWAYS BEFORE
© 1985 PAWS, INC. All Rights Reserved.

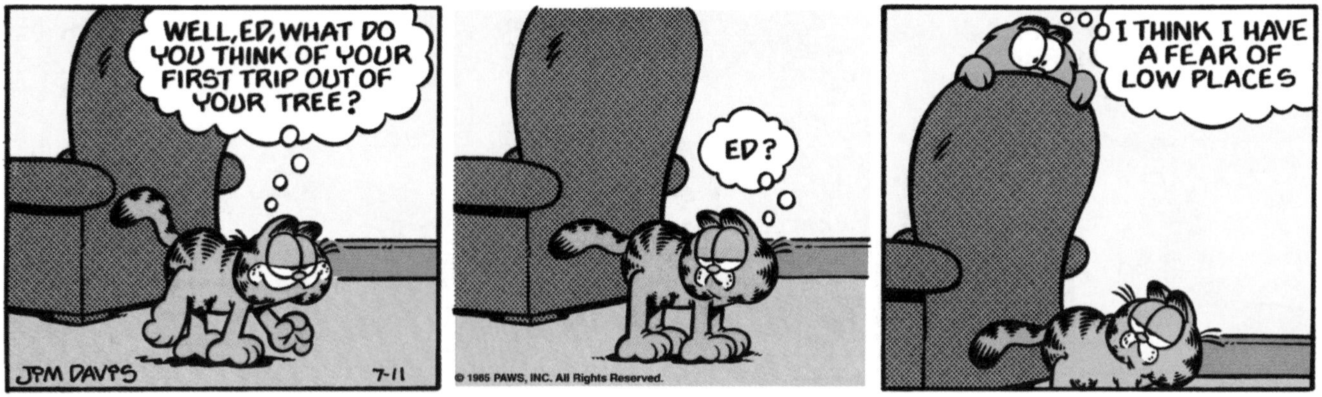
WELL, ED, WHAT DO YOU THINK OF YOUR FIRST TRIP OUT OF YOUR TREE?
JIM DAVIS
7-11
ED?
© 1985 PAWS, INC. All Rights Reserved.
I THINK I HAVE A FEAR OF LOW PLACES

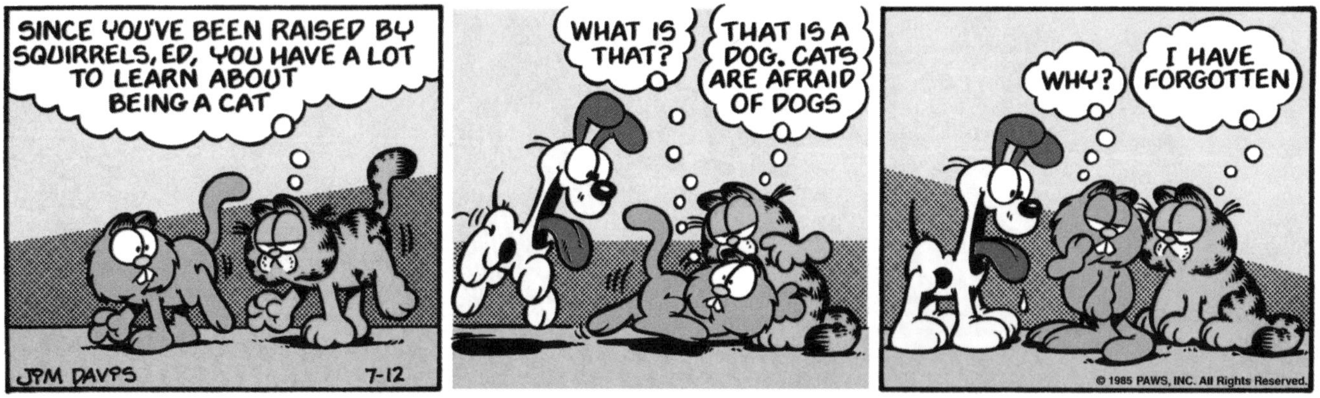
SINCE YOU'VE BEEN RAISED BY SQUIRRELS, ED, YOU HAVE A LOT TO LEARN ABOUT BEING A CAT
JIM DAVIS
7-12
WHAT IS THAT?
THAT IS A DOG. CATS ARE AFRAID OF DOGS
WHY?
I HAVE FORGOTTEN
© 1985 PAWS, INC. All Rights Reserved.

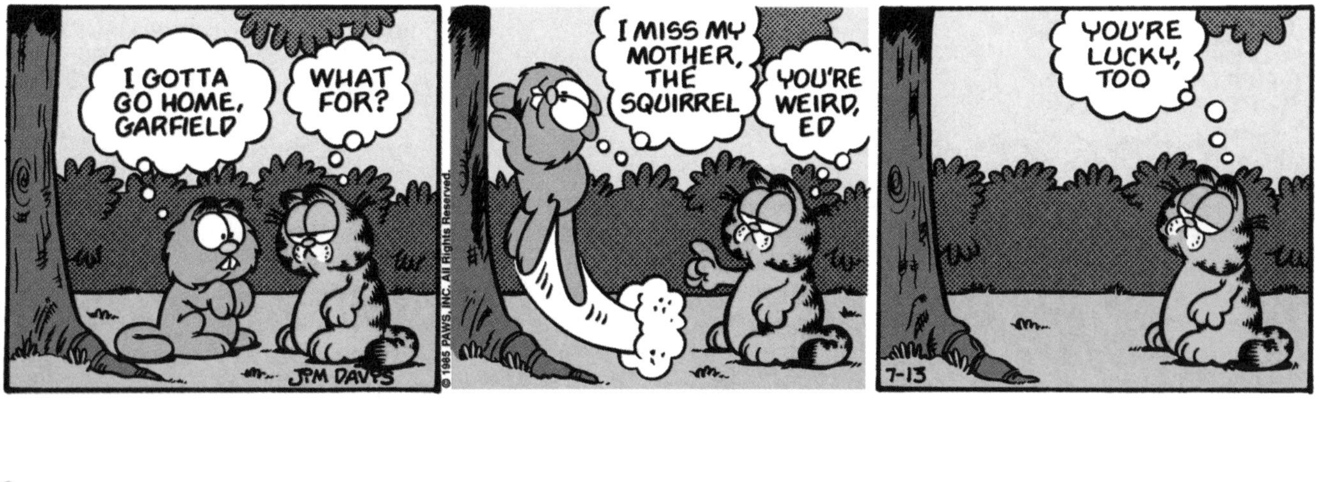
I GOTTA GO HOME, GARFIELD
WHAT FOR?
JIM DAVIS
© 1985 PAWS, INC. All Rights Reserved.
I MISS MY MOTHER, THE SQUIRREL
YOU'RE WEIRD, ED
YOU'RE LUCKY, TOO
7-13

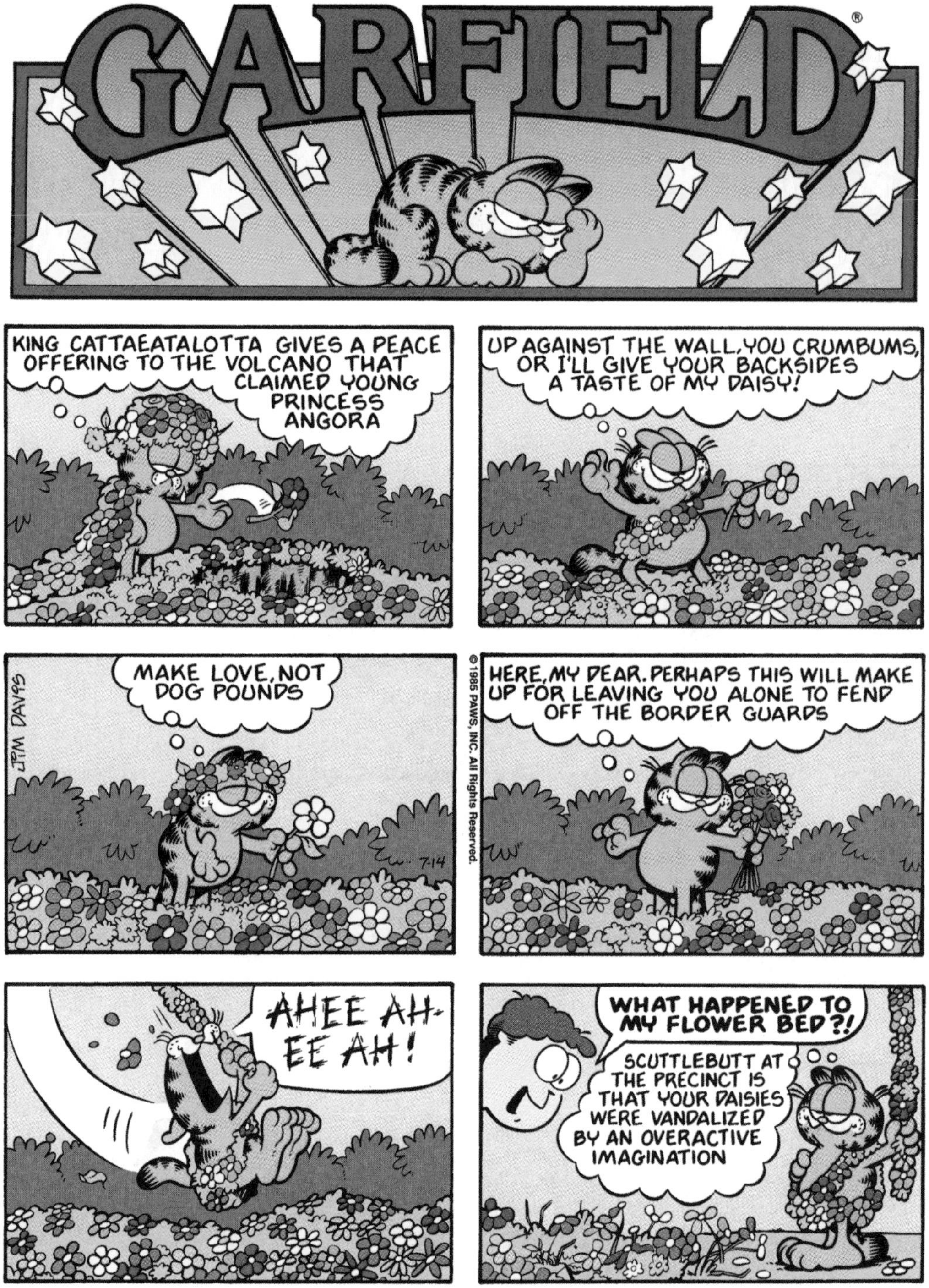
GARFIELD
KING CATTAEATALOTTA GIVES A PEACE OFFERING TO THE VOLCANO THAT CLAIMED YOUNG PRINCESS ANGORA
UP AGAINST THE WALL, YOU CRUMBUMS, OR I'LL GIVE YOUR BACKSIDES A TASTE OF MY DAISY!
MAKE LOVE, NOT DOG POUNDS
JIM DAVIS
7-14
HERE, MY DEAR. PERHAPS THIS WILL MAKE UP FOR LEAVING YOU ALONE TO FEND OFF THE BORDER GUARDS
AHEE AH-EE AH!
WHAT HAPPENED TO MY FLOWER BED?!
SCUTTLEBUTT AT THE PRECINCT IS THAT YOUR DAISIES WERE VANDALIZED BY AN OVERACTIVE IMAGINATION

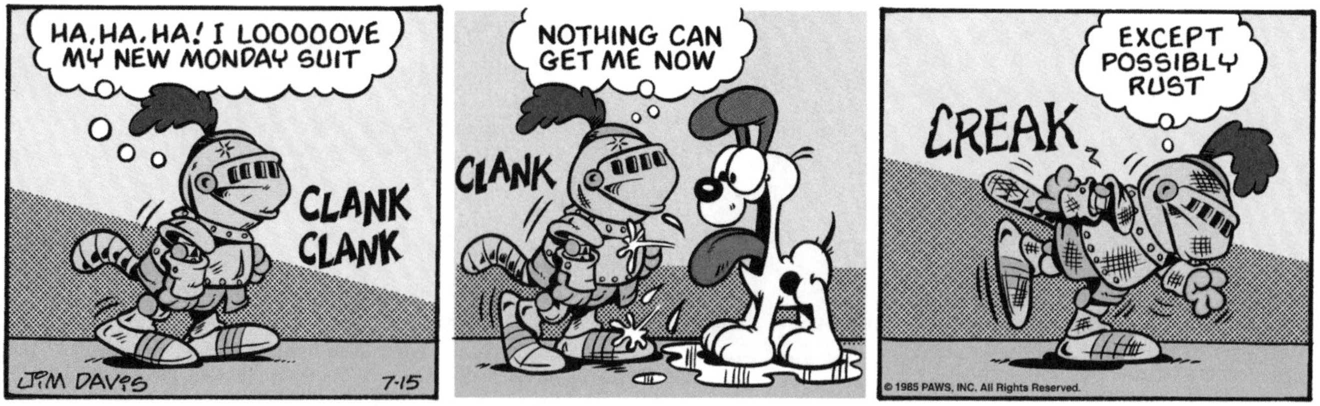
HA, HA, HA! I LOOOOOVE MY NEW MONDAY SUIT
CLANK CLANK
JIM DAVIS 7-15
CLANK
NOTHING CAN GET ME NOW
CREAK
EXCEPT POSSIBLY RUST
© 1985 PAWS, INC. All Rights Reserved.

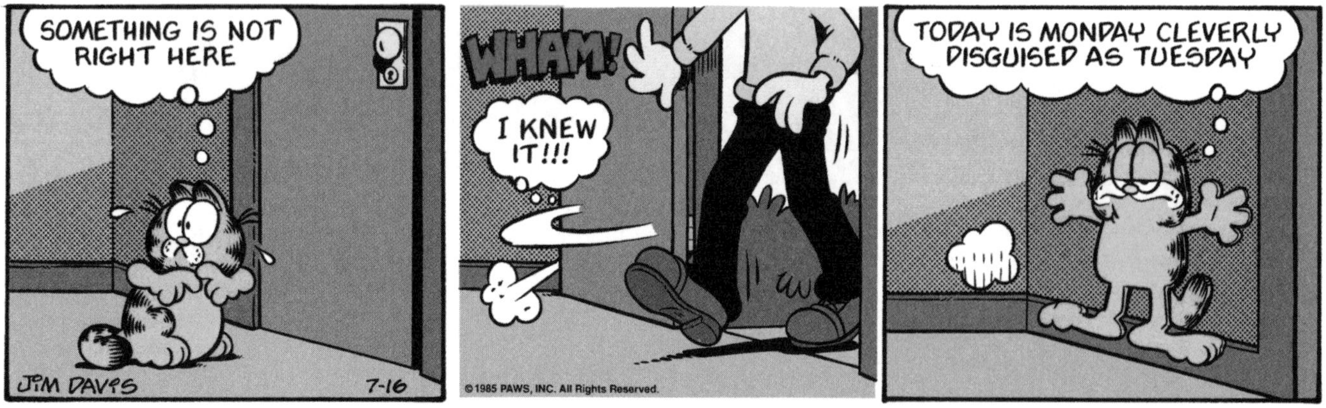
SOMETHING IS NOT RIGHT HERE
JIM DAVIS 7-16
WHAM!
I KNEW IT!!!
© 1985 PAWS, INC. All Rights Reserved.
TODAY IS MONDAY CLEVERLY DISGUISED AS TUESDAY

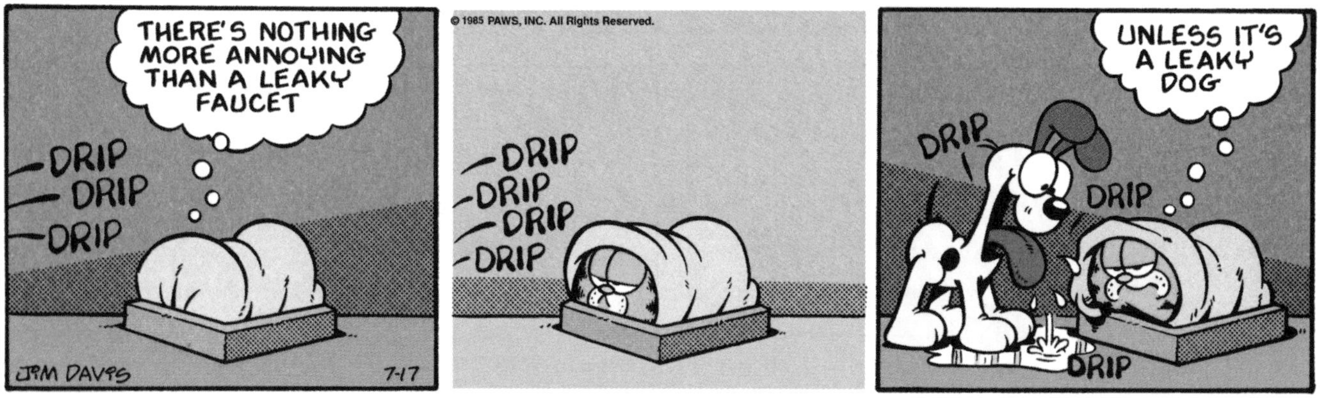
THERE'S NOTHING MORE ANNOYING THAN A LEAKY FAUCET
DRIP
DRIP
DRIP
JIM DAVIS 7-17
© 1985 PAWS, INC. All Rights Reserved.
DRIP
DRIP
DRIP
DRIP
UNLESS IT'S A LEAKY DOG
DRIP
DRIP
DRIP

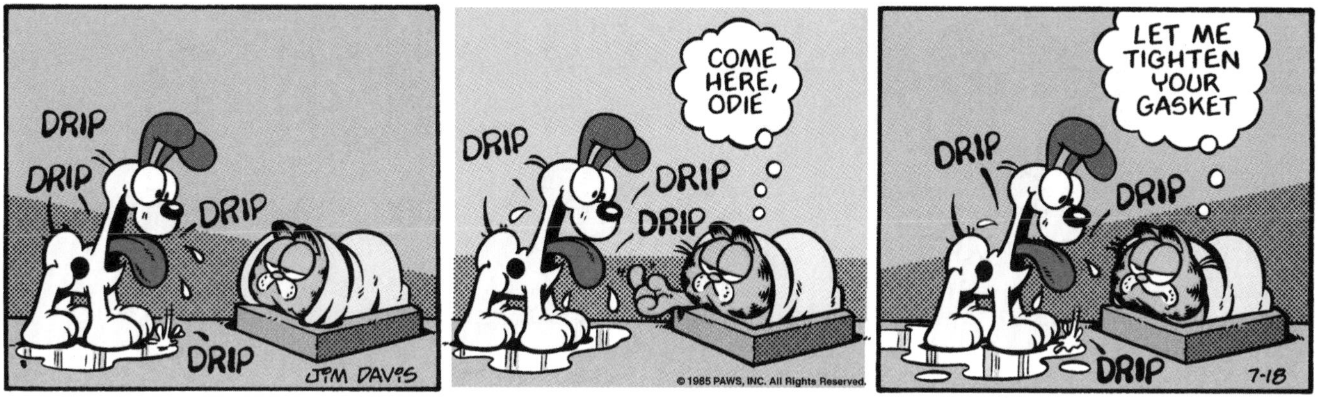
DRIP
DRIP
DRIP
DRIP
JIM DAVIS
DRIP
DRIP
DRIP
COME HERE, ODIE
© 1985 PAWS, INC. All Rights Reserved.
DRIP
DRIP
LET ME TIGHTEN YOUR GASKET
DRIP
7-18

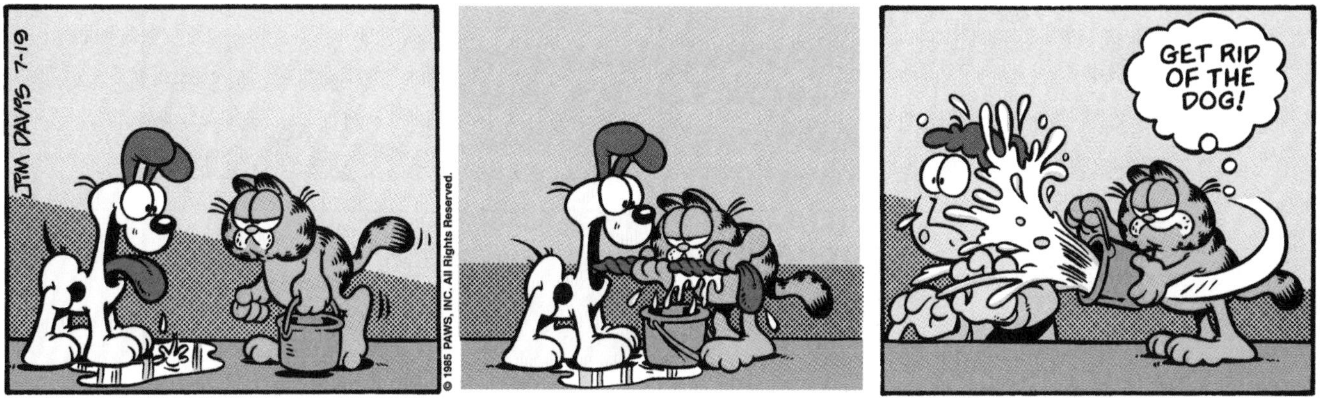
JIM DAVIS 7-19
© 1985 PAWS, INC. All Rights Reserved.
GET RID OF THE DOG!

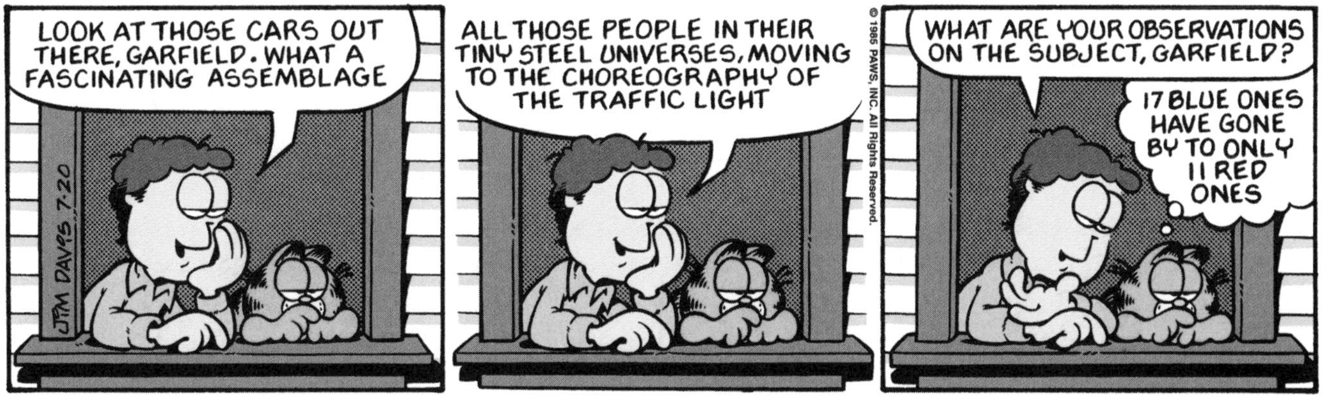
LOOK AT THOSE CARS OUT THERE, GARFIELD. WHAT A FASCINATING ASSEMBLAGE
JIM DAVIS 7-20
ALL THOSE PEOPLE IN THEIR TINY STEEL UNIVERSES, MOVING TO THE CHOREOGRAPHY OF THE TRAFFIC LIGHT
© 1985 PAWS, INC. All Rights Reserved.
WHAT ARE YOUR OBSERVATIONS ON THE SUBJECT, GARFIELD?
17 BLUE ONES HAVE GONE BY TO ONLY 11 RED ONES

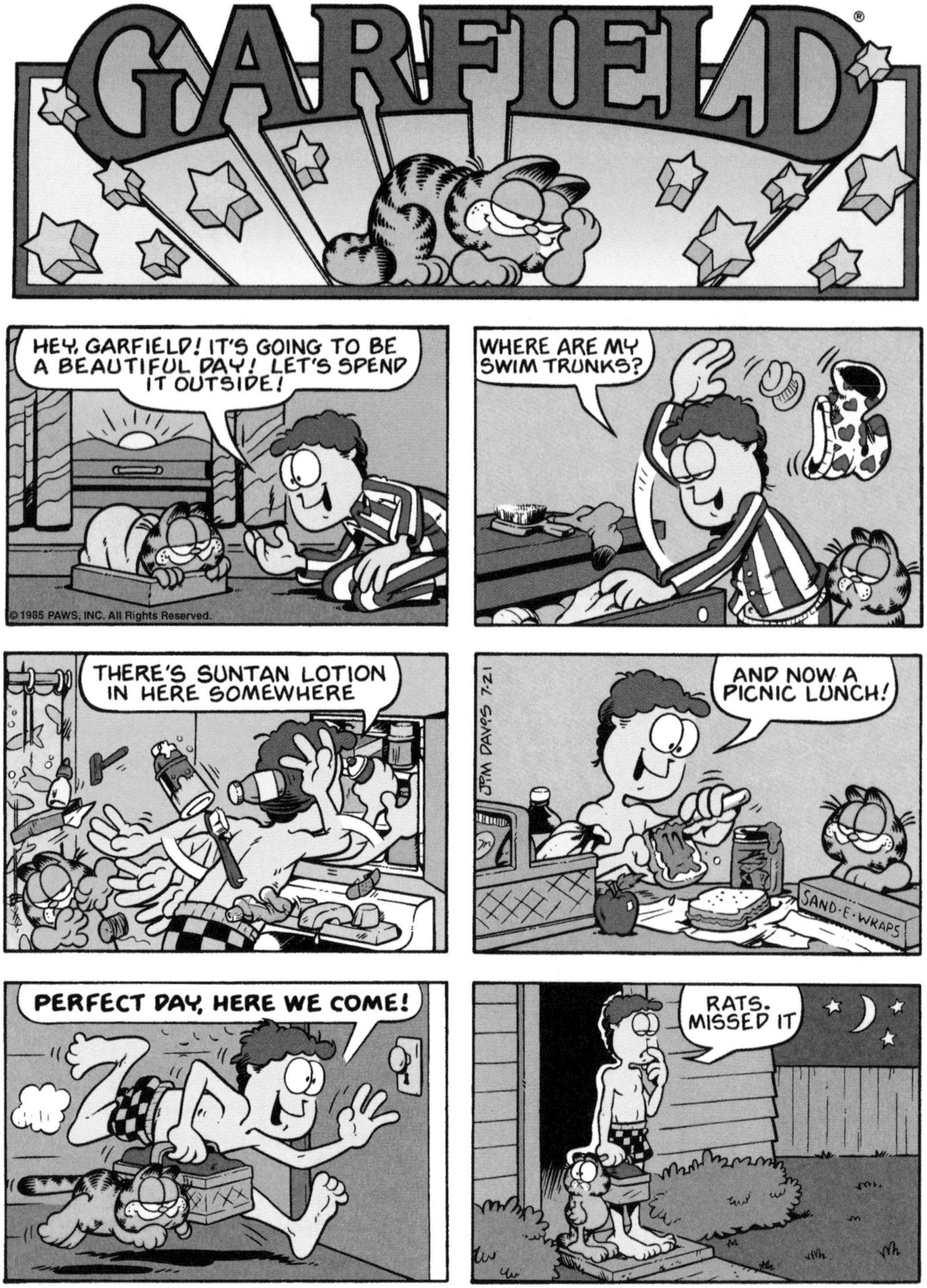
GARFIELD
HEY, GARFIELD! IT'S GOING TO BE A BEAUTIFUL DAY! LET'S SPEND IT OUTSIDE!
© 1985 PAWS, INC. All Rights Reserved.
WHERE ARE MY SWIM TRUNKS?
THERE'S SUNTAN LOTION IN HERE SOMEWHERE
JIM DAVIS 7-21
AND NOW A PICNIC LUNCH!
SAND-E-WRAPS
PERFECT DAY, HERE WE COME!
RATS. MISSED IT

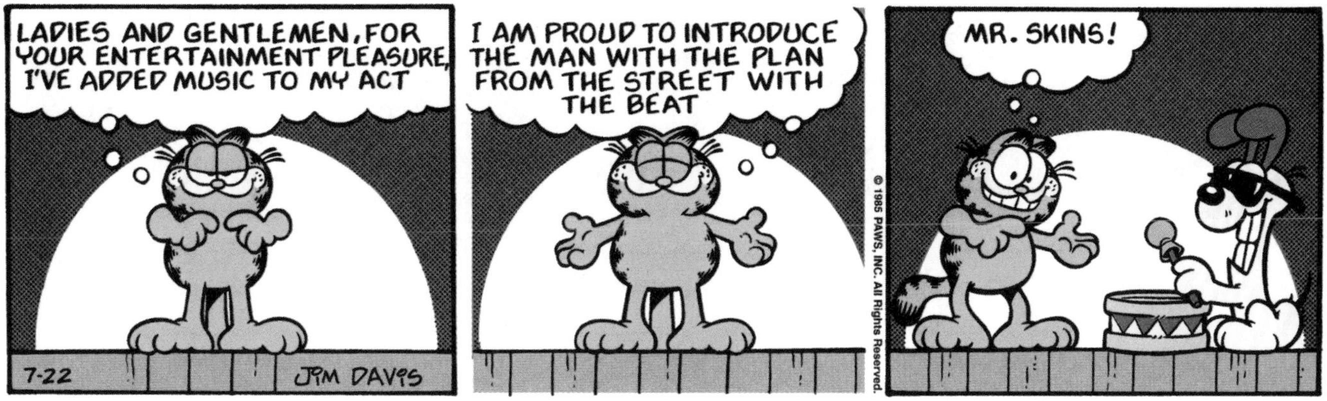
LADIES AND GENTLEMEN, FOR YOUR ENTERTAINMENT PLEASURE, I'VE ADDED MUSIC TO MY ACT
7-22
JIM DAVIS
I AM PROUD TO INTRODUCE THE MAN WITH THE PLAN FROM THE STREET WITH THE BEAT
© 1985 PAWS, INC. All Rights Reserved.
MR. SKINS!

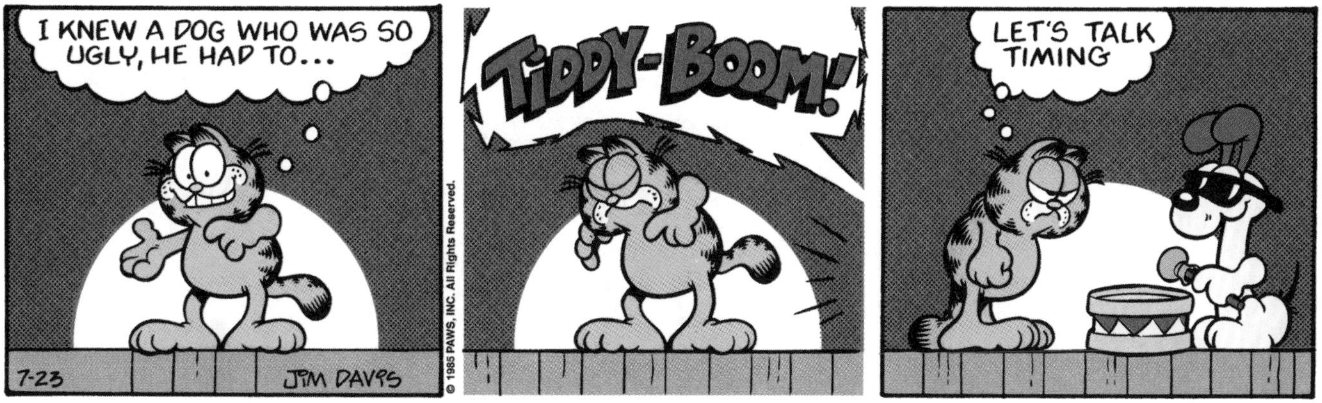
I KNEW A DOG WHO WAS SO UGLY, HE HAD TO...
7-23
JIM DAVIS
© 1985 PAWS, INC. All Rights Reserved.
TIDDY-BOOM!
LET'S TALK TIMING

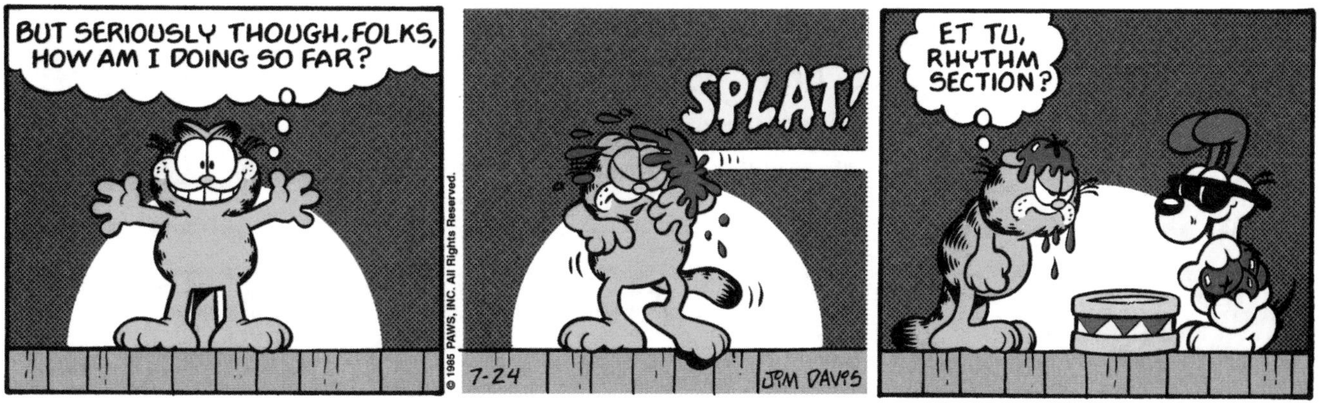
BUT SERIOUSLY THOUGH, FOLKS, HOW AM I DOING SO FAR?
© 1985 PAWS, INC. All Rights Reserved.
SPLAT!
7-24
JIM DAVIS
ET TU, RHYTHM SECTION?

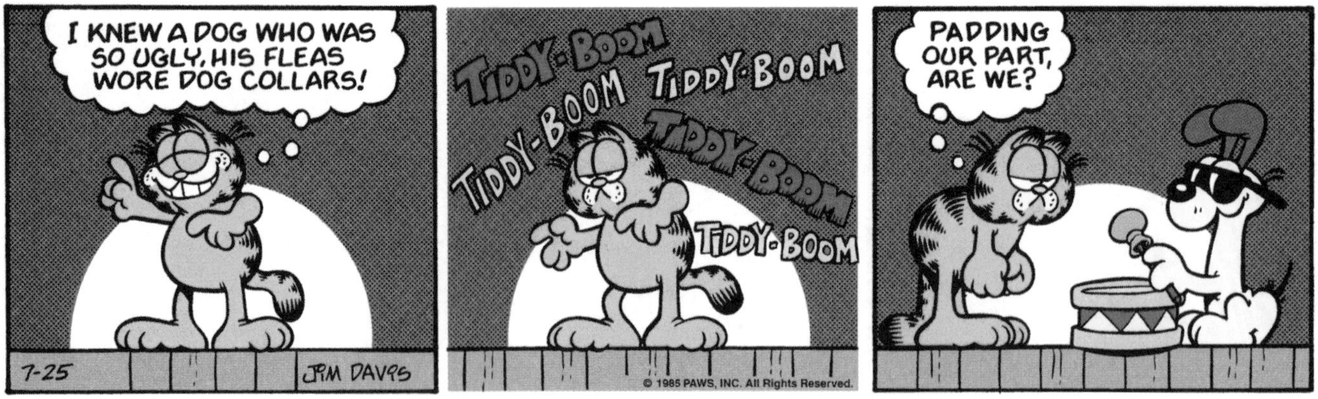
I KNEW A DOG WHO WAS SO UGLY, HIS FLEAS WORE DOG COLLARS!
7-25
JIM DAVIS
TIDDY-BOOM TIDDY-BOOM TIDDY-BOOM TIDDY-BOOM TIDDY-BOOM
© 1985 PAWS, INC. All Rights Reserved.
PADDING OUR PART, ARE WE?

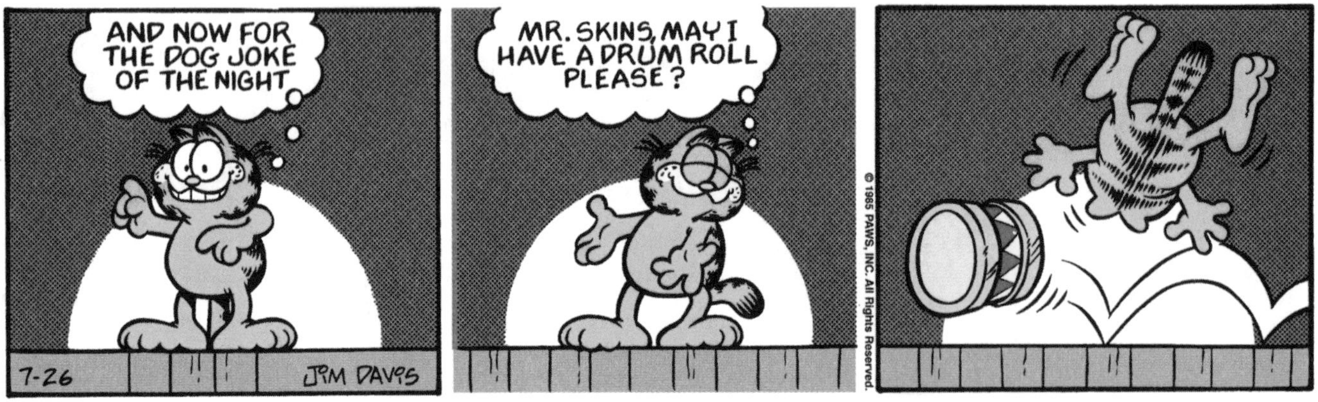
AND NOW FOR THE DOG JOKE OF THE NIGHT
7-26
JIM DAVIS
MR. SKINS, MAY I HAVE A DRUM ROLL PLEASE?
© 1985 PAWS, INC. All Rights Reserved.

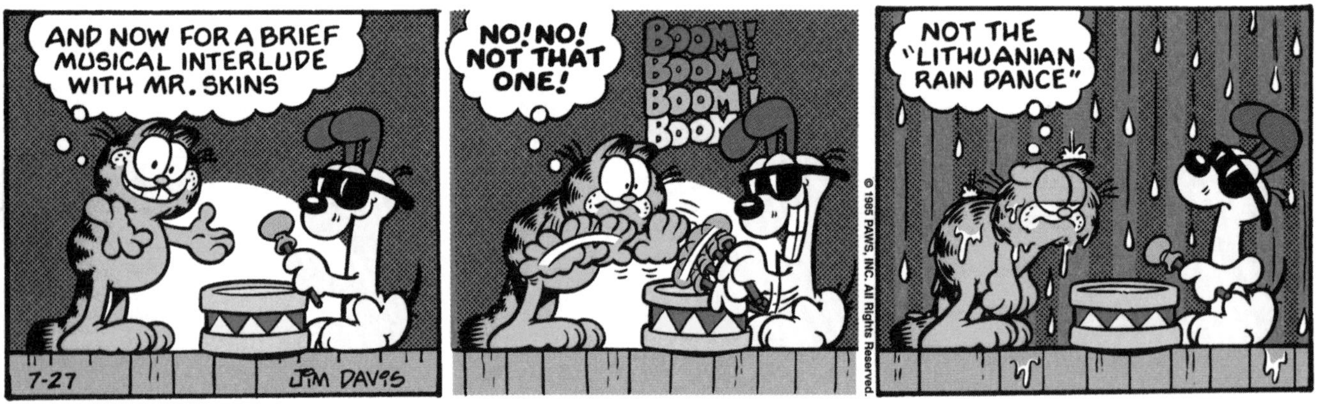
AND NOW FOR A BRIEF MUSICAL INTERLUDE WITH MR. SKINS
7-27
JIM DAVIS
NO! NO! NOT THAT ONE!
BOOM! BOOM! BOOM! BOOM
© 1985 PAWS, INC. All Rights Reserved.
NOT THE "LITHUANIAN RAIN DANCE"

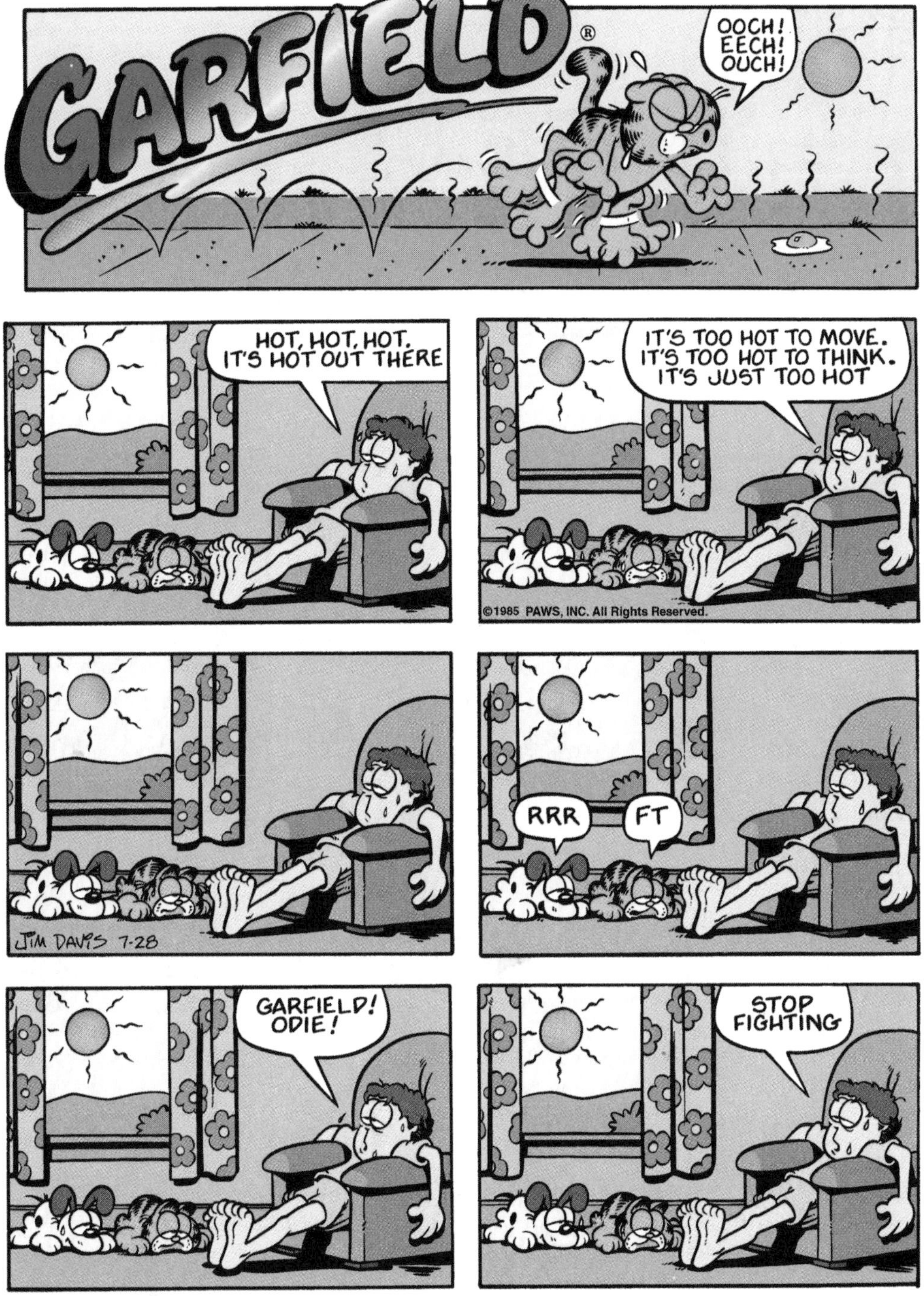
GARFIELD®
OOCH! EECH! OUCH!
HOT, HOT, HOT. IT'S HOT OUT THERE
IT'S TOO HOT TO MOVE. IT'S TOO HOT TO THINK. IT'S JUST TOO HOT
©1985 PAWS, INC. All Rights Reserved.
JIM DAVIS 7-28
RRR
FT
GARFIELD! ODIE!
STOP FIGHTING

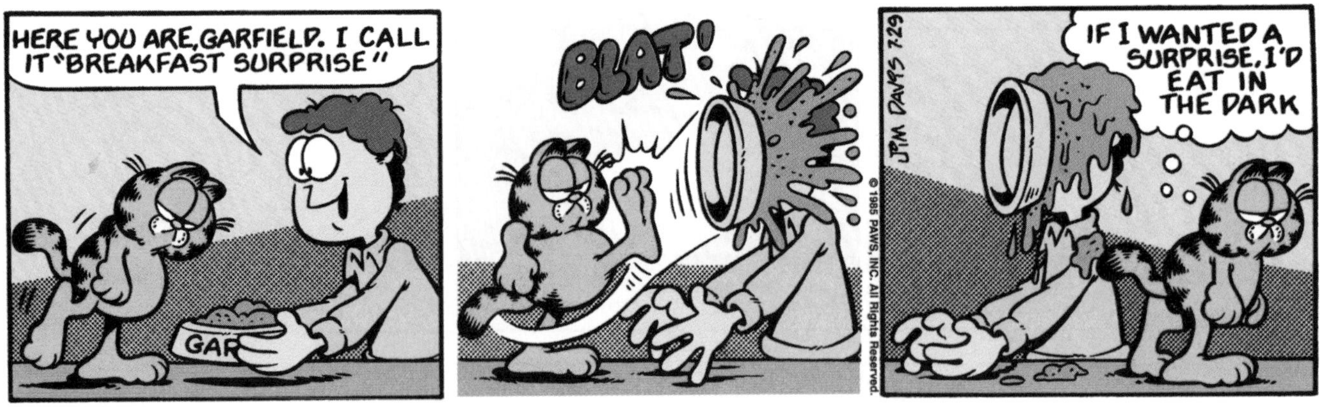
HERE YOU ARE, GARFIELD. I CALL IT "BREAKFAST SURPRISE"
GAR
BLAT!
JIM DAVIS 7-29
© 1985 PAWS, INC. All Rights Reserved.
IF I WANTED A SURPRISE, I'D EAT IN THE DARK

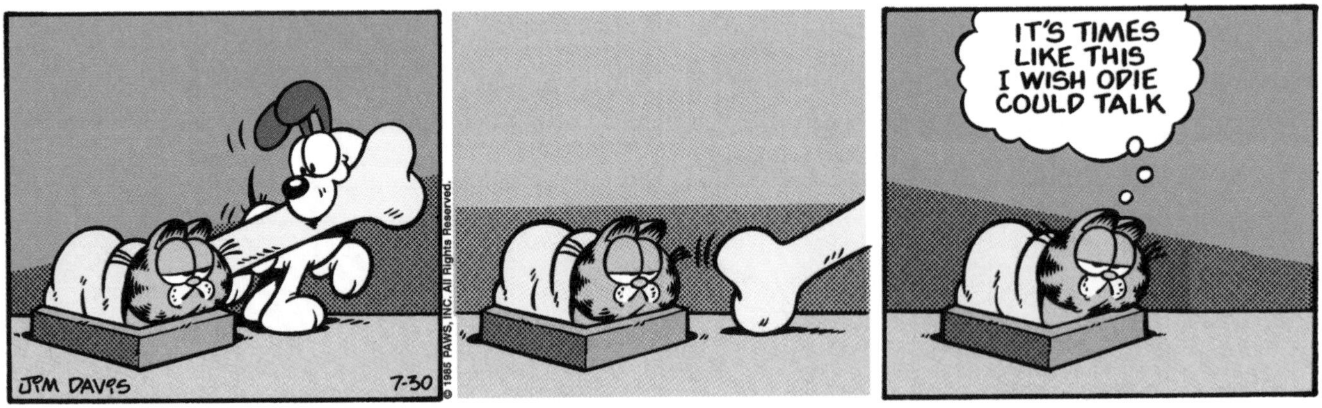
JIM DAVIS 7-30
© 1985 PAWS, INC. All Rights Reserved.
IT'S TIMES LIKE THIS I WISH ODIE COULD TALK

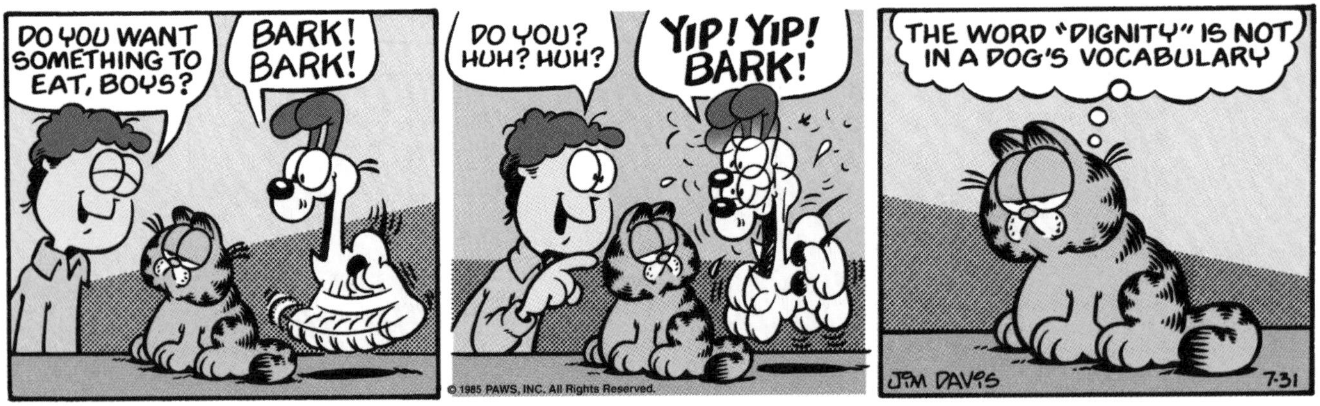
DO YOU WANT SOMETHING TO EAT, BOYS?
BARK! BARK!
DO YOU? HUH? HUH?
YIP! YIP! BARK!
© 1985 PAWS, INC. All Rights Reserved.
THE WORD "DIGNITY" IS NOT IN A DOG'S VOCABULARY
JIM DAVIS 7-31

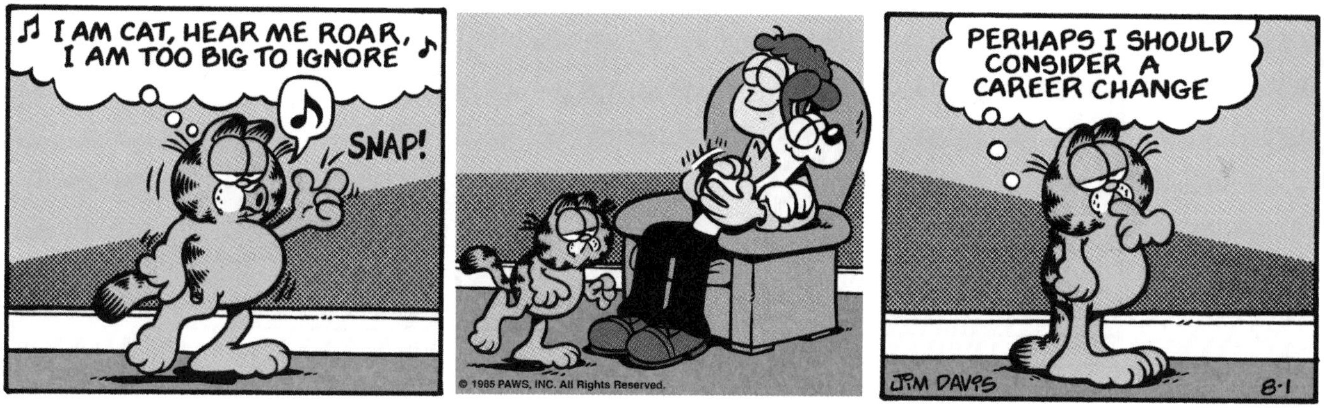
♫ I AM CAT, HEAR ME ROAR, I AM TOO BIG TO IGNORE ♪
SNAP!
© 1985 PAWS, INC. All Rights Reserved.
PERHAPS I SHOULD CONSIDER A CAREER CHANGE
JIM DAVIS
8-1

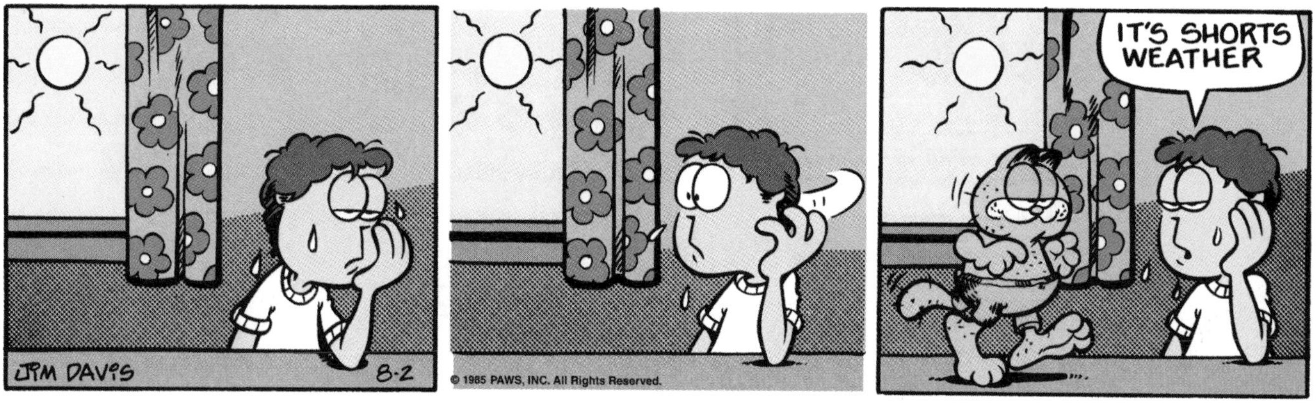
JIM DAVIS
8-2
© 1985 PAWS, INC. All Rights Reserved.
IT'S SHORTS WEATHER

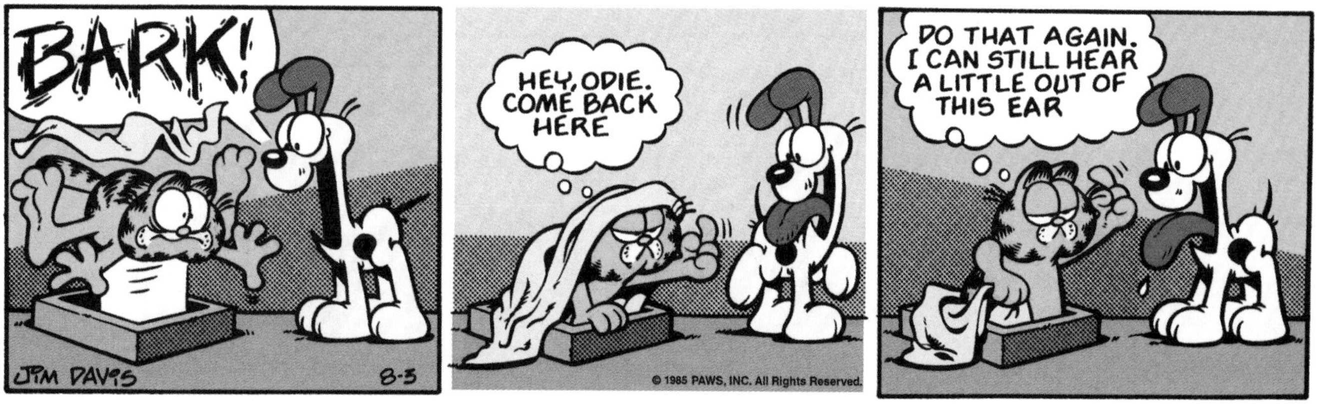
BARK!
JIM DAVIS
8-3
HEY, ODIE. COME BACK HERE
© 1985 PAWS, INC. All Rights Reserved.
DO THAT AGAIN. I CAN STILL HEAR A LITTLE OUT OF THIS EAR

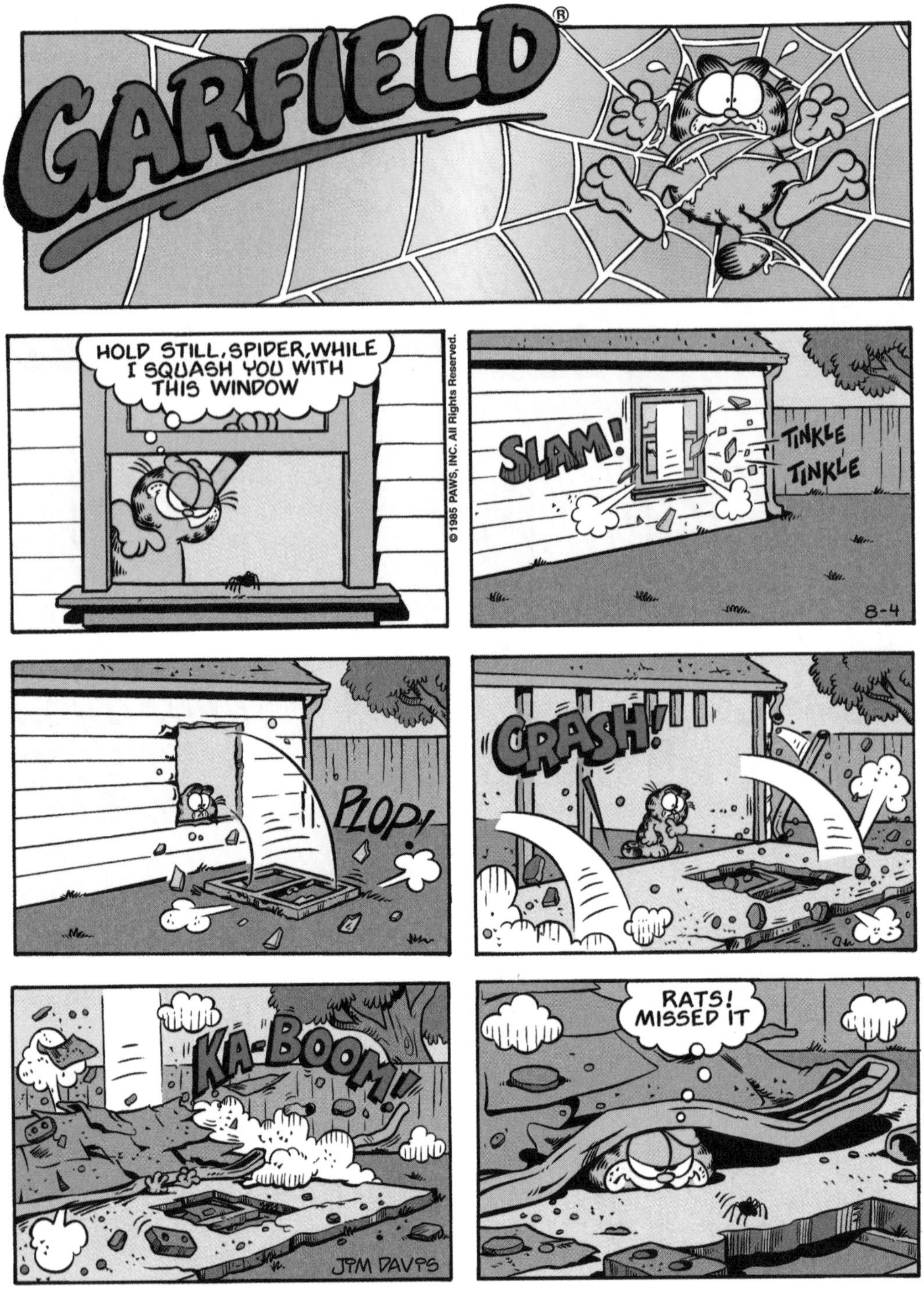
GARFIELD®
HOLD STILL, SPIDER, WHILE I SQUASH YOU WITH THIS WINDOW
©1985 PAWS, INC. All Rights Reserved.
SLAM!
TINKLE
TINKLE
8-4
PLOP!
CRASH!
KA-BOOM!
RATS! MISSED IT
JIM DAVIS